SHEKHAR KAPUR'S

DEVI™

Created by
SHEKHAR KAPUR

Script
SIDDHARTH KOTIAN (#0-#2)
SAMIT BASU (#3-#5)

Art
MUKESH SINGH

Cover Art
GREG HORN

Additional Covers
MUKESH SINGH
AMANDA CONNER
ADITYA CHARI & SURESH SEETHARAMAN

Colors
NANJAN J. (#1-#4)
NANJAN & MUKESH SINGH (#5)
SUNDARAKANNAN (#0)

Letters
RAVIKIRAN B. S.
and NILESH S. MAHADIK

Project Manager
REUBEN THOMAS

Assistant Editors
MAHESH KAMATH &
SANA AMANAT

Editor
MACKENZIE CADENHEAD

SHEKHAR KAPUR'S

DEVI™

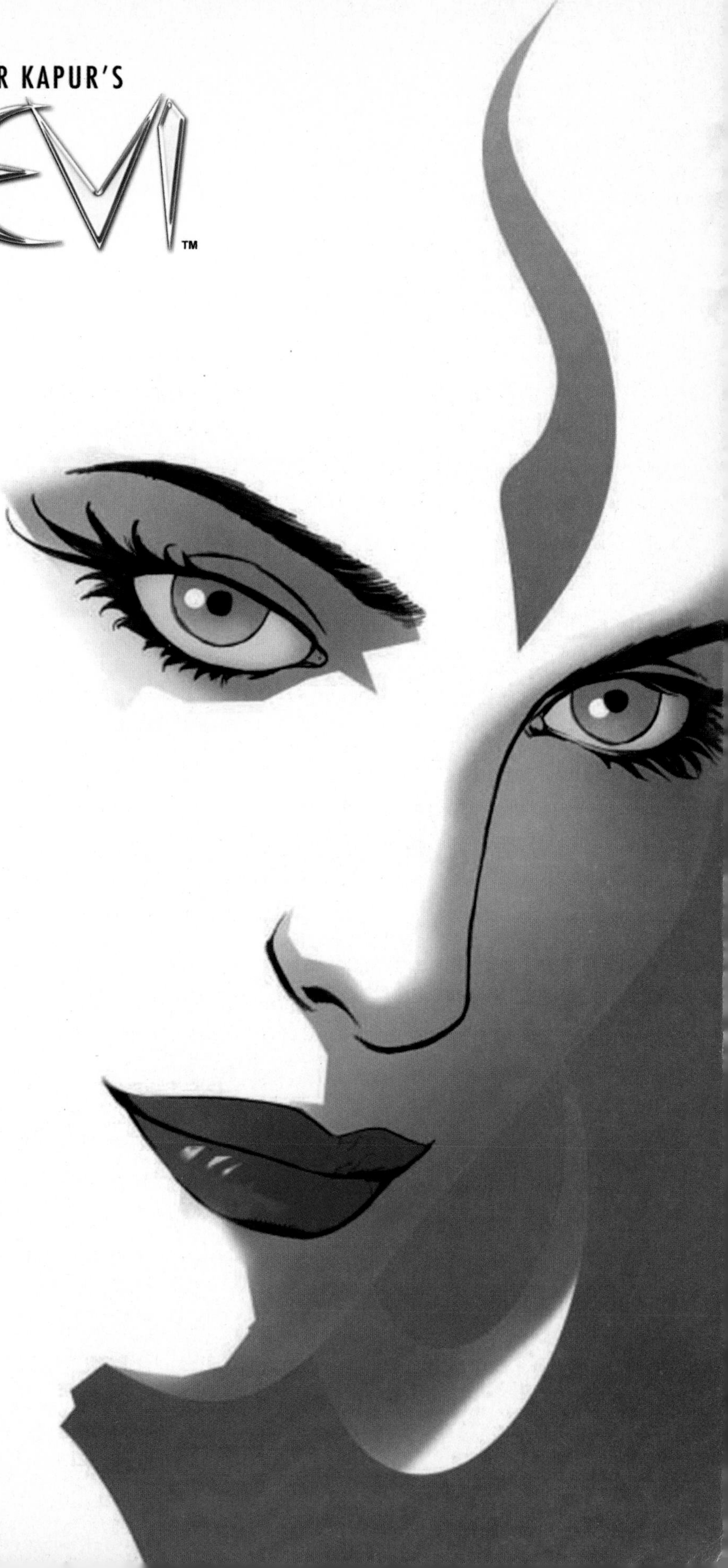

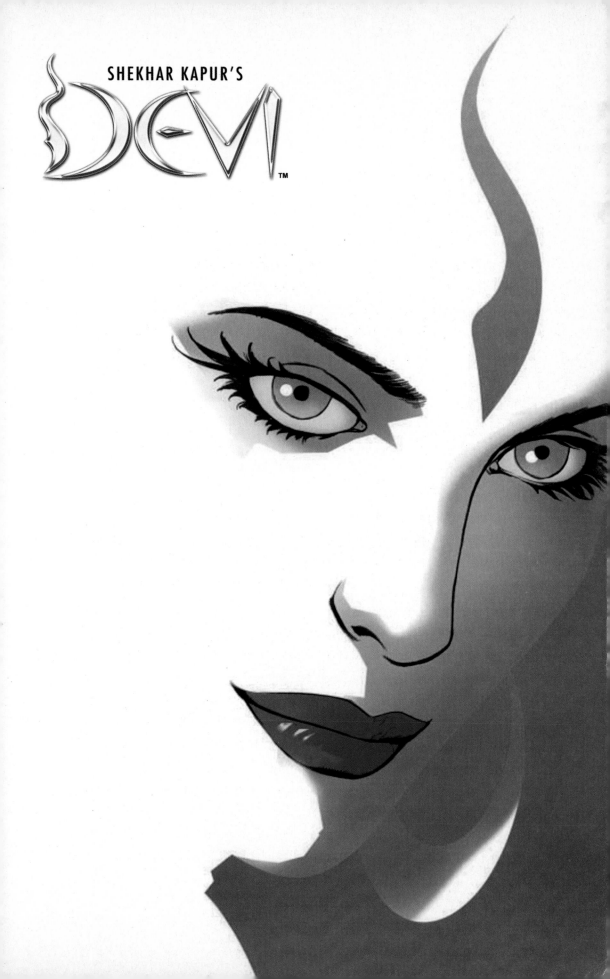

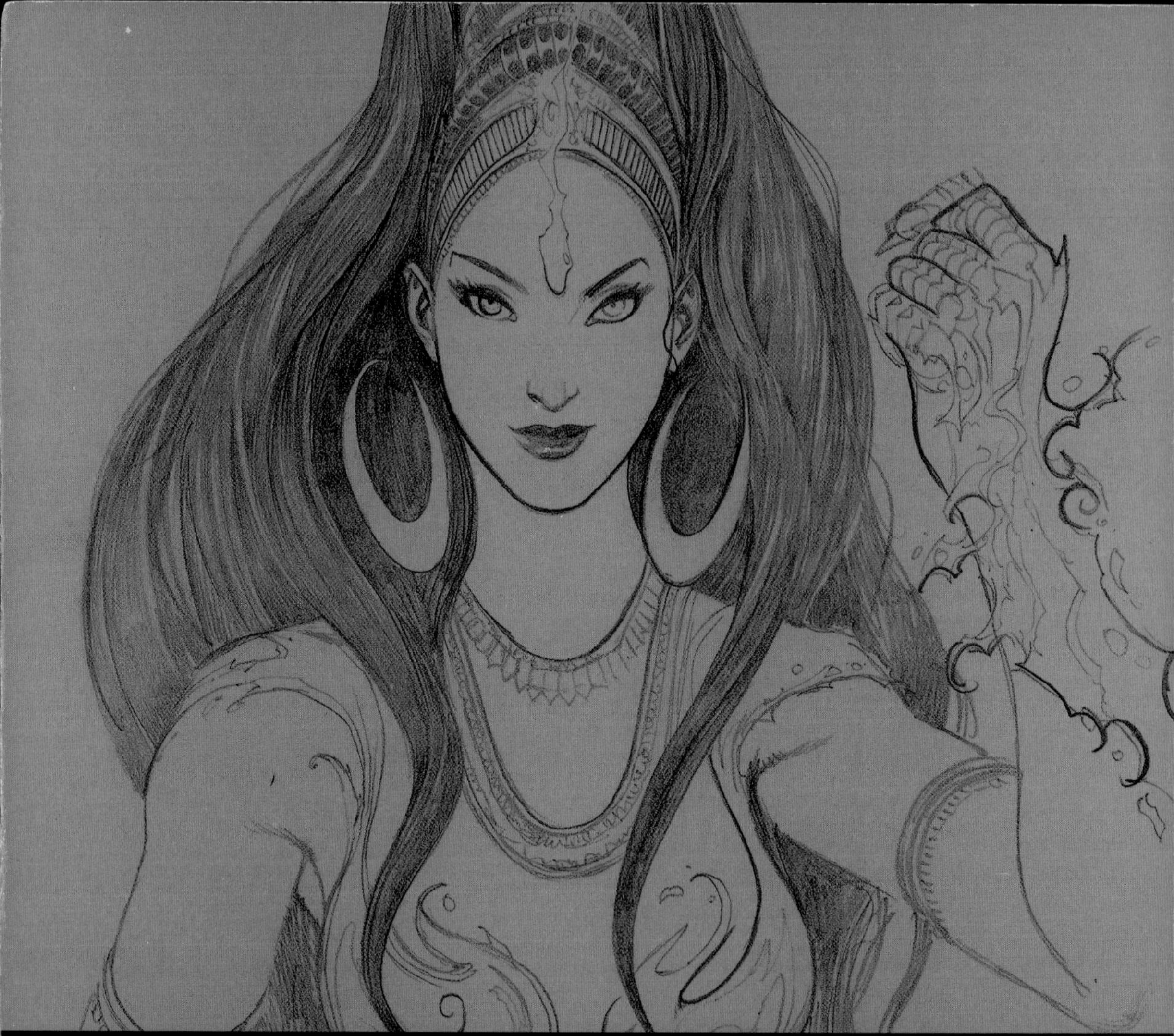

SHEKHAR KAPUR'S

DEVI™

VIRGIN COMICS

Chief Executive Officer and Publisher
SHARAD DEVARAJAN

Chief Creative Officer and Editor-in-Chief
GOTHAM CHOPRA

President & Studio Chief
SURESH SEETHARAMAN

Chief Marketing Officer
LARRY LIEBERMAN

SRVP - Studio
JEEVAN KANG

Chief Visionaries
DEEPAK CHOPRA,
SHEKHAR KAPUR,
SIR RICHARD BRANSON

Head Of Operations
ALAGAPPAN KANNAN

Director of Development
MACKENZIE CADENHEAD

Special Thanks to:
Frances Farrow, Dan Porter,
Christopher Linen, Peter Feldman,
Raju Puthukarai and Mallika Chopra

DEVI Vol. 1, May 2007 published by VIRGIN COMICS L.L.C. OFFICE OF PUBLICATION: 594 Broadway, New York, NY 10012.

"PIONEERS GET SHOT IN THE BACK."

Two years ago, when Gotham Chopra, Suresh Seetharaman, Deepak Chopra, Shekhar Kapur and I began our collective dream to redefine the Indian entertainment industry, that's the message we resoundingly heard from skeptics and nay-sayers. We were told that if there was any interest in Indian-character entertainment (think Indian superheroes) someone would have done it already. Indeed, until then, India had never produced any original characters that were of a quality and appeal to make it on the international level. Clearly, the skeptics argued, there was little interest in such characters, nor was there the skilled talent to create them. One investor after another suggested we would be better off setting up an outsourcing outfit and forgetting our foolish dreams of actually building and creating something new.

Despite this well-intended advice, we obstinately proceeded with our plans, slowly attracting and training a small group of artists, all the while making it clear we weren't interested in technicians. Our mission was to recruit a group of like-minded individuals who shared our intention to "reverse the funnel" and pioneer a new wave of Indian content to share with audiences across the globe. Similar to the phenomenon of Japanese Anime and Manga, which has influenced virtually every aspect of popular media in the world today, our mission, then and now, is to give modern Indian youth a platform to create new stories and characters, allowing their distinct creative voice to be heard around the globe.

Eventually, we found our way to one of the greatest pioneers of them all, maverick businessman Sir Richard Branson. Unlike many of his contemporaries, Sir Richard instantly recognized that India was far more than a back office—that it could be a source of incredible and unique creativity, tapping a vault of centuries' worth of myth and storytelling. Together, we formed Virgin Comics and Virgin Animation to define a new type of global entertainment company, seamlessly developing new stories to resonate with audiences from Boston to Beijing to Bangalore.

A friend once told me that beginnings are arbitrary, that any singular point in time is both the start and the end of the story—that we choose our beginnings and choose where to carve out our endings. If we are truly able to pick our starting points, then what you hold in your hands today is certainly our beginning—the start of a story that is much bigger than just the illustrated panels and written words in this book. What you are holding is the beginning of the story of Virgin Comics and the international Indian-character entertainment revolution. Devi #1 is the first book of the first series produced by Virgin Comics, and this volume is our first collection. Our hope is that it's also the start of a paradigm shift for South Asian creators, who will look at this book as a call to action—that it will spark a creative renaissance in the region and will reshape the entertainment industry for decades to come.

Already our studio of artists and writers, which has grown from a handful to a hundred, is using the medium of graphic novels to challenge the status quo of their country. The comics they are creating—such as *Devi, Ramayan 3392AD* and *The Sadhu*—are unlike anything that has been produced in India before now. The unique vision of these young creators has already captivated audiences worldwide, their stories have already been translated into over a half-dozen languages and are serving as the source for new Hollywood films, video games and animation projects. Creators such as the team on *Devi*, including Mukesh Singh, Samit Basu and Siddharth Kotian, are championing a new Golden Age for the Indian comics industry. We like to think that with *Devi*, an industry was born.

Though the road ahead still has many challenges, for all of us here at Virgin, those challenges are far outweighed by the rewards. Our vision is embodied in this book: we allow new voices to be heard, whether it is the voice of one person, or the voice of a country.

Some pioneers may get shot in the back... but the successful ones plant their flags, pitch their tents, and create a legacy.

Sharad Devarajan
CEO AND PUBLISHER
Virgin Comics / Virgin Animation

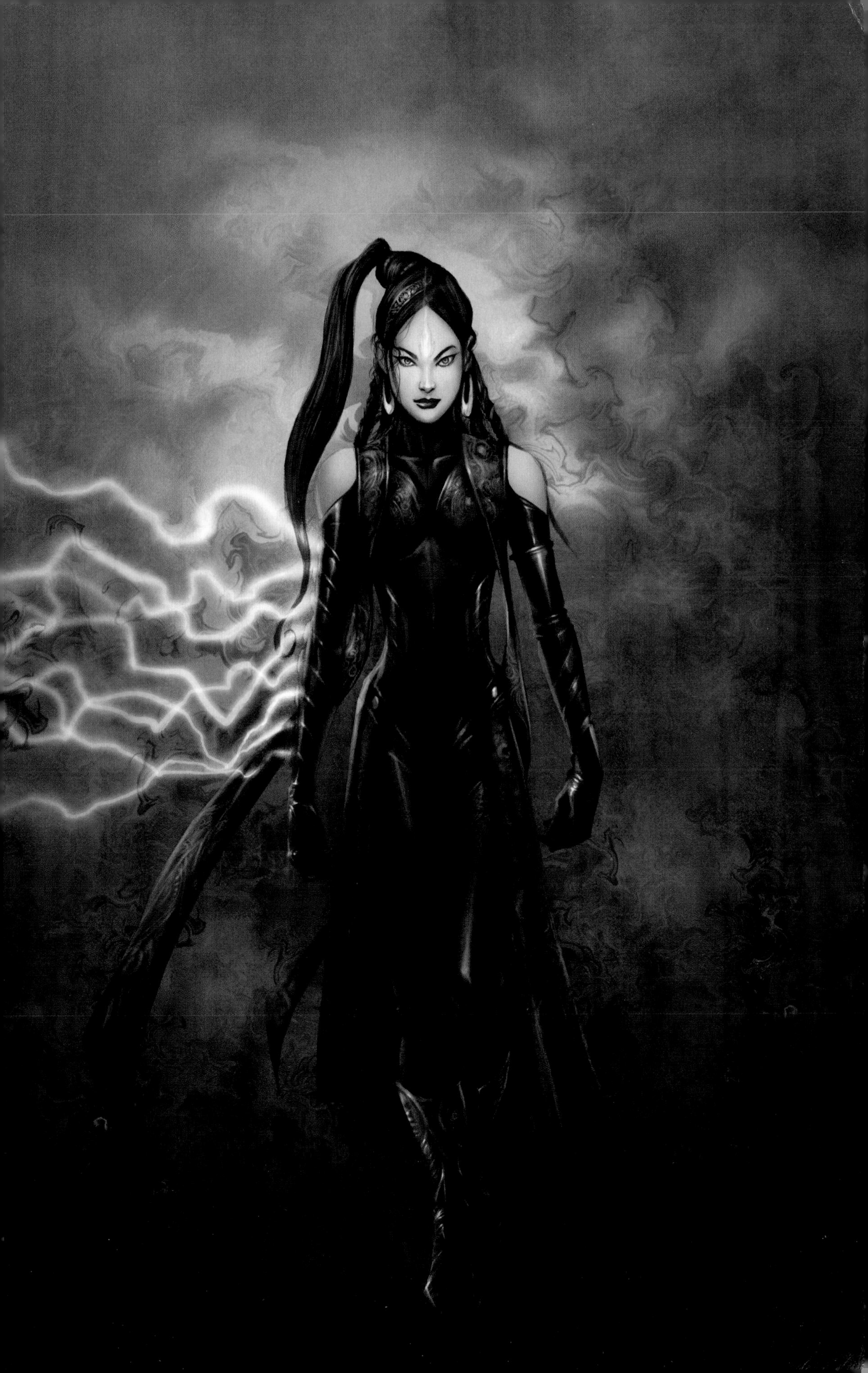

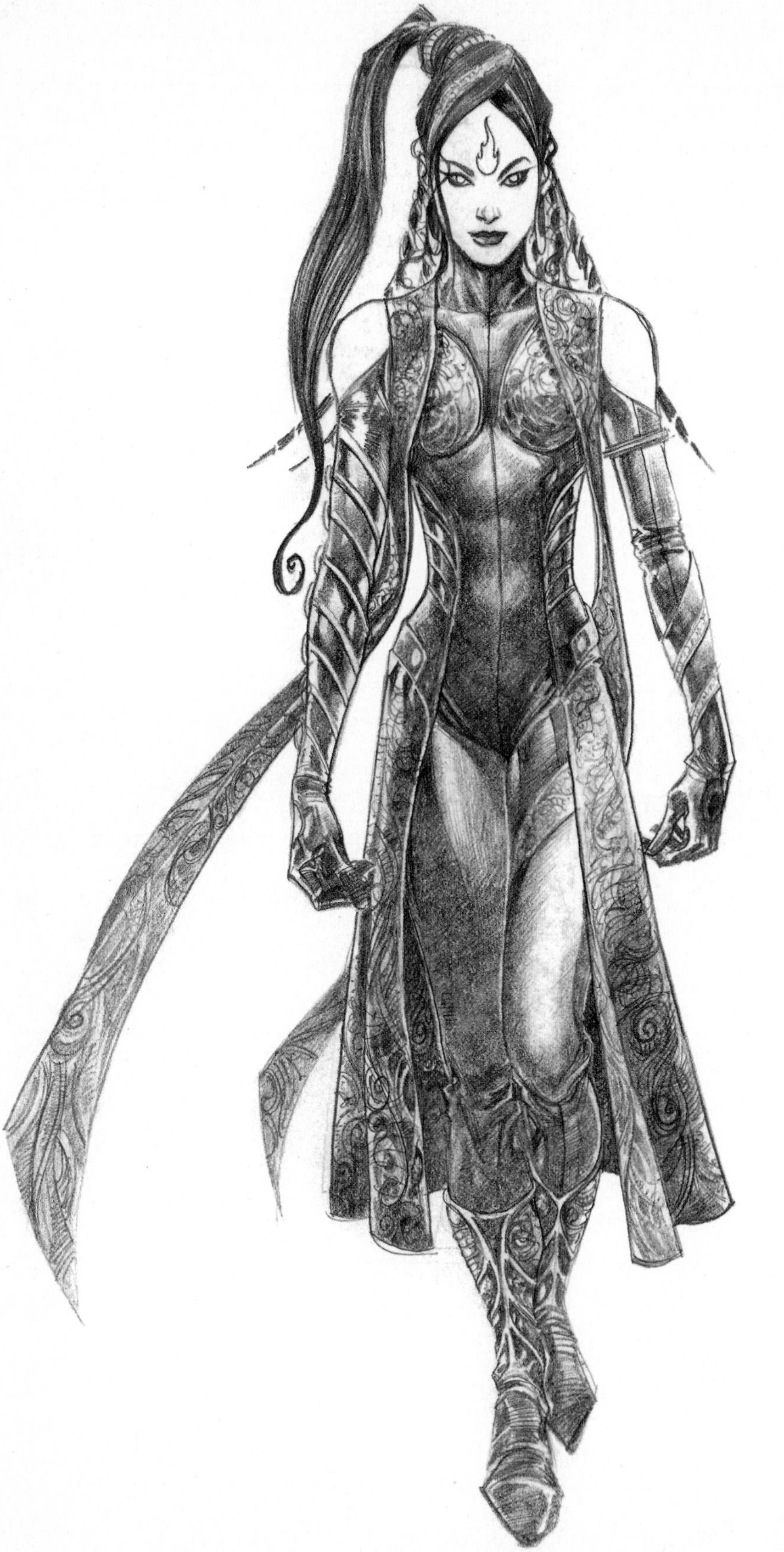

It was the second century of mankind's arrival on earth when the Gods of Light took up arms against one of their own. Bala, a fallen God, had rejected the old ways of the Pantheon and sought to impose his dominion over man.

Feeding off the forced worship of men, Bala had grown too powerful for the pantheon to take him on alone. So the pure Gods each sacrificed a part of themselves to create a powerful entity.

She is Devi.

STORY SO FAR...

THE DEVI ENTITY HAS BEEN PLACED IN A WARRIOR WOMAN OF THE DURAPASYA-- THE HUMANS WHO FIGHT ALONGSIDE THE PURE GODS. SHE HAS TAKEN ON THE NAMESAKE OF THE DIVINE ENTITY AND LED THE ARMIES OF GODS AND MEN ON AN ALL-OUT ASSAULT ON BALA'S FORTRESS.

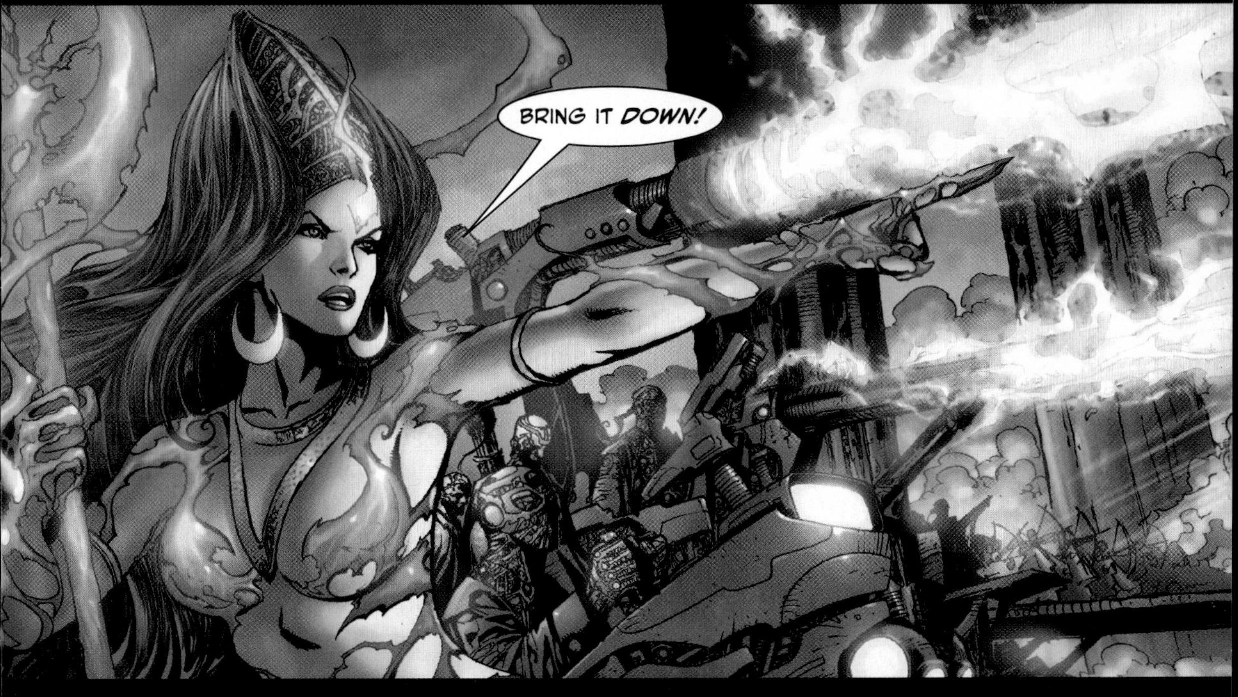
BRING IT DOWN!

Part One
BHAIRAVI

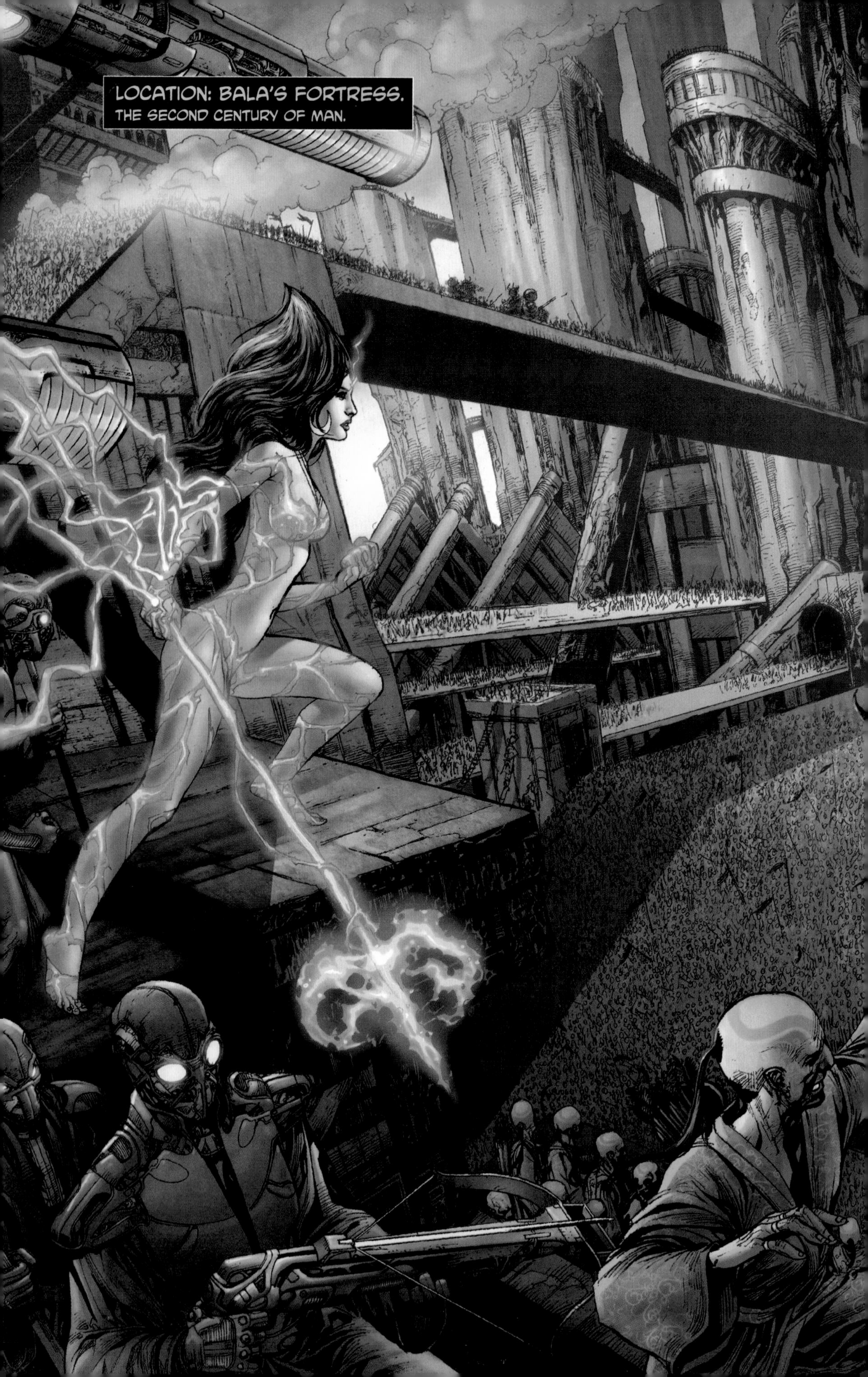
LOCATION: BALA'S FORTRESS.
THE SECOND CENTURY OF MAN.

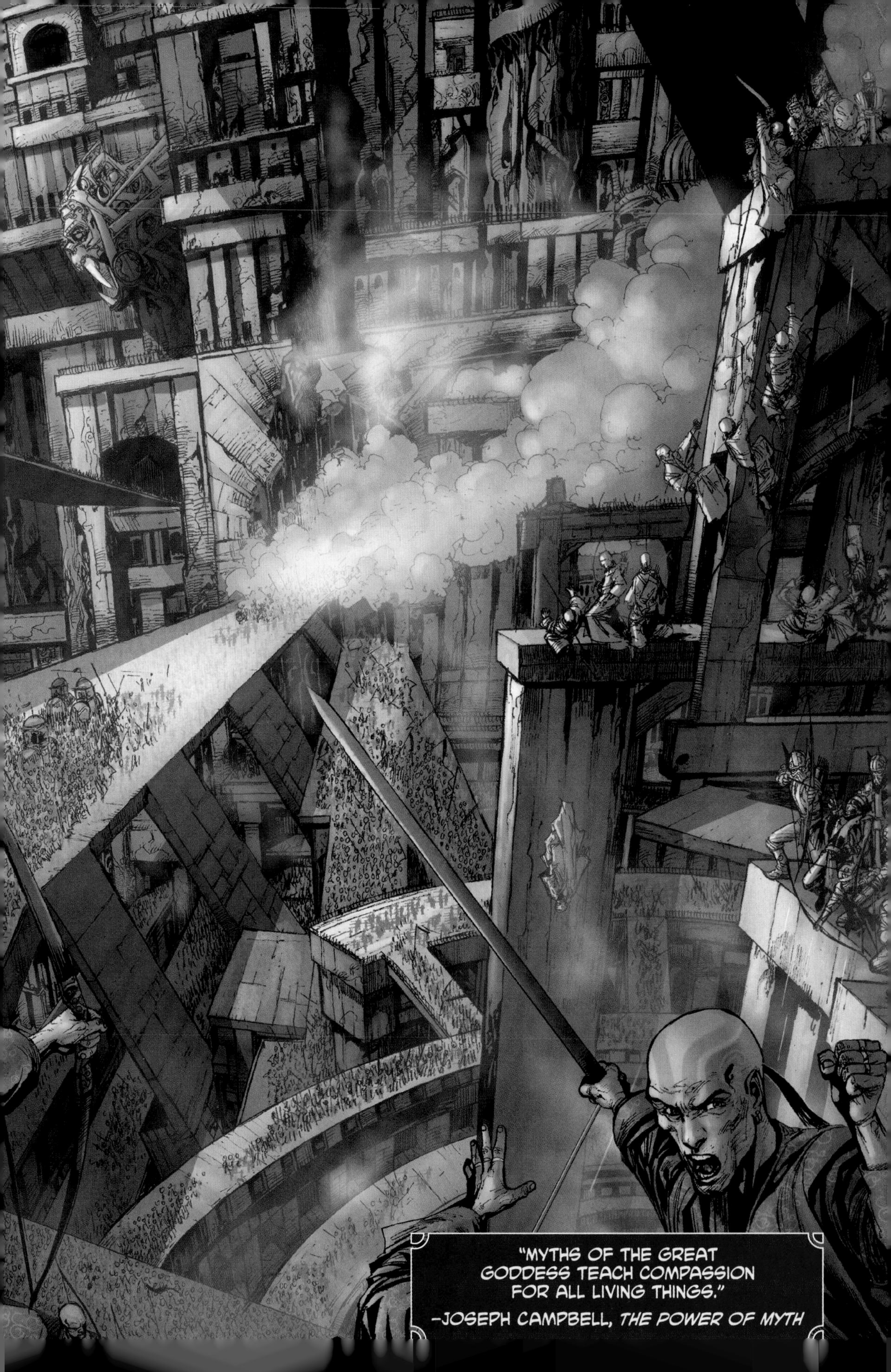
"MYTHS OF THE GREAT GODDESS TEACH COMPASSION FOR ALL LIVING THINGS."
–JOSEPH CAMPBELL, *THE POWER OF MYTH*

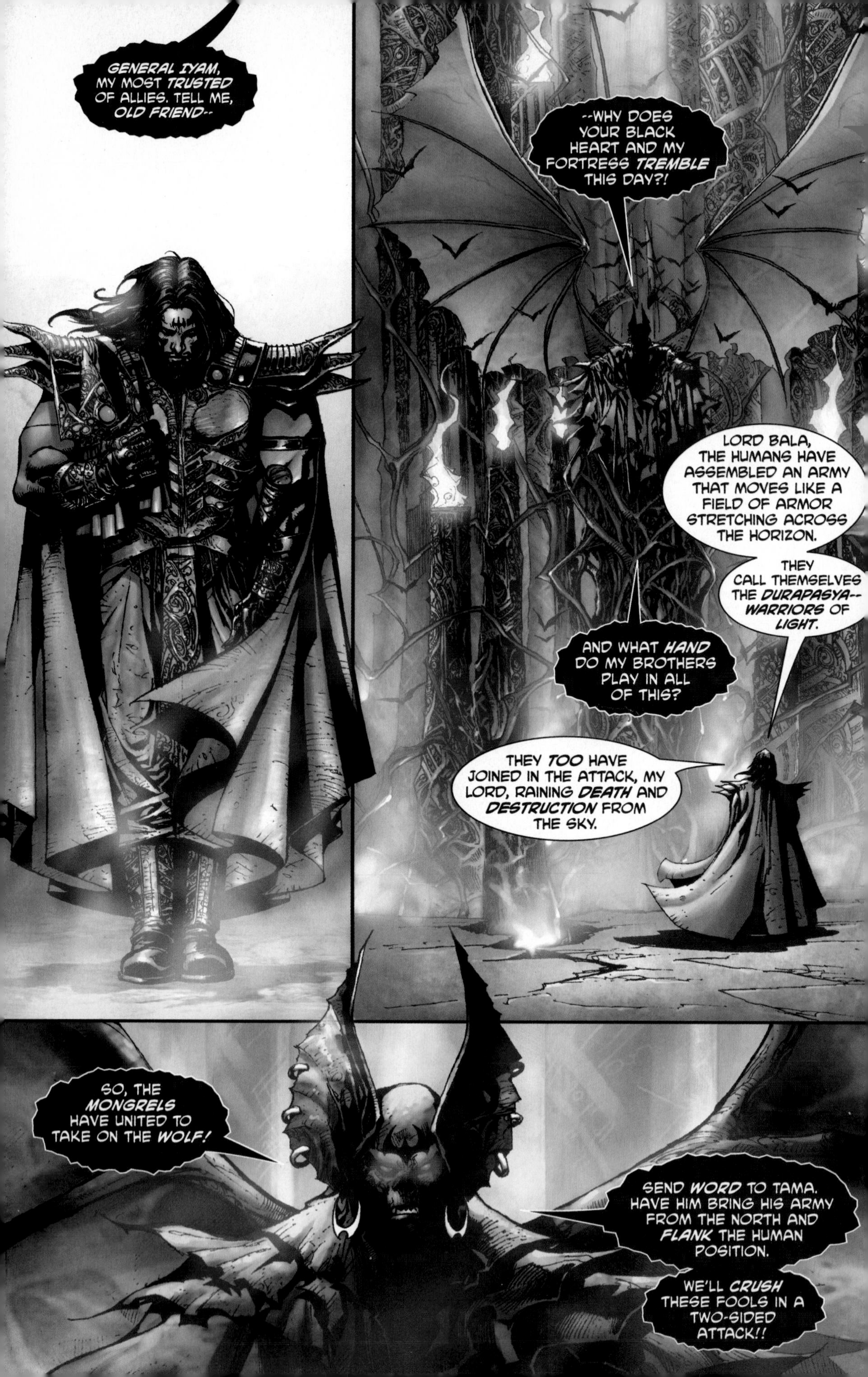
GENERAL IYAM, MY MOST TRUSTED OF ALLIES. TELL ME, OLD FRIEND--
--WHY DOES YOUR BLACK HEART AND MY FORTRESS TREMBLE THIS DAY?!
LORD BALA, THE HUMANS HAVE ASSEMBLED AN ARMY THAT MOVES LIKE A FIELD OF ARMOR STRETCHING ACROSS THE HORIZON.
THEY CALL THEMSELVES THE DURAPASYA-- WARRIORS OF LIGHT.
AND WHAT HAND DO MY BROTHERS PLAY IN ALL OF THIS?
THEY TOO HAVE JOINED IN THE ATTACK, MY LORD, RAINING DEATH AND DESTRUCTION FROM THE SKY.
SO, THE MONGRELS HAVE UNITED TO TAKE ON THE WOLF!
SEND WORD TO TAMA. HAVE HIM BRING HIS ARMY FROM THE NORTH AND FLANK THE HUMAN POSITION.
WE'LL CRUSH THESE FOOLS IN A TWO-SIDED ATTACK!!

THERE SHALL BE NO REINFORCEMENTS COMING IN FROM THE NORTH, MY LORD. I TRIED SENDING WORD TO TAMA WHEN THE SIEGE WAS *FIRST* LAID. THE BLACK WIND MESSENGERS REPORT THAT THE STRONGHOLD HAS BEEN DESTROYED--TAMA IS CAPTURED.

THE ATTACK CAME SO SWIFT AND FIERCE THAT THE BATTLE TOOK NOT A *QUARTER-HOUR* TO RAZE HIS BASTION TO THE GROUND.

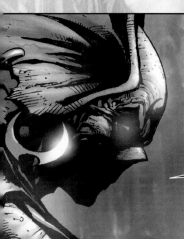

EH?! HOW COULD THE TIDE OF WAR TURN SO *SUDDENLY?* THESE *DOGS* HAVE *WAGED* BATTLE AGAINST ME BEFORE AND LOST.

WHAT IS SO *DIFFERENT* THIS TIME, *GENERAL?*

"LORD BALA, THE HUMANS HAVE A NEW CHAMPION AND NONE CAN WITHSTAND THE FURY OF HER BLADE.

"THEY CALL HER-- *DEVI...*"

AHAHAHAHAHA!

DEVI? A WOMAN?!! THEY SEND *A WOMAN* TO DEFEAT *ME?!!!*

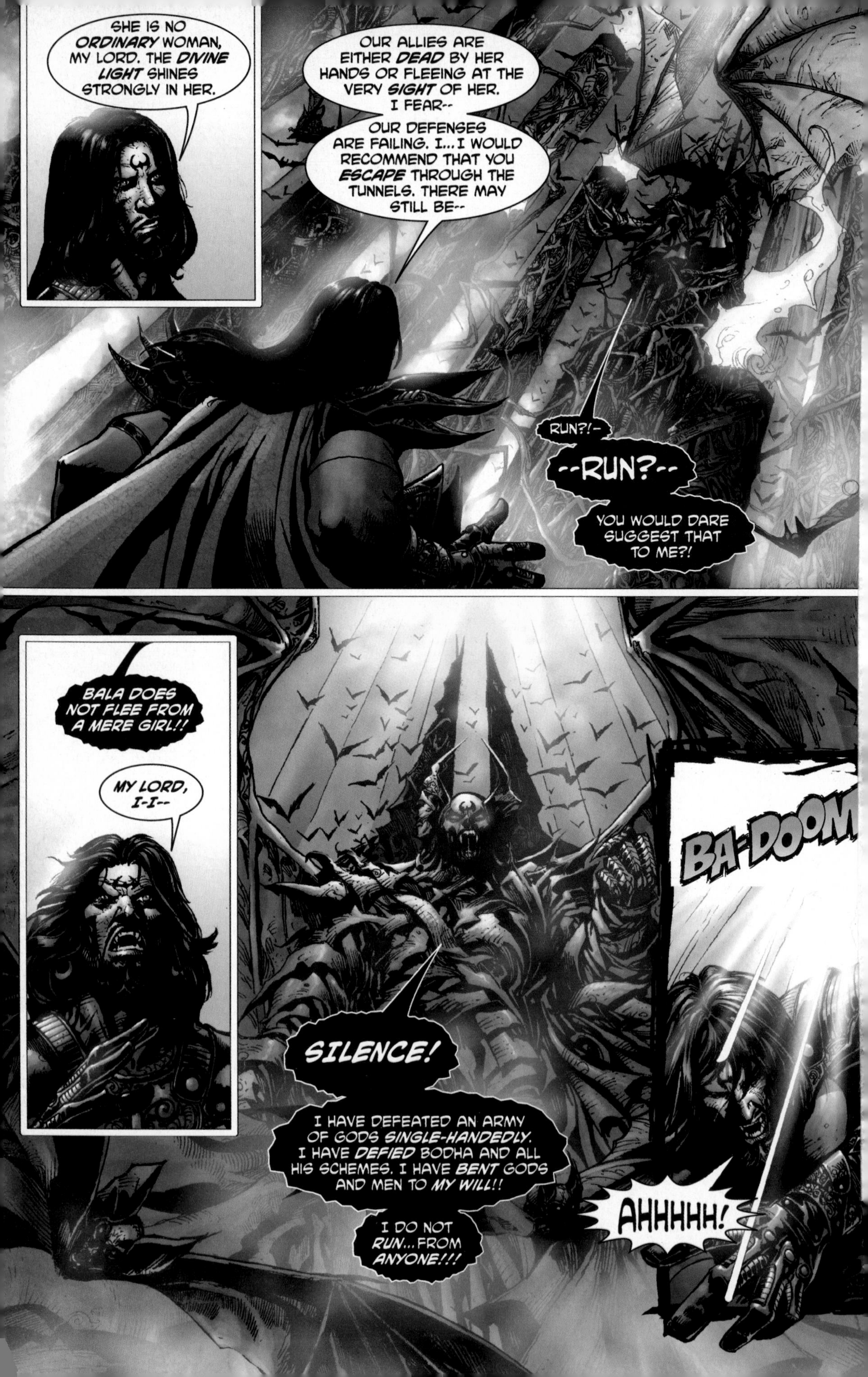
SHE IS NO ORDINARY WOMAN, MY LORD. THE DIVINE LIGHT SHINES STRONGLY IN HER.
OUR ALLIES ARE EITHER DEAD BY HER HANDS OR FLEEING AT THE VERY SIGHT OF HER. I FEAR--
OUR DEFENSES ARE FAILING. I...I WOULD RECOMMEND THAT YOU ESCAPE THROUGH THE TUNNELS. THERE MAY STILL BE--
RUN?!-
--RUN?--
YOU WOULD DARE SUGGEST THAT TO ME?!
BALA DOES NOT FLEE FROM A MERE GIRL!!
MY LORD, I-I--
BA-DOOM
SILENCE!
I HAVE DEFEATED AN ARMY OF GODS SINGLE-HANDEDLY. I HAVE DEFIED BODHA AND ALL HIS SCHEMES. I HAVE BENT GODS AND MEN TO MY WILL!!
I DO NOT RUN...FROM ANYONE!!!
AHHHHH!

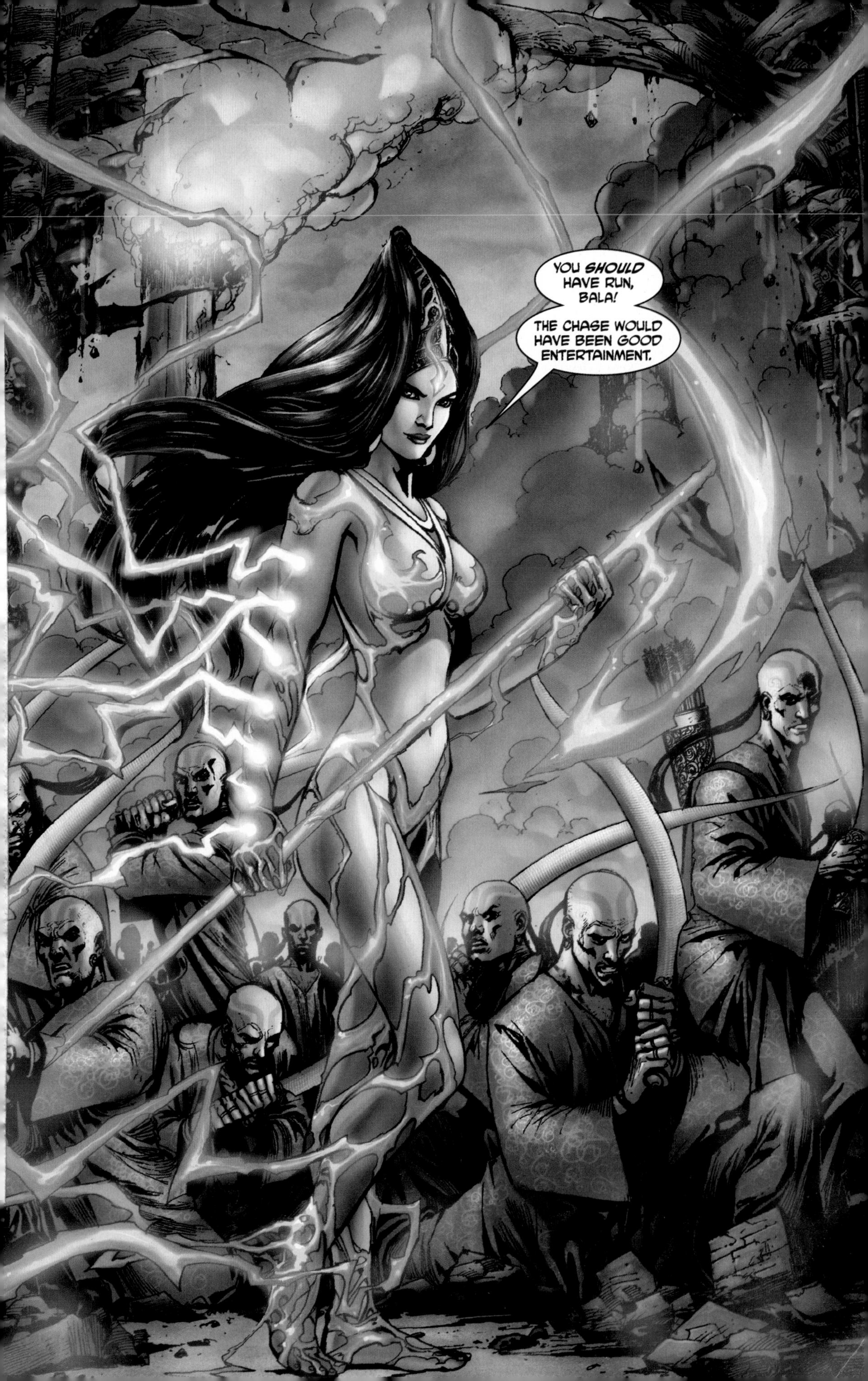
YOU *SHOULD* HAVE RUN, BALA!
THE CHASE WOULD HAVE BEEN GOOD ENTERTAINMENT.

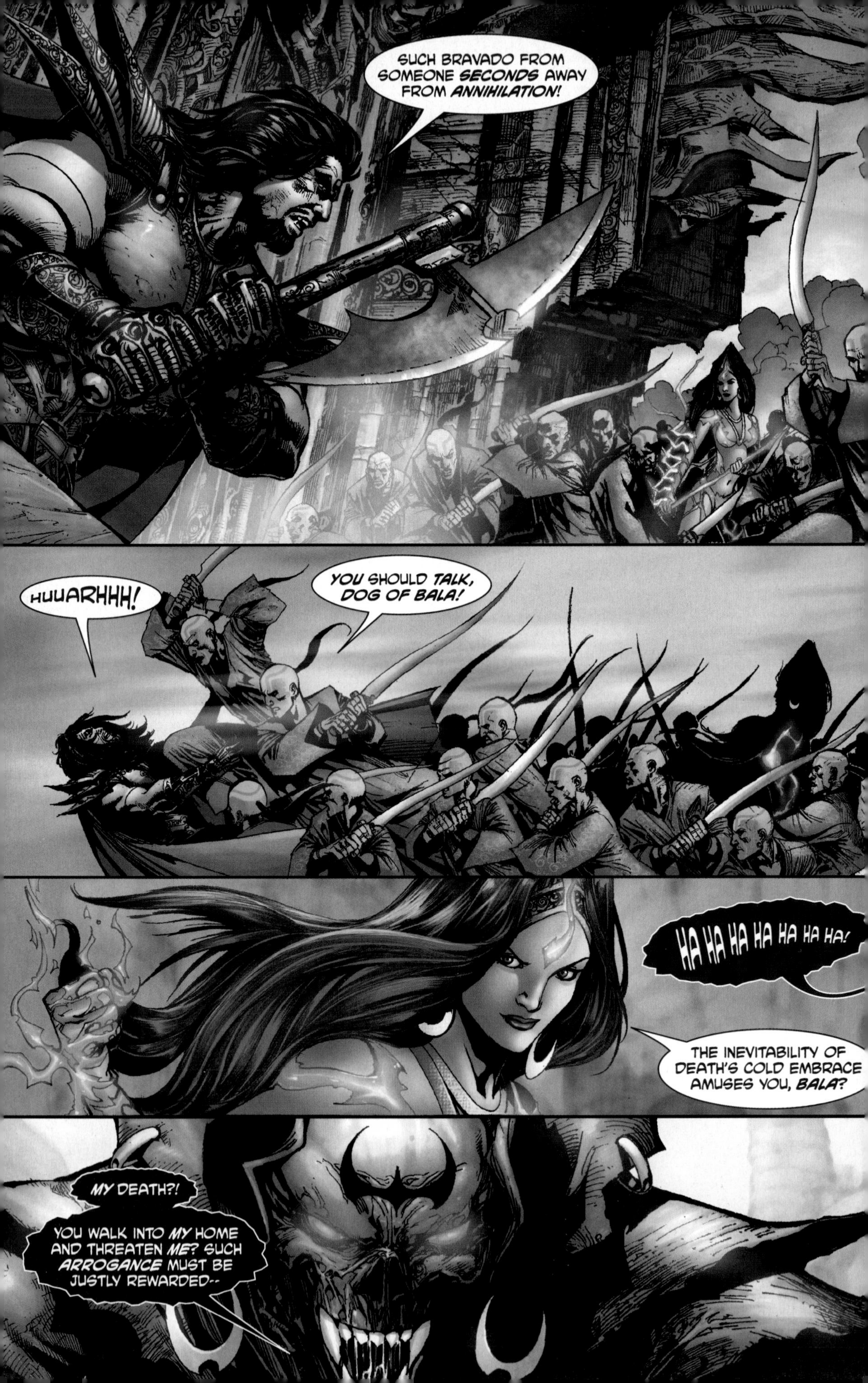
SUCH BRAVADO FROM SOMEONE SECONDS AWAY FROM ANNIHILATION!
HUUARHHH!
YOU SHOULD TALK, DOG OF BALA!
HA HA HA HA HA HA HA!
THE INEVITABILITY OF DEATH'S COLD EMBRACE AMUSES YOU, BALA?
MY DEATH?!
YOU WALK INTO MY HOME AND THREATEN ME? SUCH ARROGANCE MUST BE JUSTLY REWARDED--

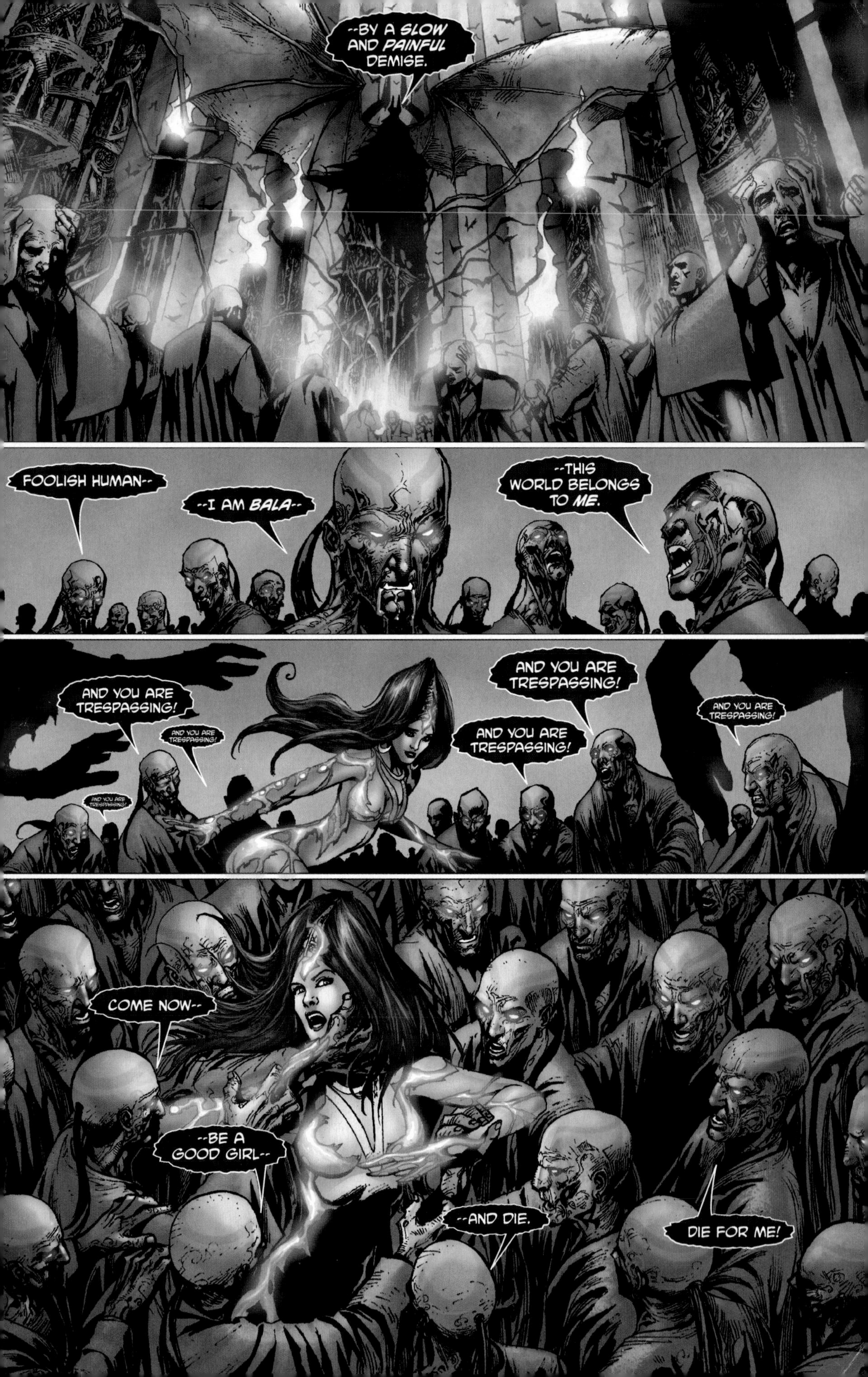

--BY A SLOW AND PAINFUL DEMISE.
FOOLISH HUMAN--
--I AM BALA--
--THIS WORLD BELONGS TO ME.
AND YOU ARE TRESPASSING!
AND YOU ARE TRESPASSING!
AND YOU ARE TRESPASSING!
AND YOU ARE TRESPASSING!
AND YOU ARE TRESPASSING!
AND YOU ARE TRESPASSING!
COME NOW--
--BE A GOOD GIRL--
--AND DIE.
DIE FOR ME!

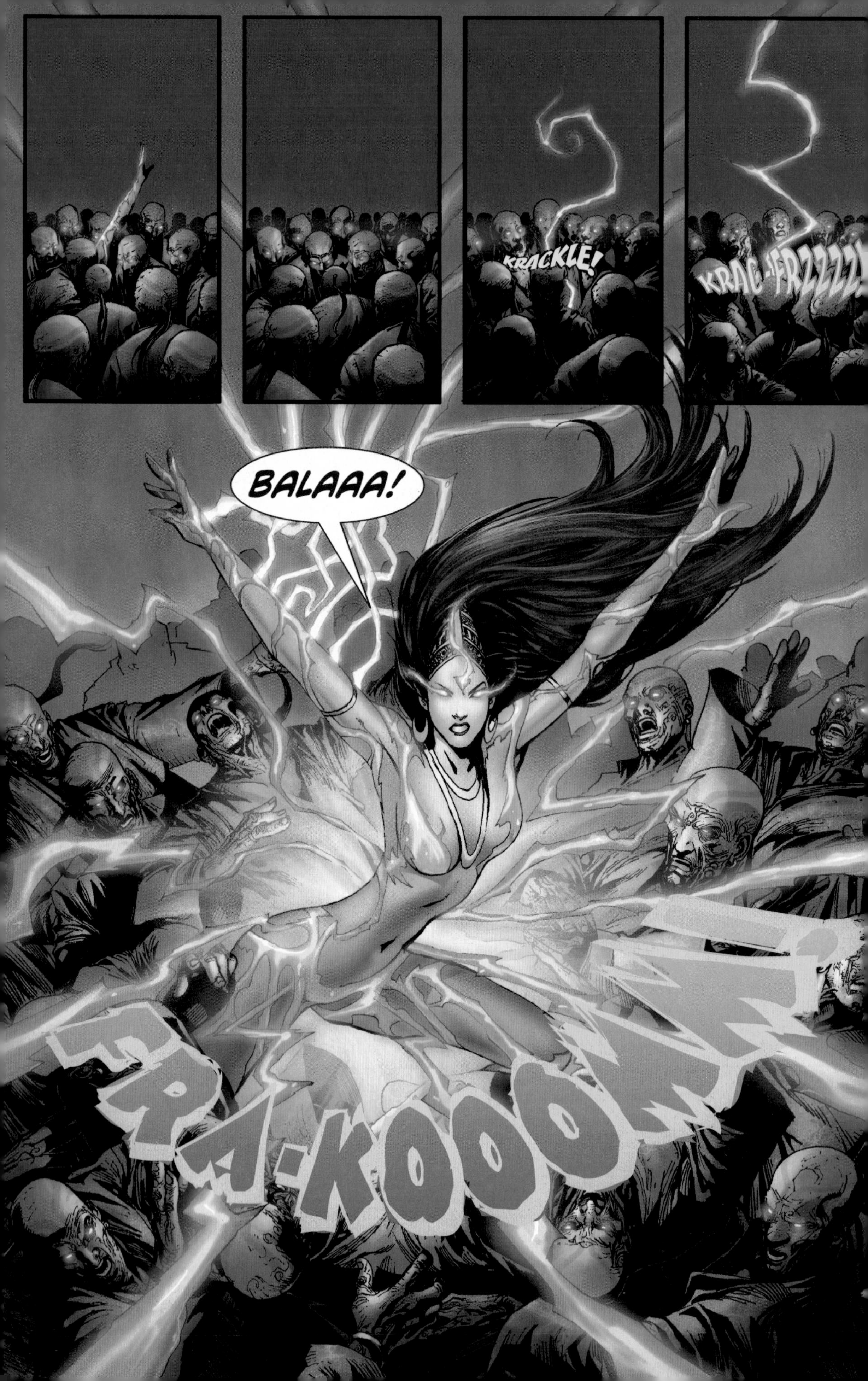
KRACKLE!
KRAC-FRZZZZ!
BALAAA!
FRA-KOOOM!

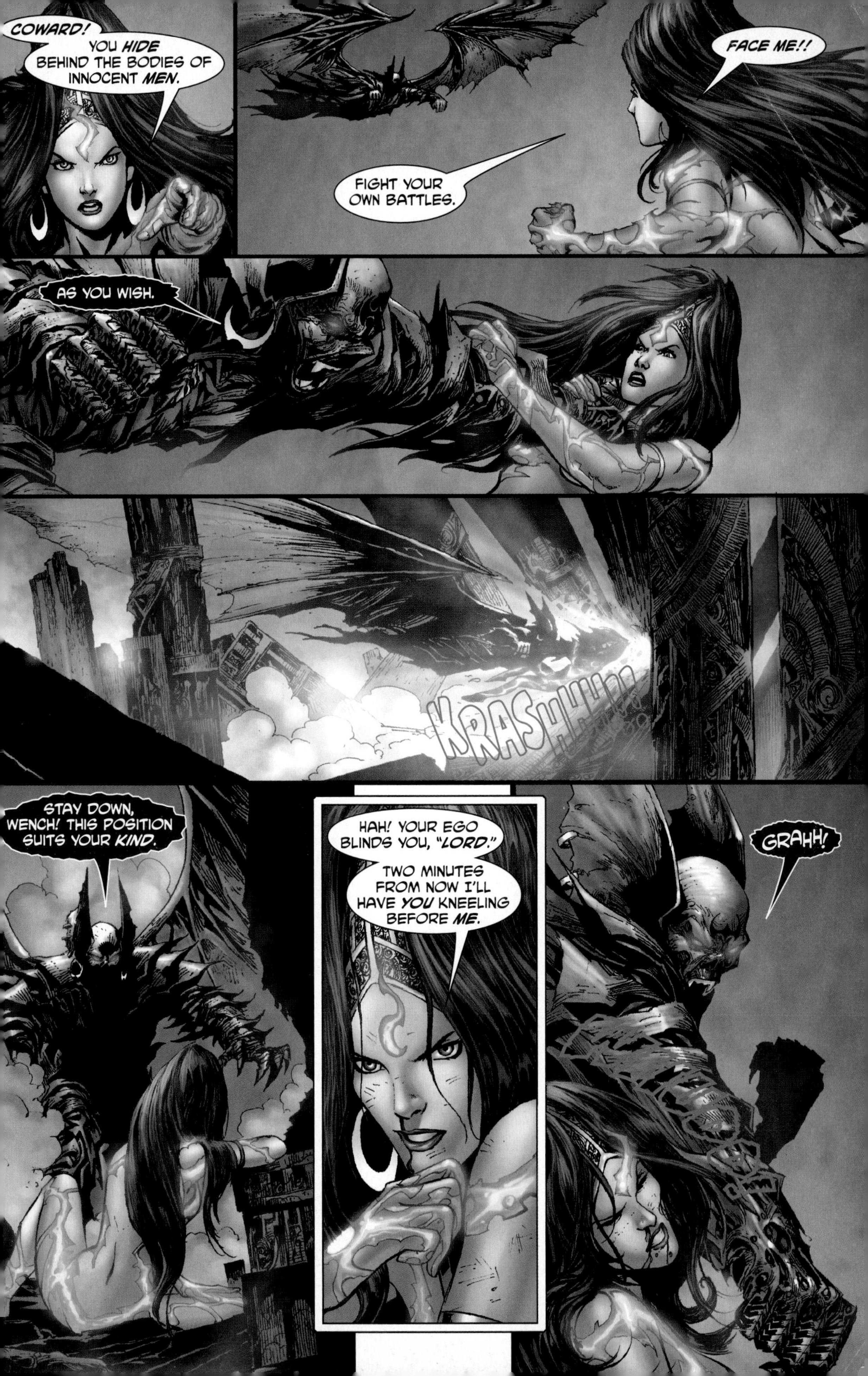
COWARD! YOU HIDE BEHIND THE BODIES OF INNOCENT MEN.
FACE ME!!
FIGHT YOUR OWN BATTLES.
AS YOU WISH.
KRASHHH!!
STAY DOWN, WENCH! THIS POSITION SUITS YOUR KIND.
HAH! YOUR EGO BLINDS YOU, "LORD."
TWO MINUTES FROM NOW I'LL HAVE YOU KNEELING BEFORE ME.
GRAHH!

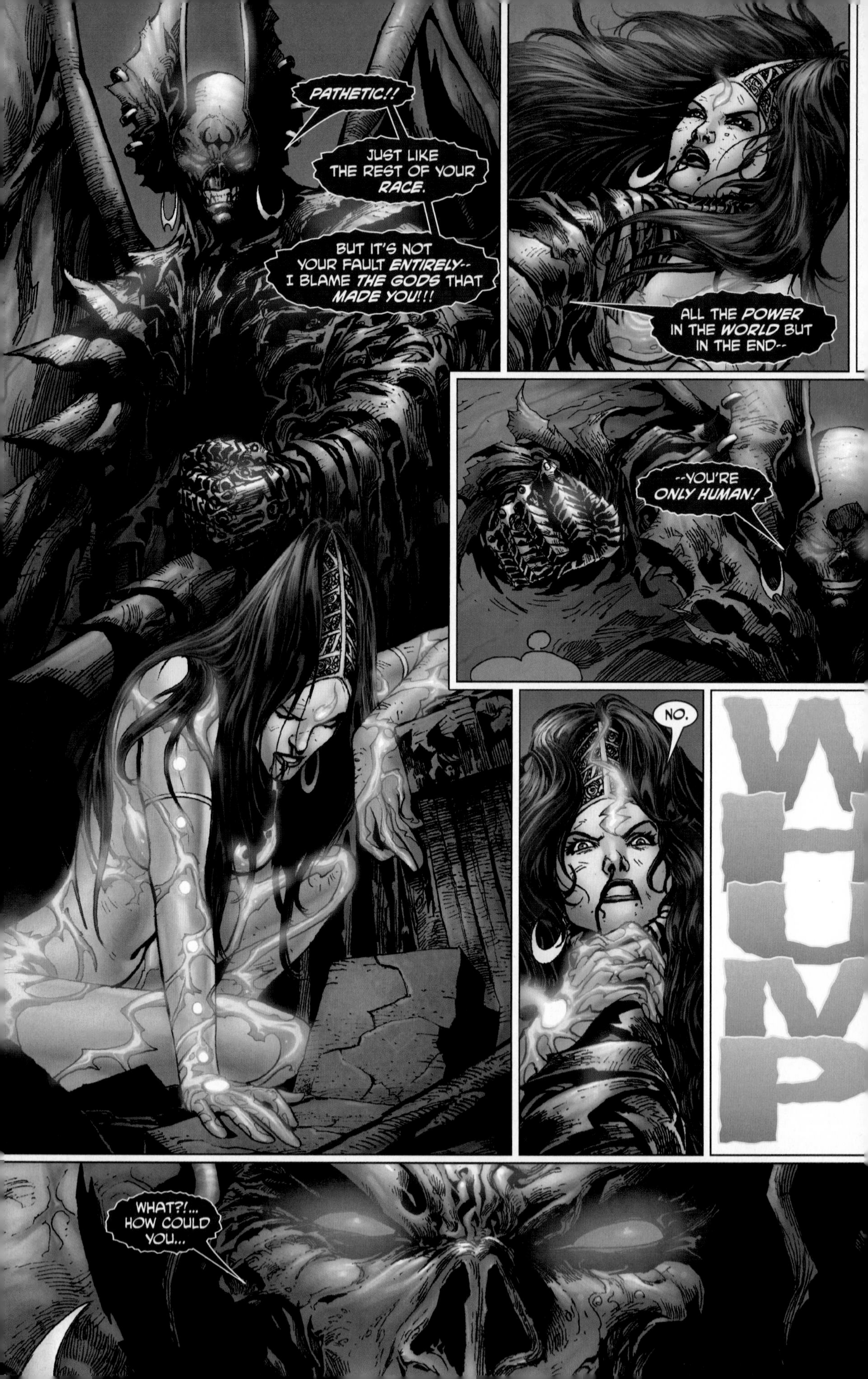
PATHETIC!!
JUST LIKE THE REST OF YOUR RACE.
BUT IT'S NOT YOUR FAULT ENTIRELY-- I BLAME THE GODS THAT MADE YOU!!!
ALL THE POWER IN THE WORLD BUT IN THE END--
--YOU'RE ONLY HUMAN!
NO.
WHUMP
WHAT?!... HOW COULD YOU...

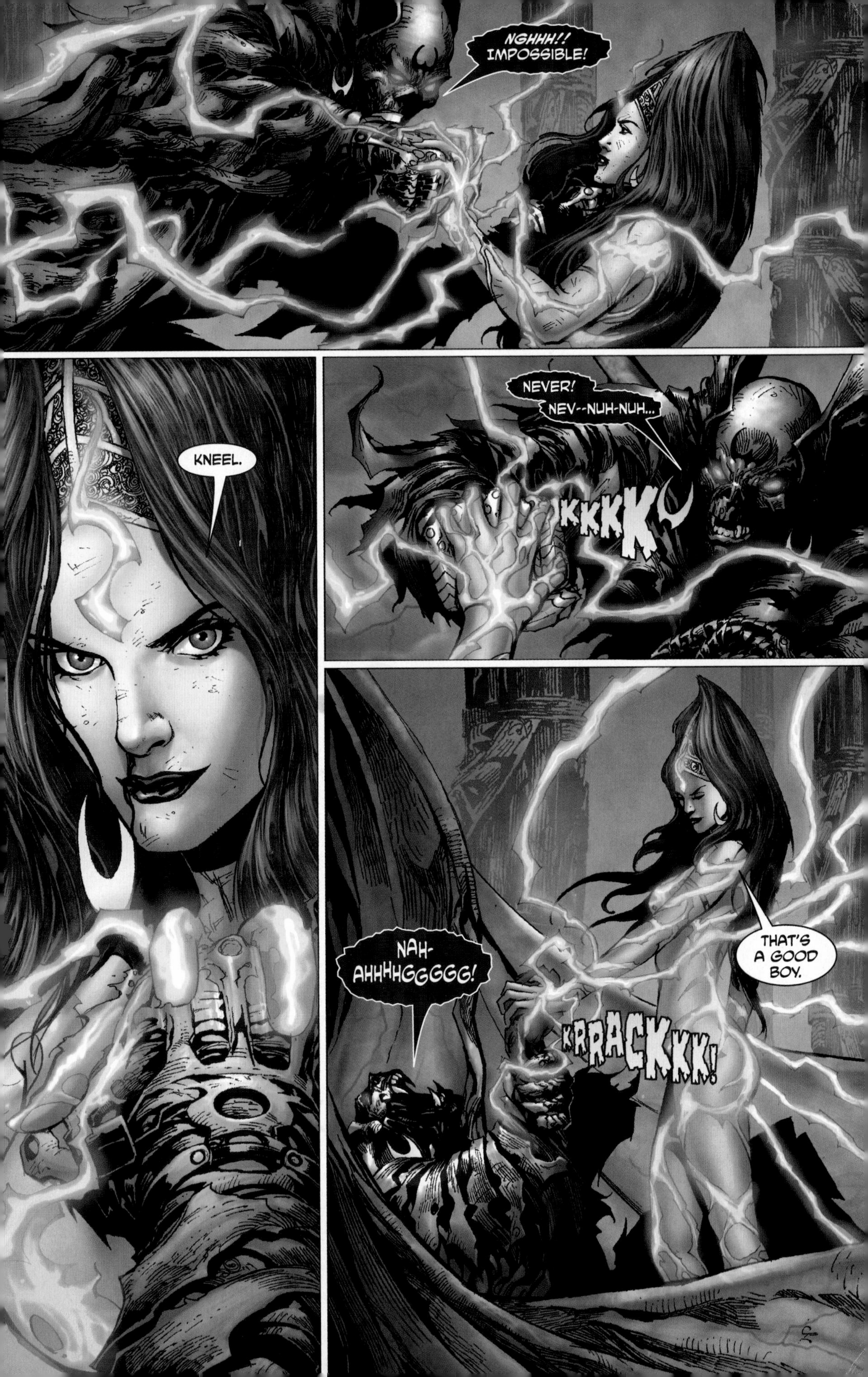
NGHHH!! IMPOSSIBLE!
KNEEL.
NEVER!
NEV--NUH-NUH...
KKKK
THAT'S A GOOD BOY.
NAH-AHHHHGGGGG!
KRRACKKK!

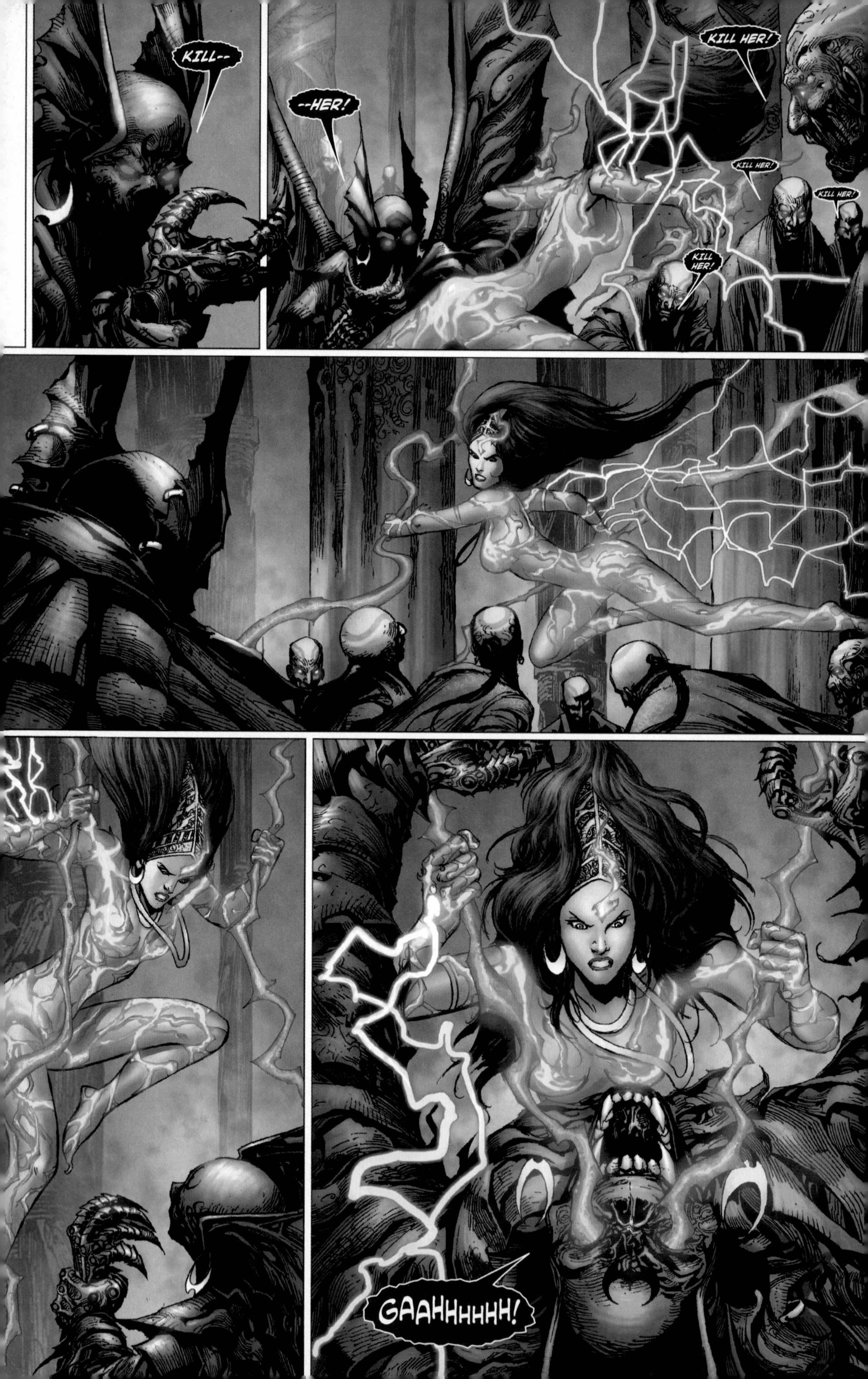
KILL--
--HER!
KILL HER!
KILL HER!
KILL HER!
KILL HER!
GAAHHHHHH!

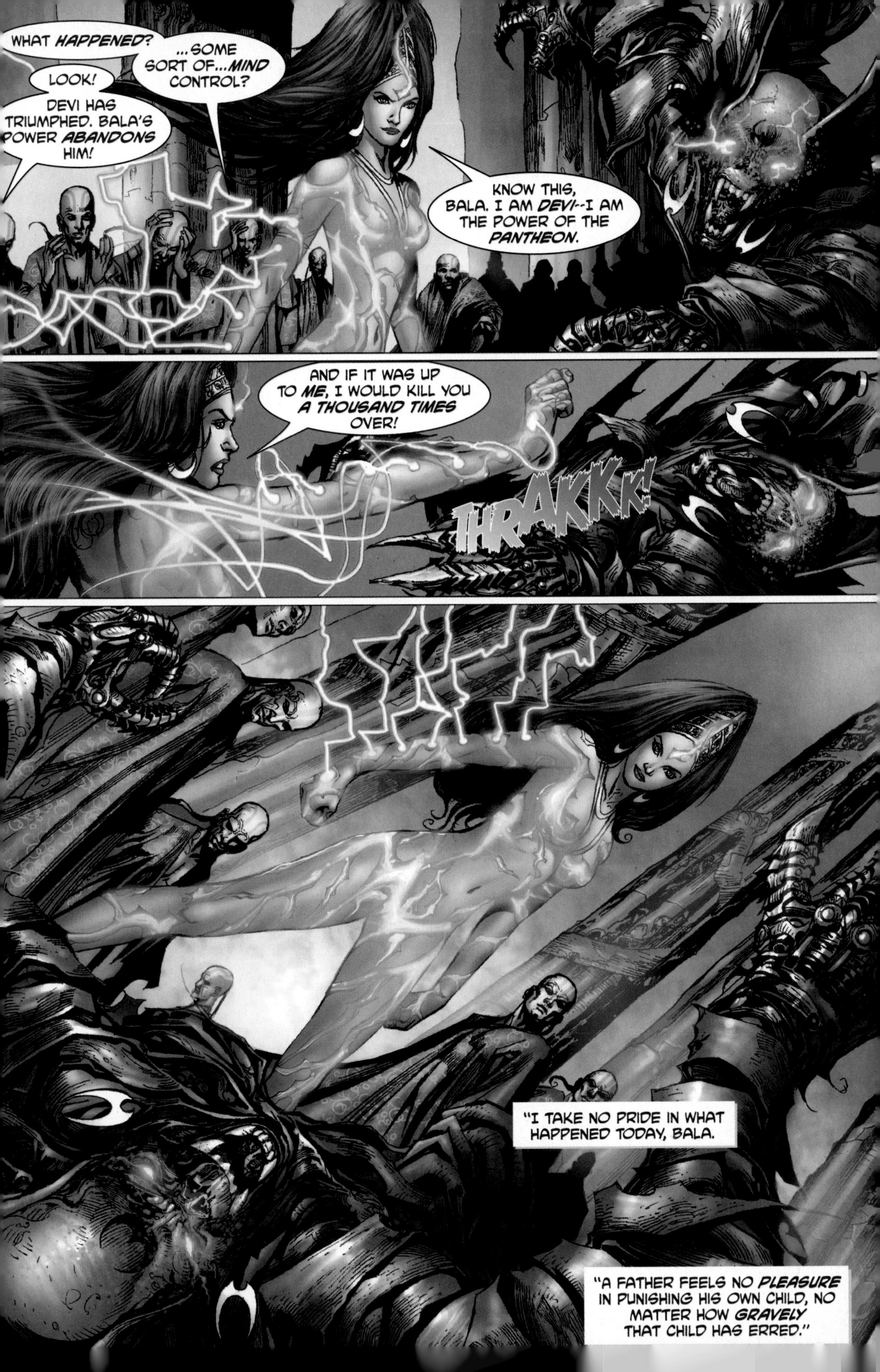
WHAT HAPPENED?
LOOK!
DEVI HAS TRIUMPHED. BALA'S POWER ABANDONS HIM!
...SOME SORT OF...MIND CONTROL?
KNOW THIS, BALA. I AM DEVI--I AM THE POWER OF THE PANTHEON.
AND IF IT WAS UP TO ME, I WOULD KILL YOU A THOUSAND TIMES OVER!
THRAKKK!
"I TAKE NO PRIDE IN WHAT HAPPENED TODAY, BALA.
"A FATHER FEELS NO PLEASURE IN PUNISHING HIS OWN CHILD, NO MATTER HOW GRAVELY THAT CHILD HAS ERRED."

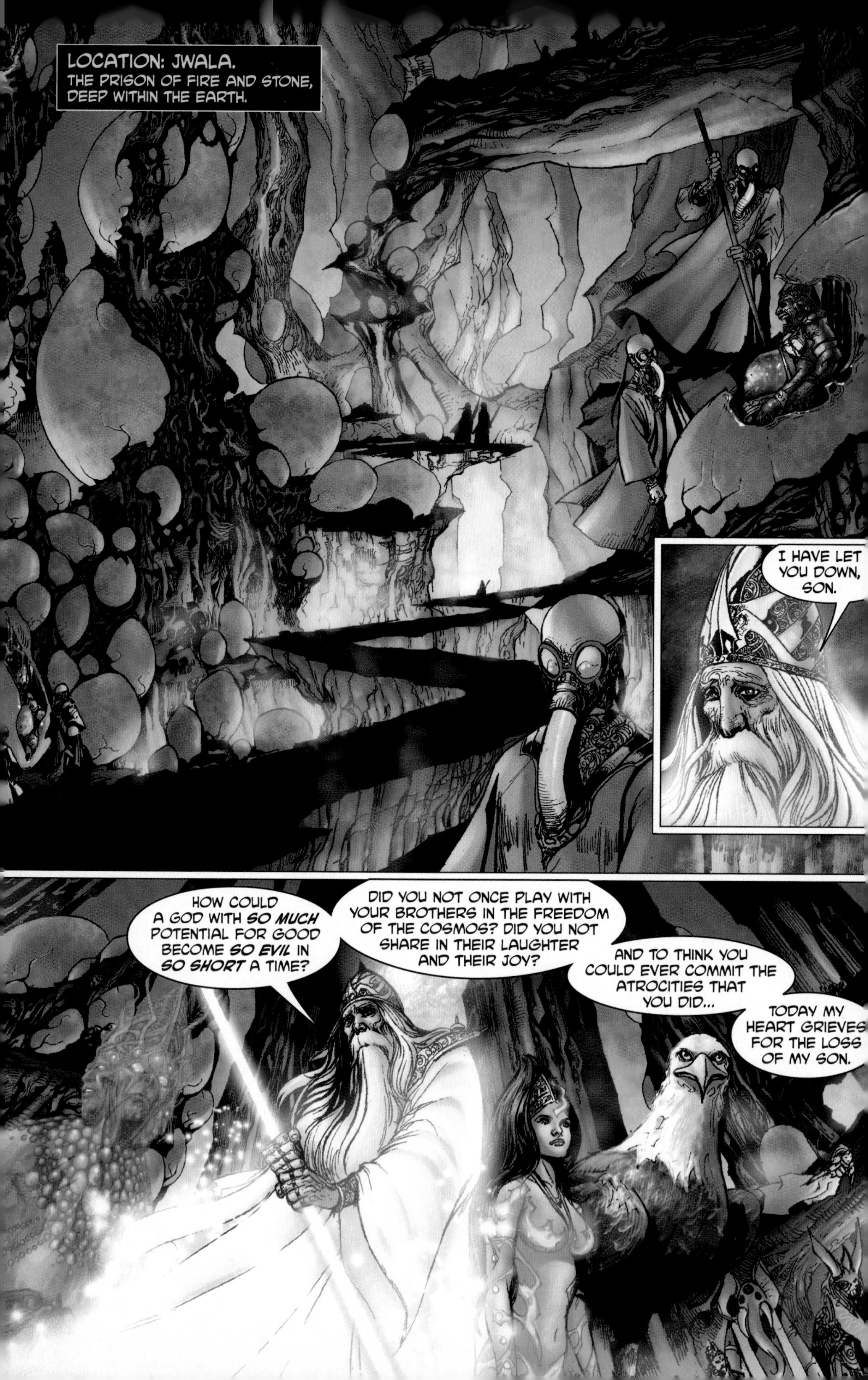
LOCATION: JWALA.
THE PRISON OF FIRE AND STONE, DEEP WITHIN THE EARTH.
I HAVE LET YOU DOWN, SON.
HOW COULD A GOD WITH SO MUCH POTENTIAL FOR GOOD BECOME SO EVIL IN SO SHORT A TIME?
DID YOU NOT ONCE PLAY WITH YOUR BROTHERS IN THE FREEDOM OF THE COSMOS? DID YOU NOT SHARE IN THEIR LAUGHTER AND THEIR JOY?
AND TO THINK YOU COULD EVER COMMIT THE ATROCITIES THAT YOU DID...
TODAY MY HEART GRIEVES FOR THE LOSS OF MY SON.

DO NOT *PITY* ME, BODHA, SO-CALLED KING OF *GODS!* FOR I HAVE DONE *NOTHING* WRONG.

YOU LOOK AT HUMANS AND SEE CHILDREN, *BRIGHT* AND *BEAUTIFUL.* I LOOK AT THEM AND SEE THE LABOR OF *FLAWED HANDS* WORKED ON BY *LACKLUSTER MINDS,* THE PRODUCT OF RECKLESS *INDIFFERENCE.*

ALL I TRIED TO DO WAS *BETTER* WHAT YOU HAD ALREADY *ABANDONED!*

THERE IS NO PRISON THAT CAN HOLD ME.

I AM *BALA!*

I WILL BE--

--FREE--

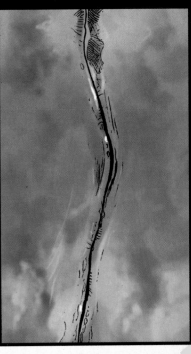

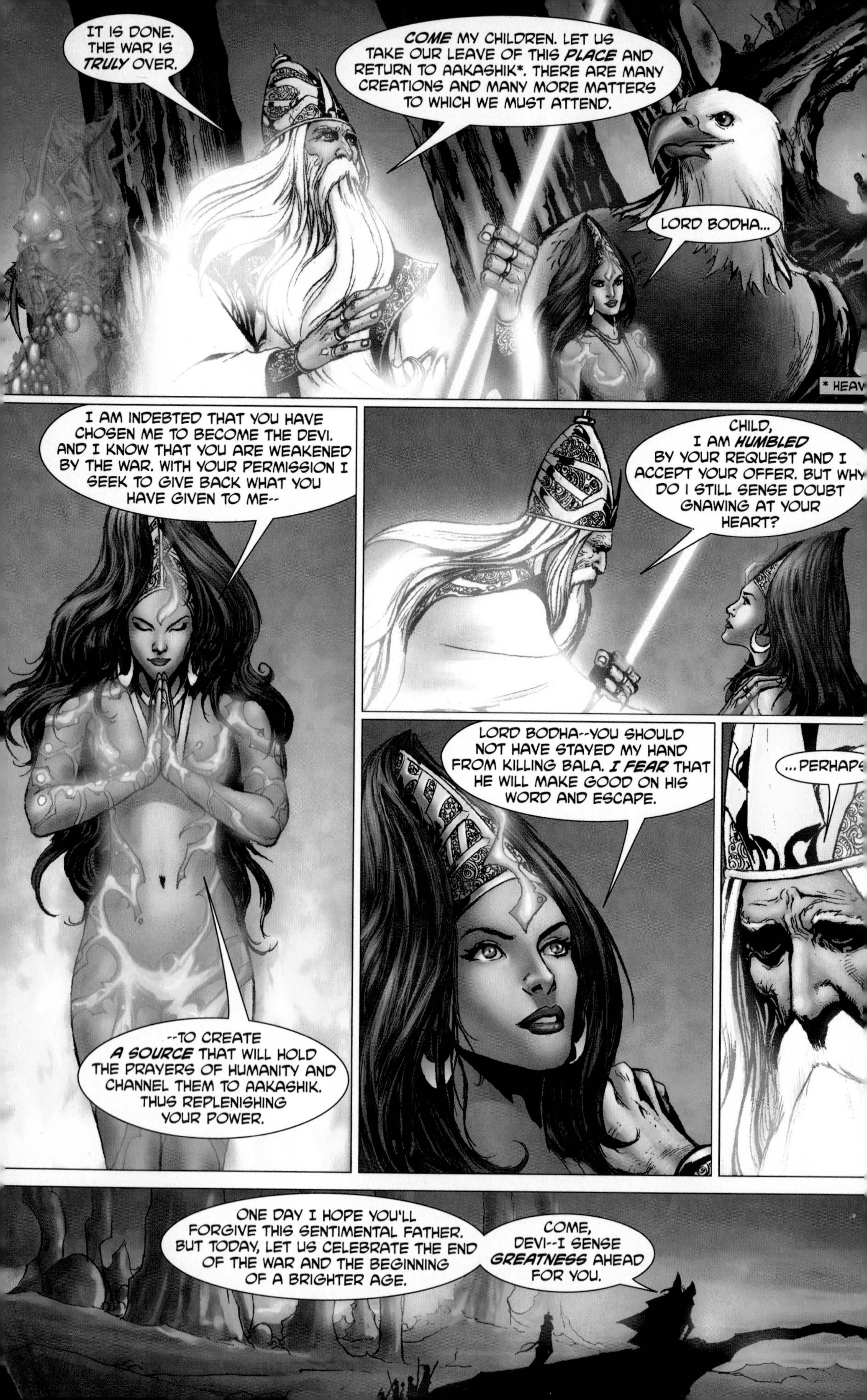
IT IS DONE. THE WAR IS TRULY OVER.
COME MY CHILDREN. LET US TAKE OUR LEAVE OF THIS PLACE AND RETURN TO AAKASHIK*. THERE ARE MANY CREATIONS AND MANY MORE MATTERS TO WHICH WE MUST ATTEND.
LORD BODHA...
* HEAV
I AM INDEBTED THAT YOU HAVE CHOSEN ME TO BECOME THE DEVI. AND I KNOW THAT YOU ARE WEAKENED BY THE WAR. WITH YOUR PERMISSION I SEEK TO GIVE BACK WHAT YOU HAVE GIVEN TO ME--
--TO CREATE A SOURCE THAT WILL HOLD THE PRAYERS OF HUMANITY AND CHANNEL THEM TO AAKASHIK. THUS REPLENISHING YOUR POWER.
CHILD, I AM HUMBLED BY YOUR REQUEST AND I ACCEPT YOUR OFFER. BUT WHY DO I STILL SENSE DOUBT GNAWING AT YOUR HEART?
LORD BODHA--YOU SHOULD NOT HAVE STAYED MY HAND FROM KILLING BALA. I FEAR THAT HE WILL MAKE GOOD ON HIS WORD AND ESCAPE.
...PERHAPS
ONE DAY I HOPE YOU'LL FORGIVE THIS SENTIMENTAL FATHER. BUT TODAY, LET US CELEBRATE THE END OF THE WAR AND THE BEGINNING OF A BRIGHTER AGE.
COME, DEVI--I SENSE GREATNESS AHEAD FOR YOU.

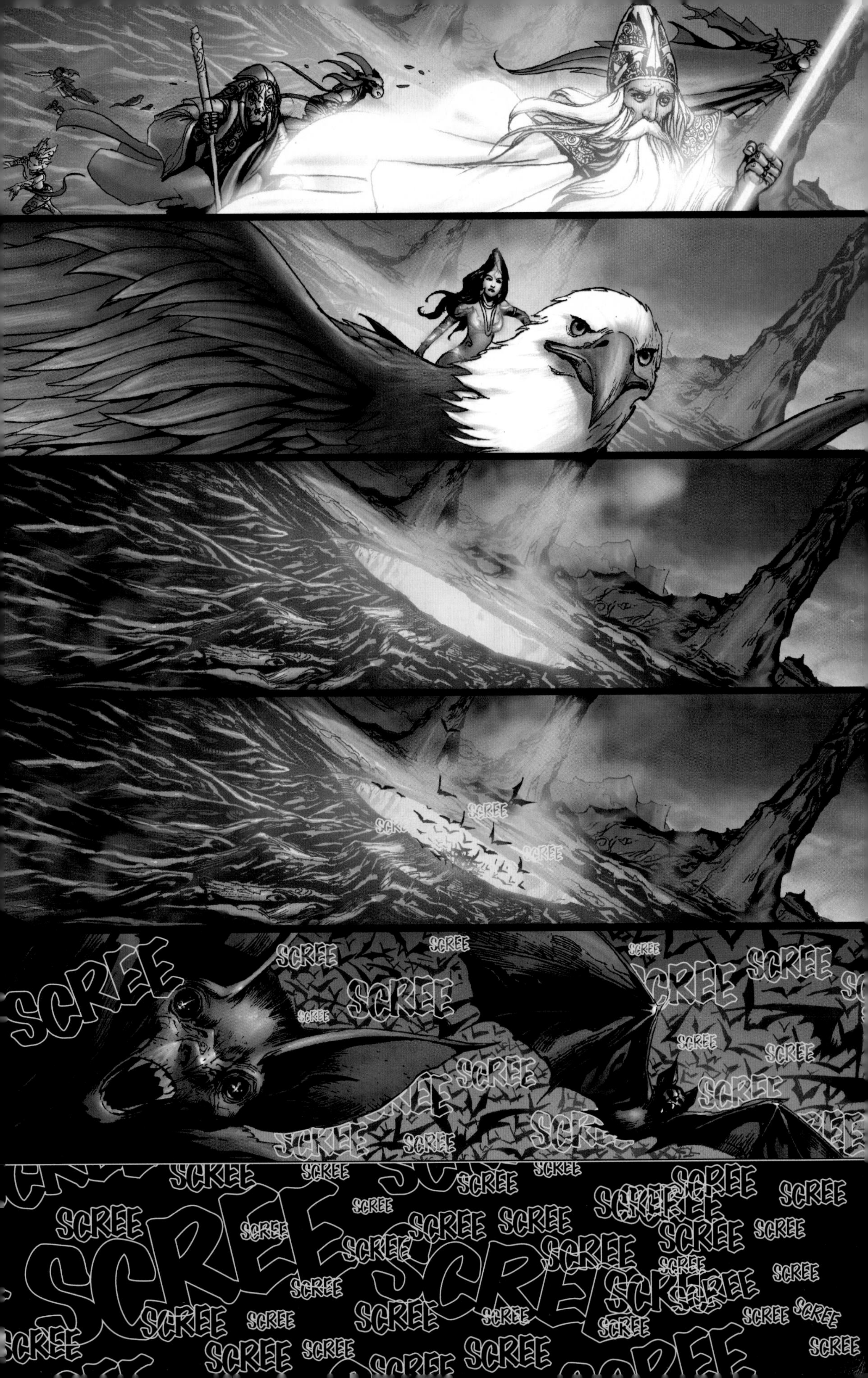
SCREE
SCREE
SCREE
SCREE
SCREE
SCREE
SCREE
SCREE
SCREE
SCREE
SCREE
SCREE
SCREE
SCREE
SCREE

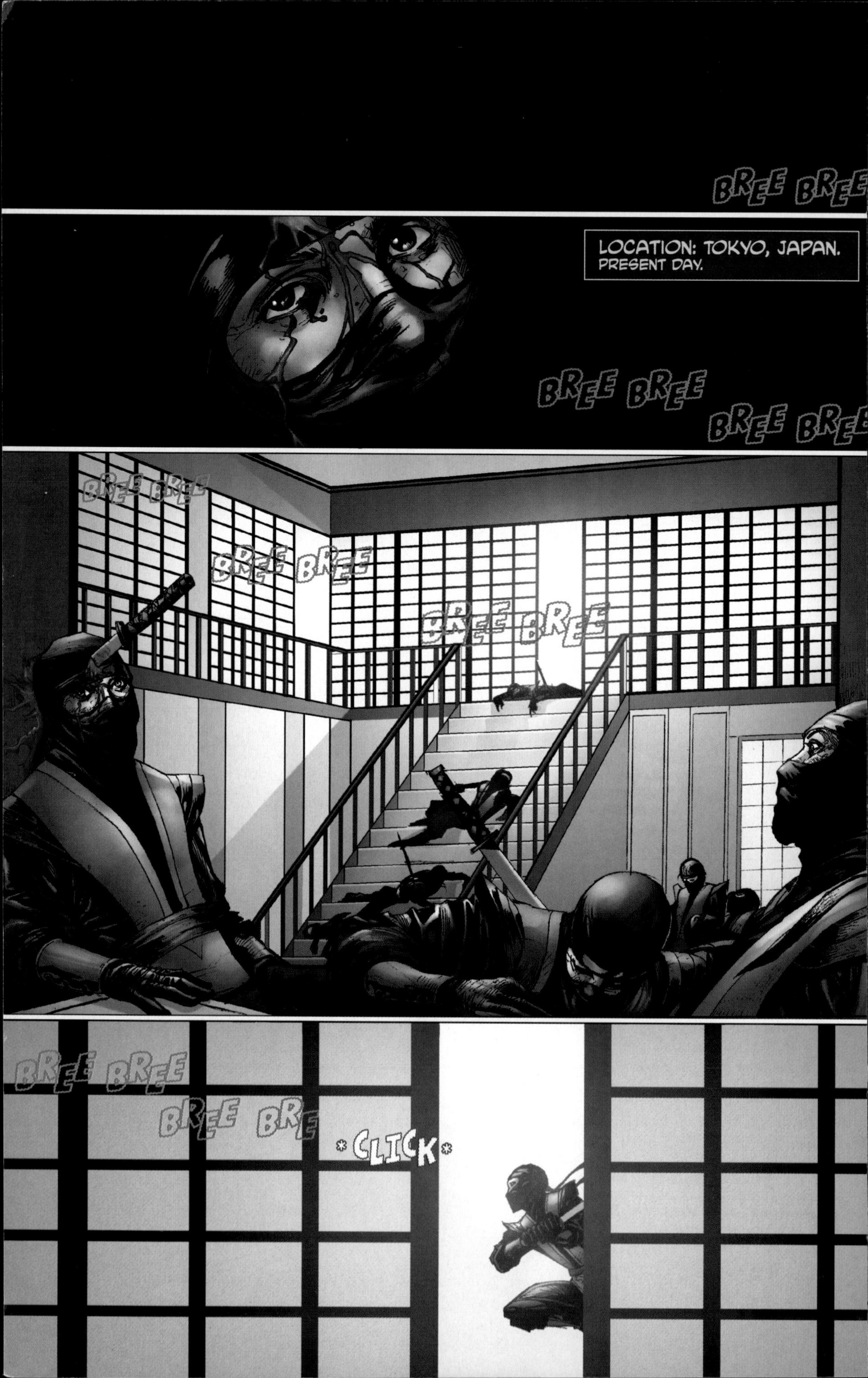
BREE BREE
LOCATION: TOKYO, JAPAN.
PRESENT DAY.
BREE BREE
BREE BREE
BREE BREE
BREE BREE
BREE BREE
BREE BREE
BREE BRE
CLICK

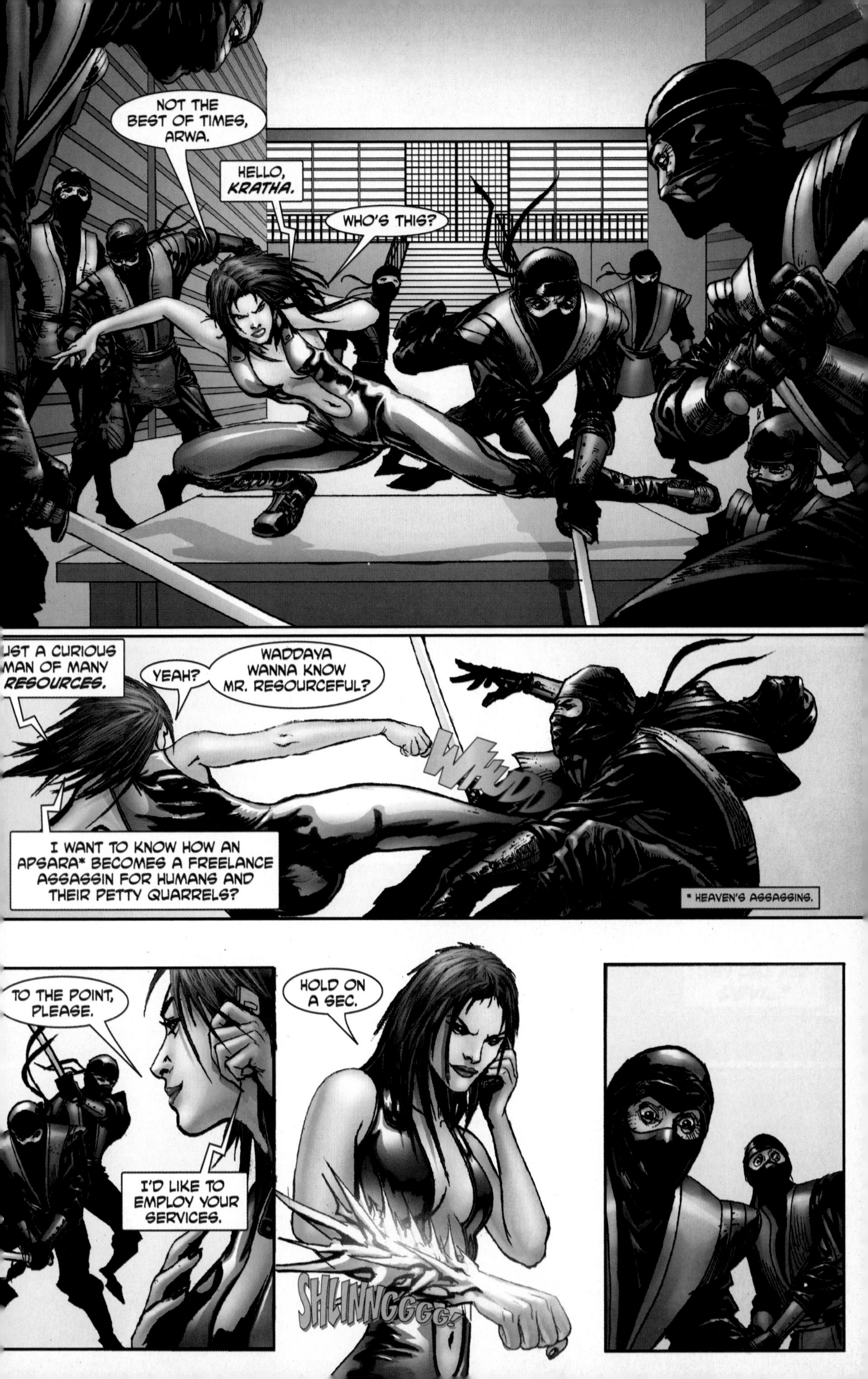
NOT THE BEST OF TIMES, ARWA.
HELLO, KRATHA.
WHO'S THIS?
UST A CURIOUS MAN OF MANY RESOURCES.
YEAH?
WADDAYA WANNA KNOW MR. RESOURCEFUL?
WHUD
I WANT TO KNOW HOW AN APSARA* BECOMES A FREELANCE ASSASSIN FOR HUMANS AND THEIR PETTY QUARRELS?
* HEAVEN'S ASSASSINS.
TO THE POINT, PLEASE.
I'D LIKE TO EMPLOY YOUR SERVICES.
HOLD ON A SEC.
SHLINNGGGG!

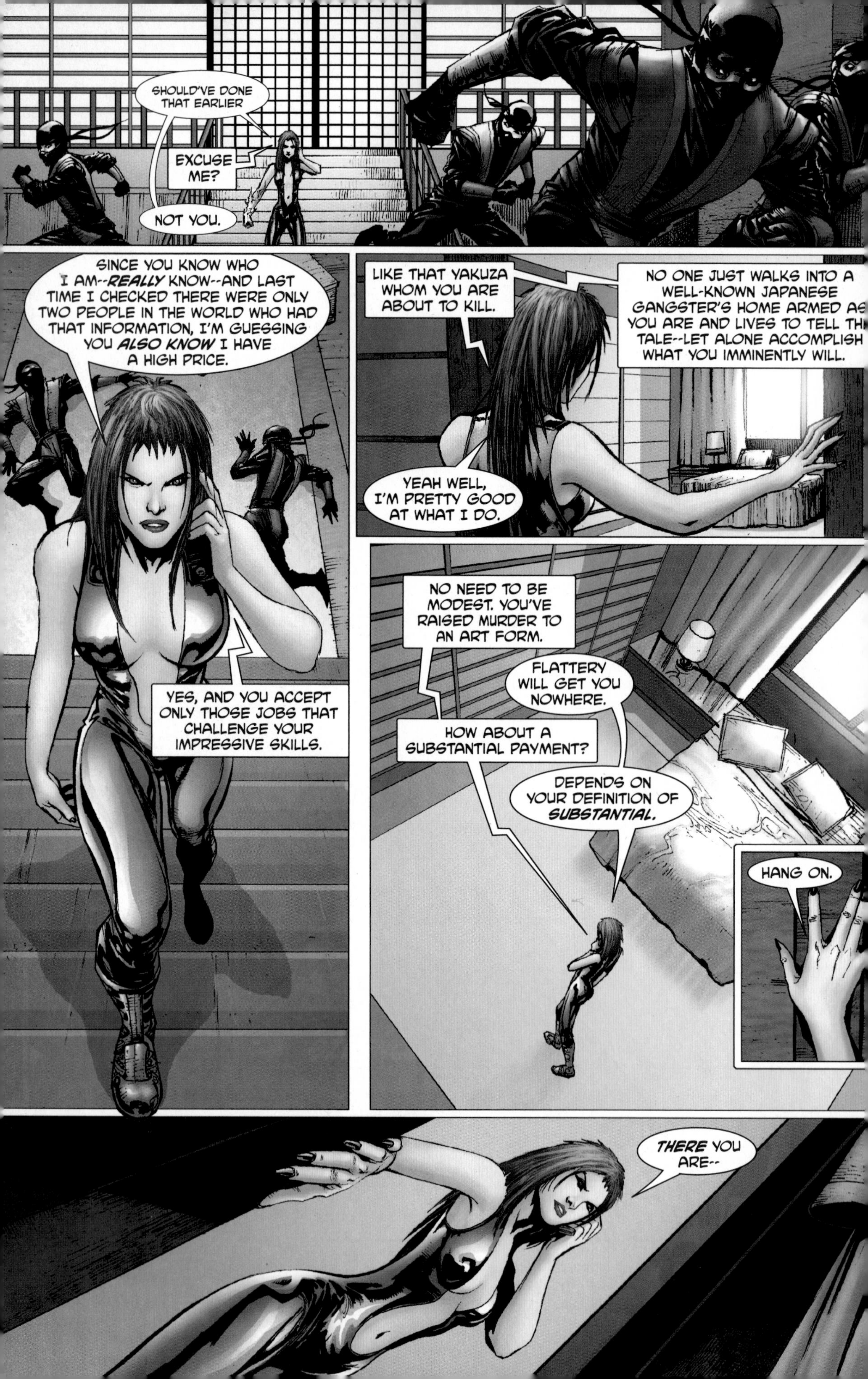
SHOULD'VE DONE THAT EARLIER
EXCUSE ME?
NOT YOU.
SINCE YOU KNOW WHO I AM--REALLY KNOW--AND LAST TIME I CHECKED THERE WERE ONLY TWO PEOPLE IN THE WORLD WHO HAD THAT INFORMATION, I'M GUESSING YOU ALSO KNOW I HAVE A HIGH PRICE.
YES, AND YOU ACCEPT ONLY THOSE JOBS THAT CHALLENGE YOUR IMPRESSIVE SKILLS.
LIKE THAT YAKUZA WHOM YOU ARE ABOUT TO KILL.
NO ONE JUST WALKS INTO A WELL-KNOWN JAPANESE GANGSTER'S HOME ARMED AS YOU ARE AND LIVES TO TELL THE TALE--LET ALONE ACCOMPLISH WHAT YOU IMMINENTLY WILL.
YEAH WELL, I'M PRETTY GOOD AT WHAT I DO.
NO NEED TO BE MODEST. YOU'VE RAISED MURDER TO AN ART FORM.
FLATTERY WILL GET YOU NOWHERE.
HOW ABOUT A SUBSTANTIAL PAYMENT?
DEPENDS ON YOUR DEFINITION OF SUBSTANTIAL.
HANG ON.
THERE YOU ARE--

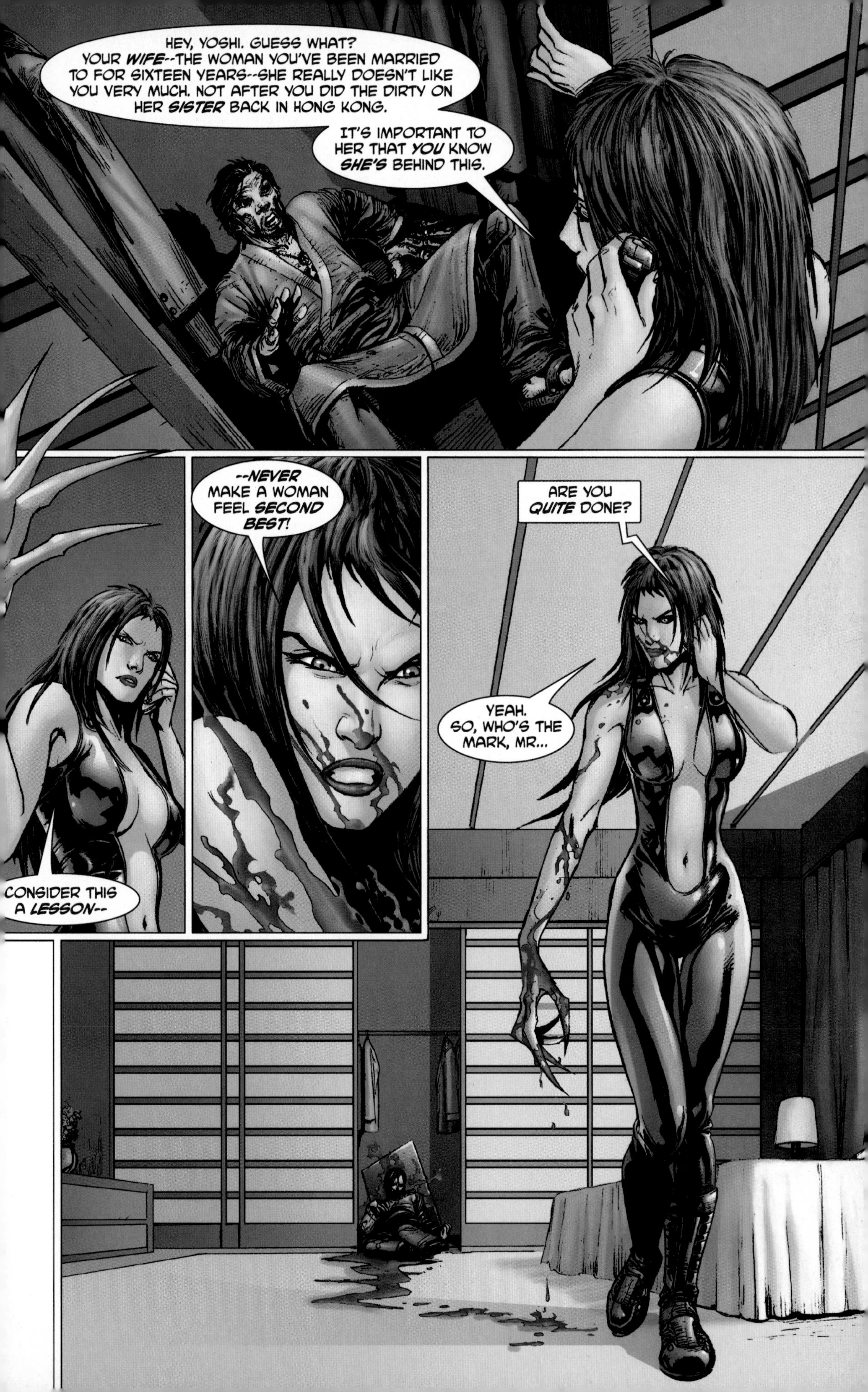
HEY, YOSHI. GUESS WHAT? YOUR WIFE--THE WOMAN YOU'VE BEEN MARRIED TO FOR SIXTEEN YEARS--SHE REALLY DOESN'T LIKE YOU VERY MUCH. NOT AFTER YOU DID THE DIRTY ON HER SISTER BACK IN HONG KONG.
IT'S IMPORTANT TO HER THAT YOU KNOW SHE'S BEHIND THIS.
CONSIDER THIS A LESSON--
--NEVER MAKE A WOMAN FEEL SECOND BEST!
ARE YOU QUITE DONE?
YEAH. SO, WHO'S THE MARK, MR...

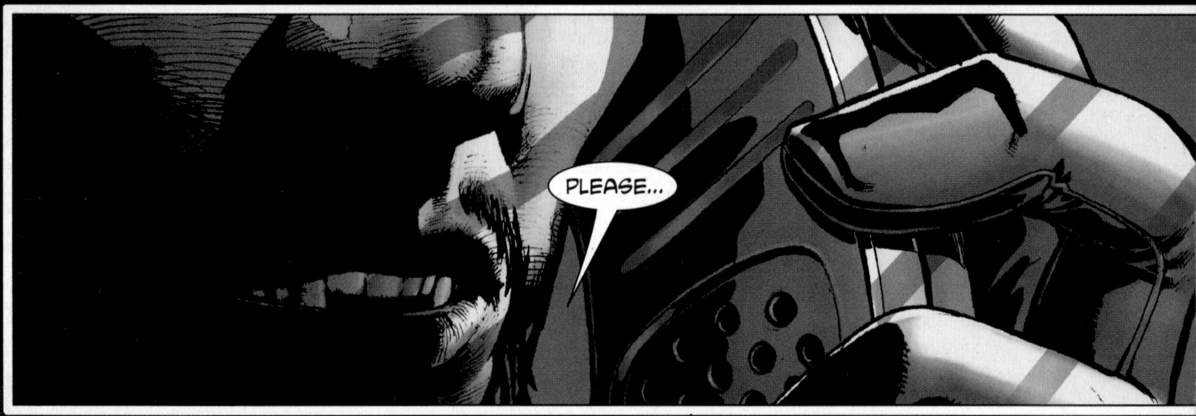
PLEASE...

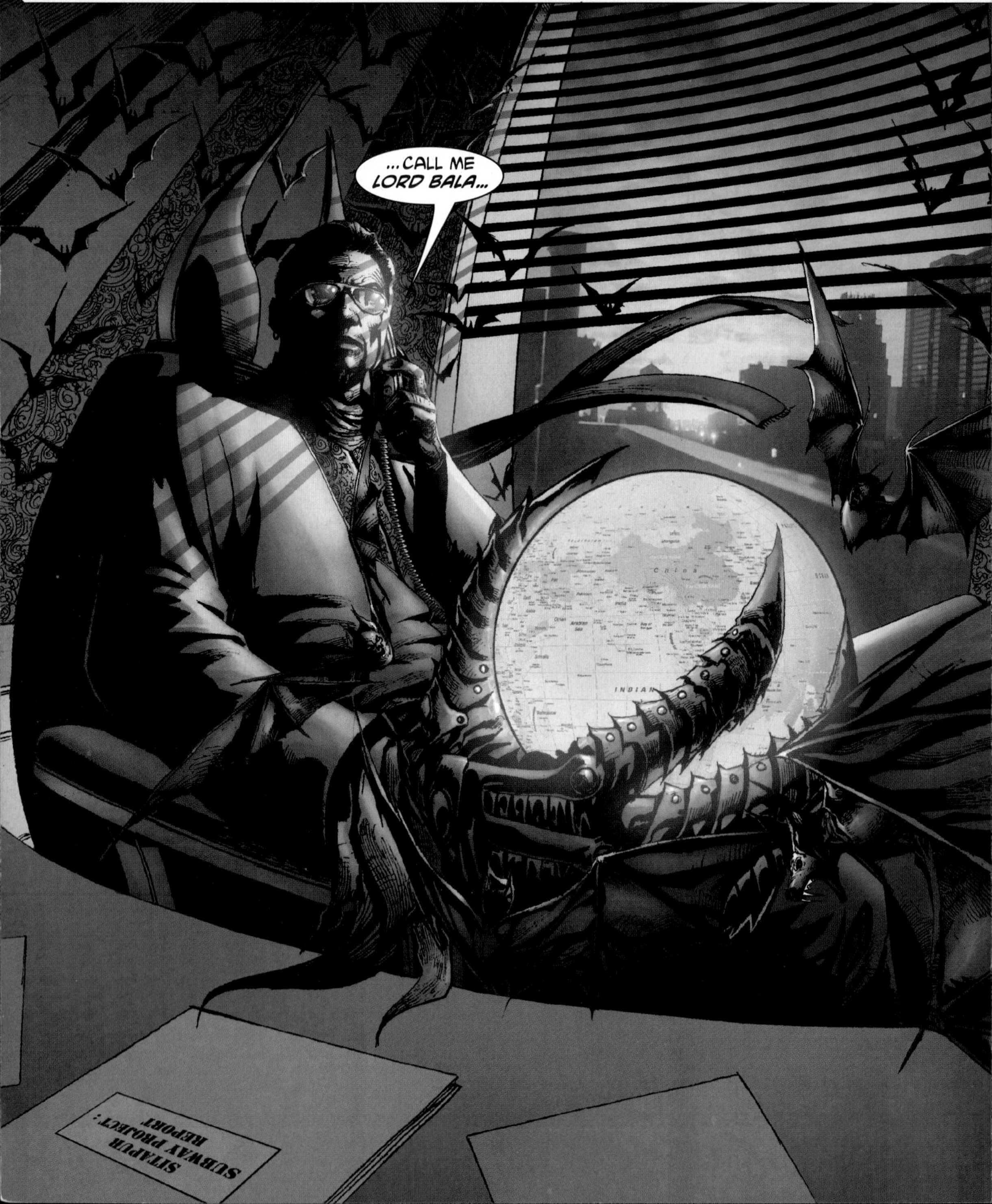
...CALL ME LORD BALA...
SITAPUR SUBWAY PROJECT: REPORT

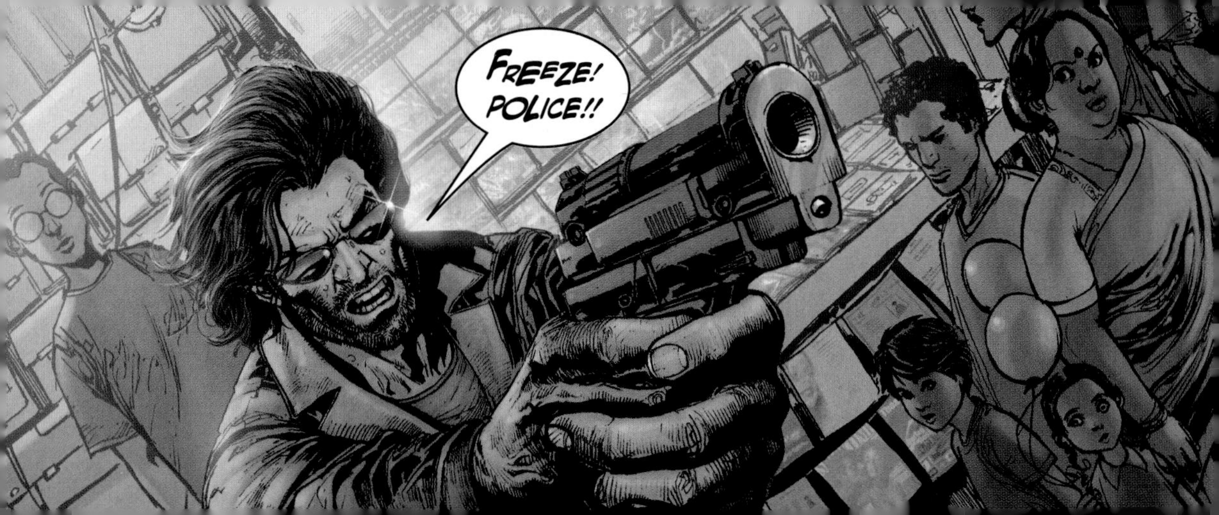
FREEZE! POLICE!!

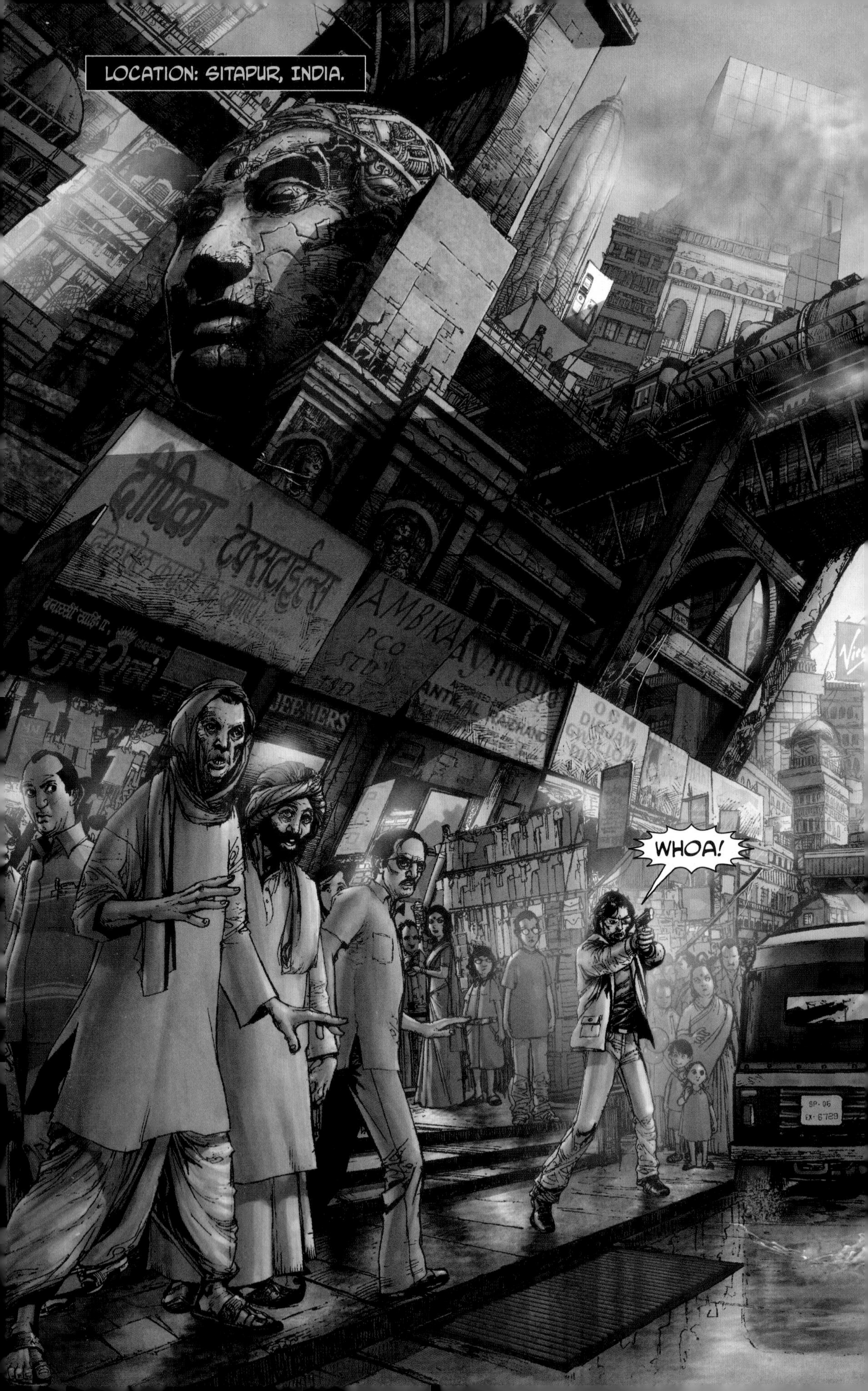
LOCATION: SITAPUR, INDIA.
WHOA!

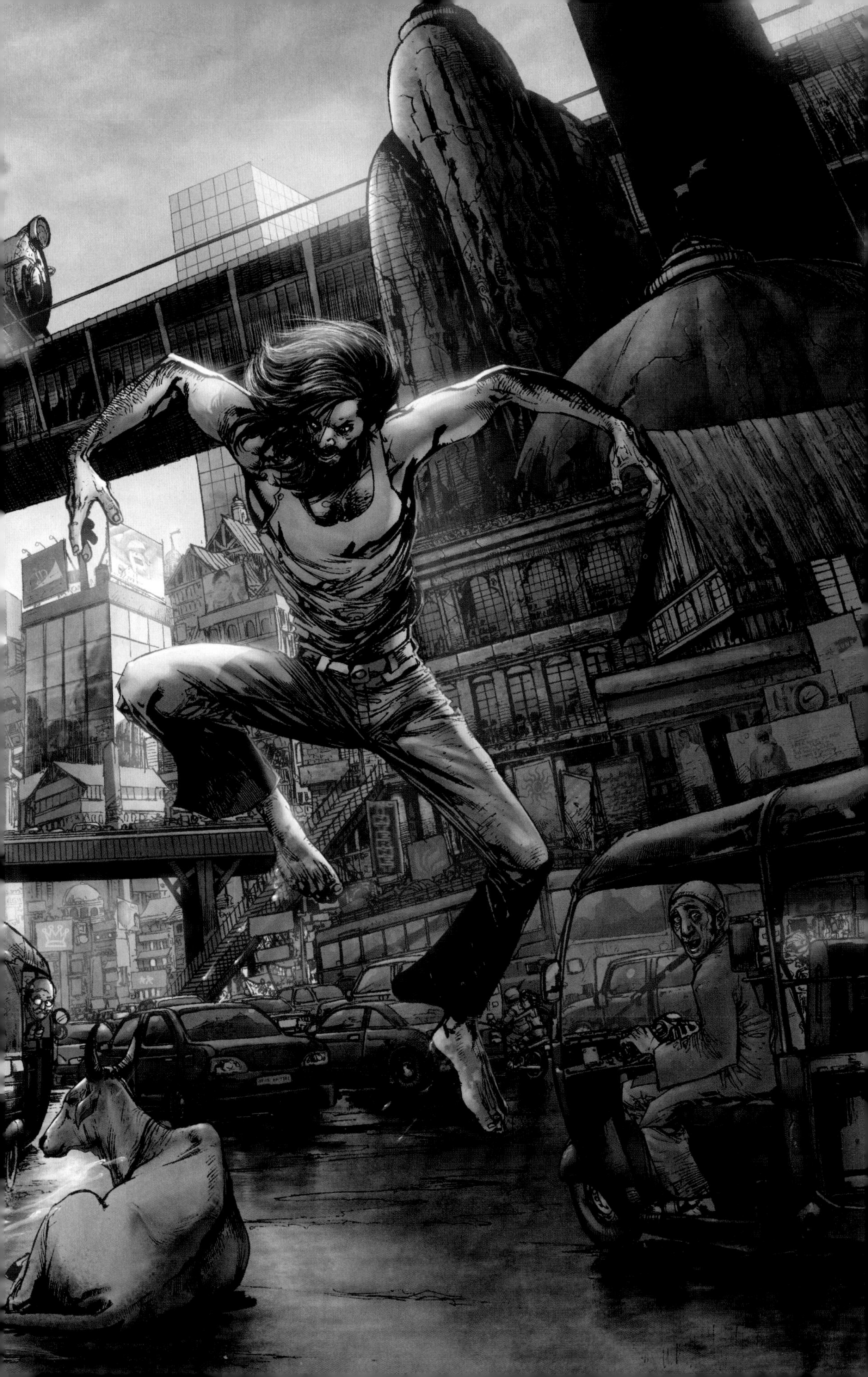

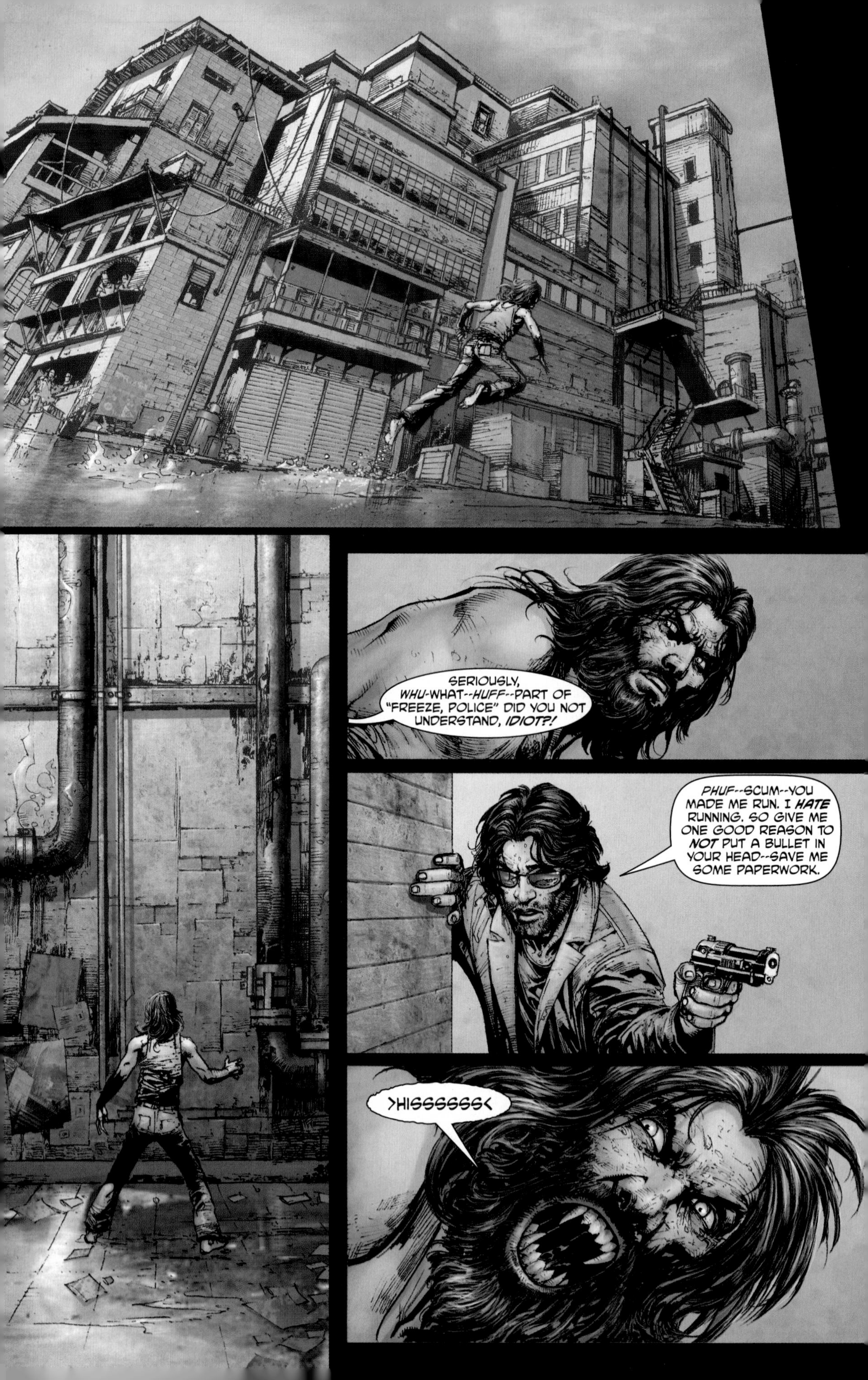
SERIOUSLY, WHU-WHAT--HUFF--PART OF "FREEZE, POLICE" DID YOU NOT UNDERSTAND, IDIOT?!
PHUF--SCUM--YOU MADE ME RUN. I HATE RUNNING. SO GIVE ME ONE GOOD REASON TO NOT PUT A BULLET IN YOUR HEAD--SAVE ME SOME PAPERWORK.
>HISSSSSS<

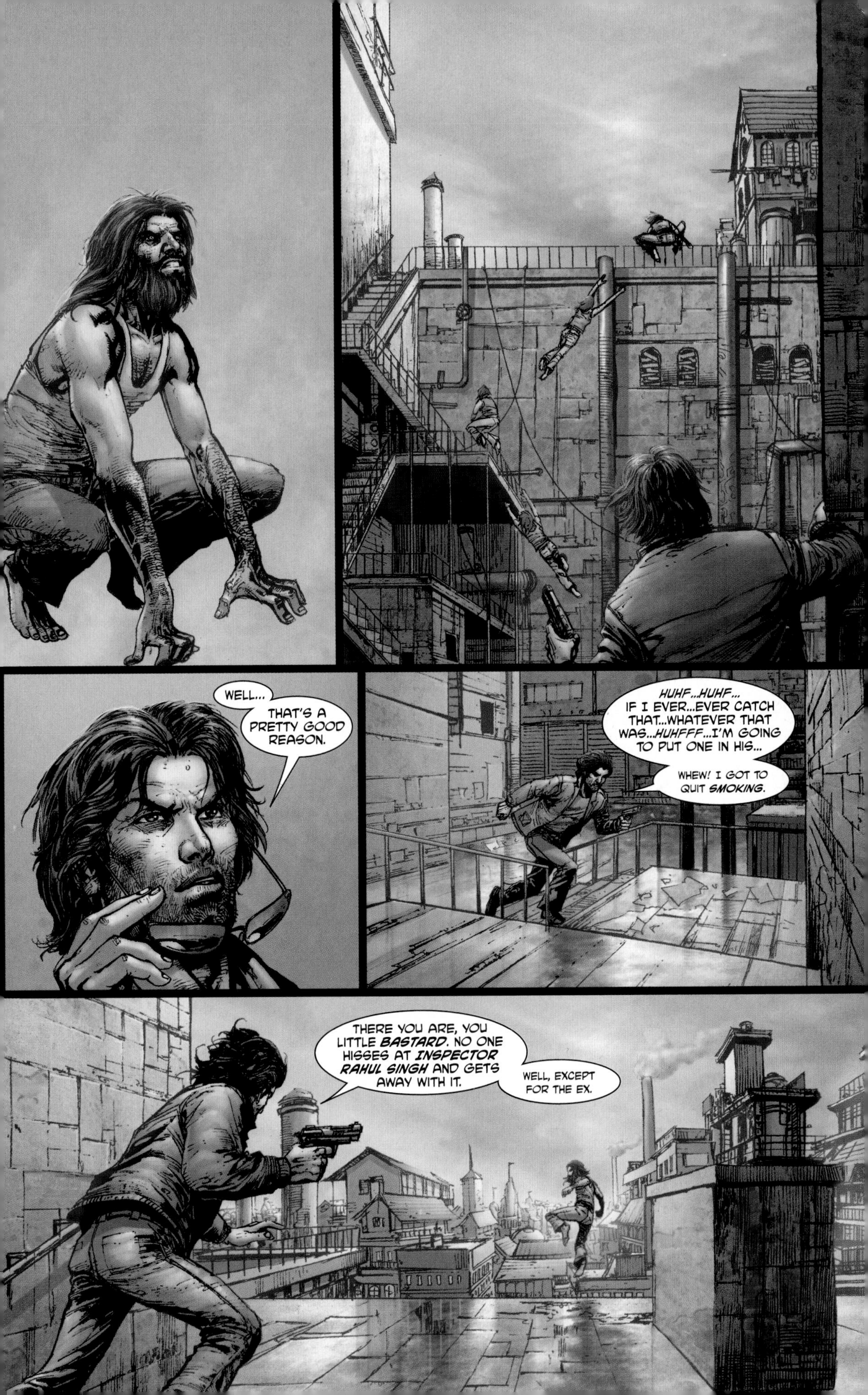
WELL... THAT'S A PRETTY GOOD REASON.
HUHF...HUHF... IF I EVER...EVER CATCH THAT...WHATEVER THAT WAS...HUHFFF...I'M GOING TO PUT ONE IN HIS...
WHEW! I GOT TO QUIT SMOKING.
THERE YOU ARE, YOU LITTLE BASTARD. NO ONE HISSES AT INSPECTOR RAHUL SINGH AND GETS AWAY WITH IT.
WELL, EXCEPT FOR THE EX.

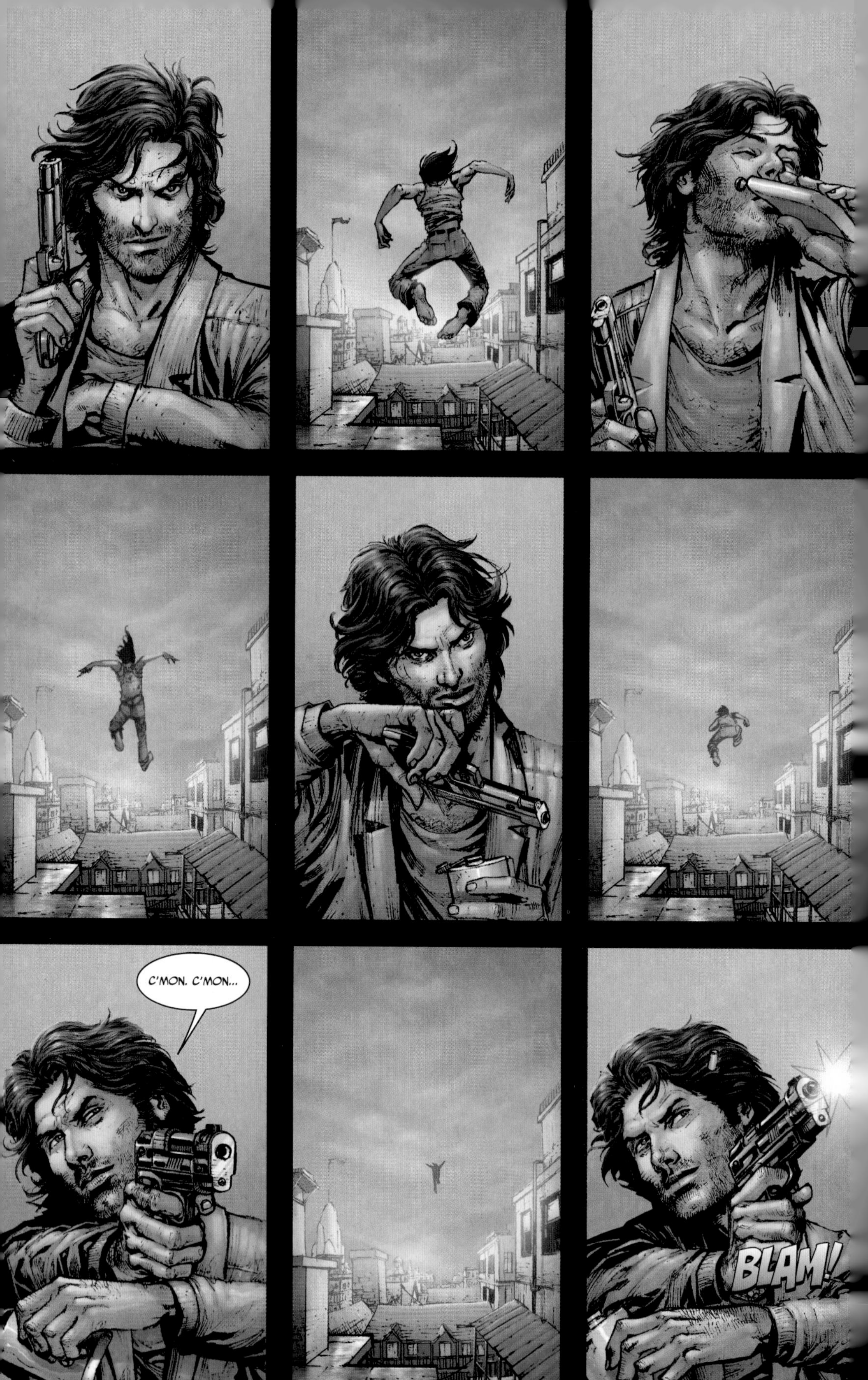
C'MON. C'MON...
BLAM!

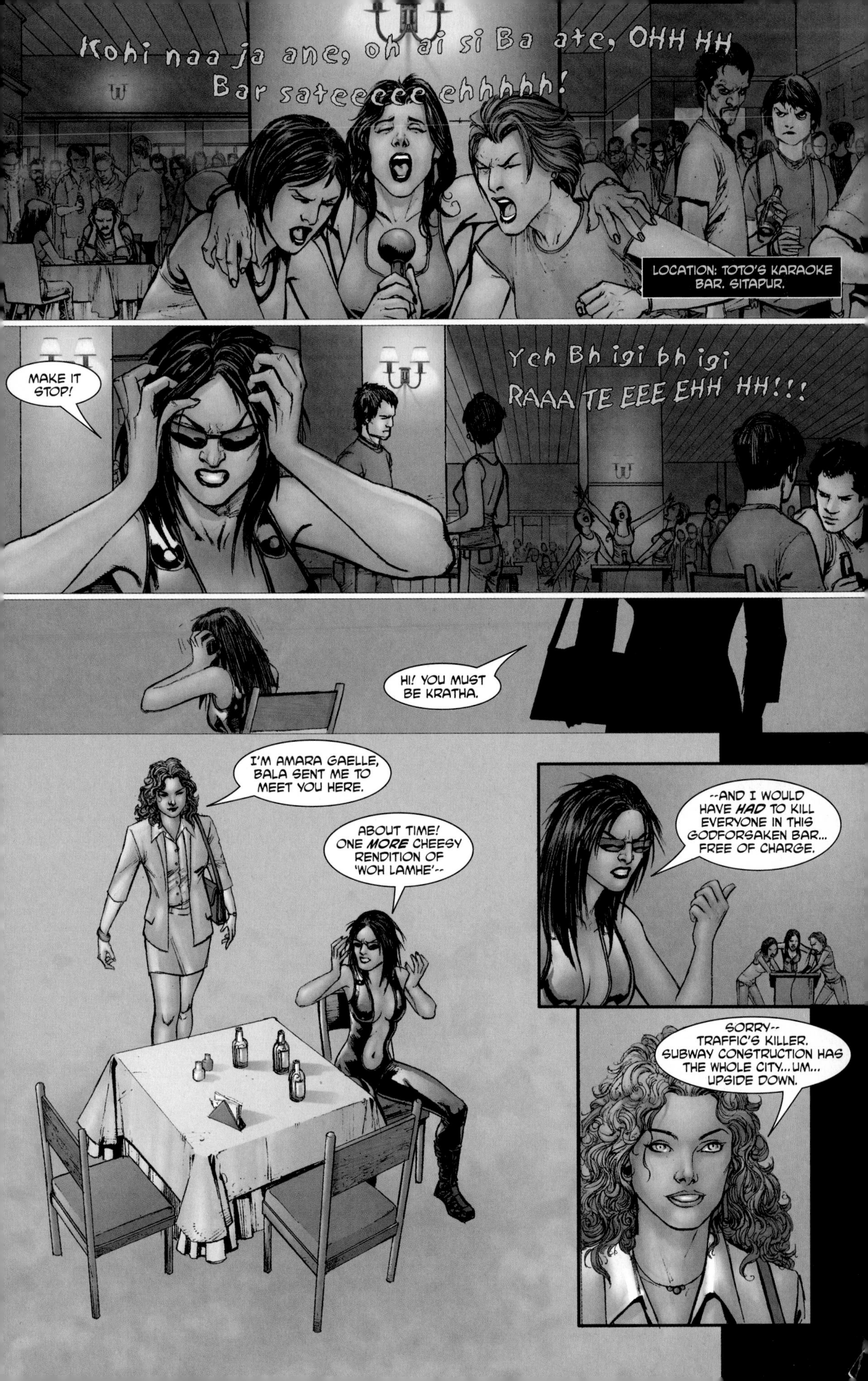
Kohi naa ja ane, oh ai si Ba ate, OHH HH
Bar sateeeeee ehhhhh!
LOCATION: TOTO'S KARAOKE BAR. SITAPUR.
MAKE IT STOP!
Yeh Bh igi bh igi
RAAA TE EEE EHH HH!!!
HI! YOU MUST BE KRATHA.
I'M AMARA GAELLE, BALA SENT ME TO MEET YOU HERE.
ABOUT TIME! ONE MORE CHEESY RENDITION OF 'WOH LAMHE'--
--AND I WOULD HAVE HAD TO KILL EVERYONE IN THIS GODFORSAKEN BAR... FREE OF CHARGE.
SORRY-- TRAFFIC'S KILLER. SUBWAY CONSTRUCTION HAS THE WHOLE CITY...UM... UPSIDE DOWN.

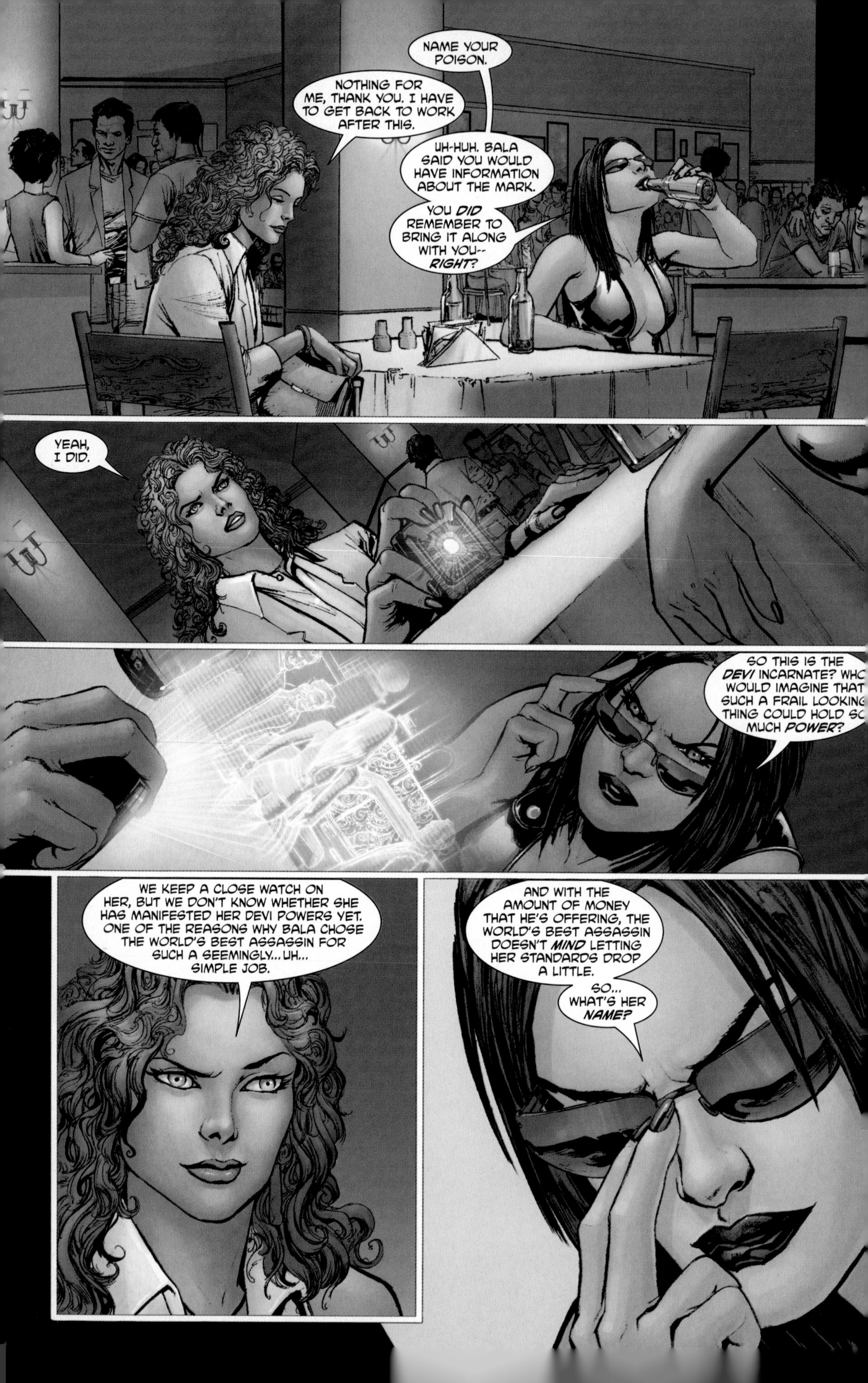
NAME YOUR POISON.
NOTHING FOR ME, THANK YOU. I HAVE TO GET BACK TO WORK AFTER THIS.
UH-HUH. BALA SAID YOU WOULD HAVE INFORMATION ABOUT THE MARK.
YOU DID REMEMBER TO BRING IT ALONG WITH YOU-- RIGHT?
YEAH, I DID.
SO THIS IS THE DEVI INCARNATE? WHO WOULD IMAGINE THAT SUCH A FRAIL LOOKING THING COULD HOLD SO MUCH POWER?
WE KEEP A CLOSE WATCH ON HER, BUT WE DON'T KNOW WHETHER SHE HAS MANIFESTED HER DEVI POWERS YET. ONE OF THE REASONS WHY BALA CHOSE THE WORLD'S BEST ASSASSIN FOR SUCH A SEEMINGLY... UH... SIMPLE JOB.
AND WITH THE AMOUNT OF MONEY THAT HE'S OFFERING, THE WORLD'S BEST ASSASSIN DOESN'T MIND LETTING HER STANDARDS DROP A LITTLE.
SO... WHAT'S HER NAME?

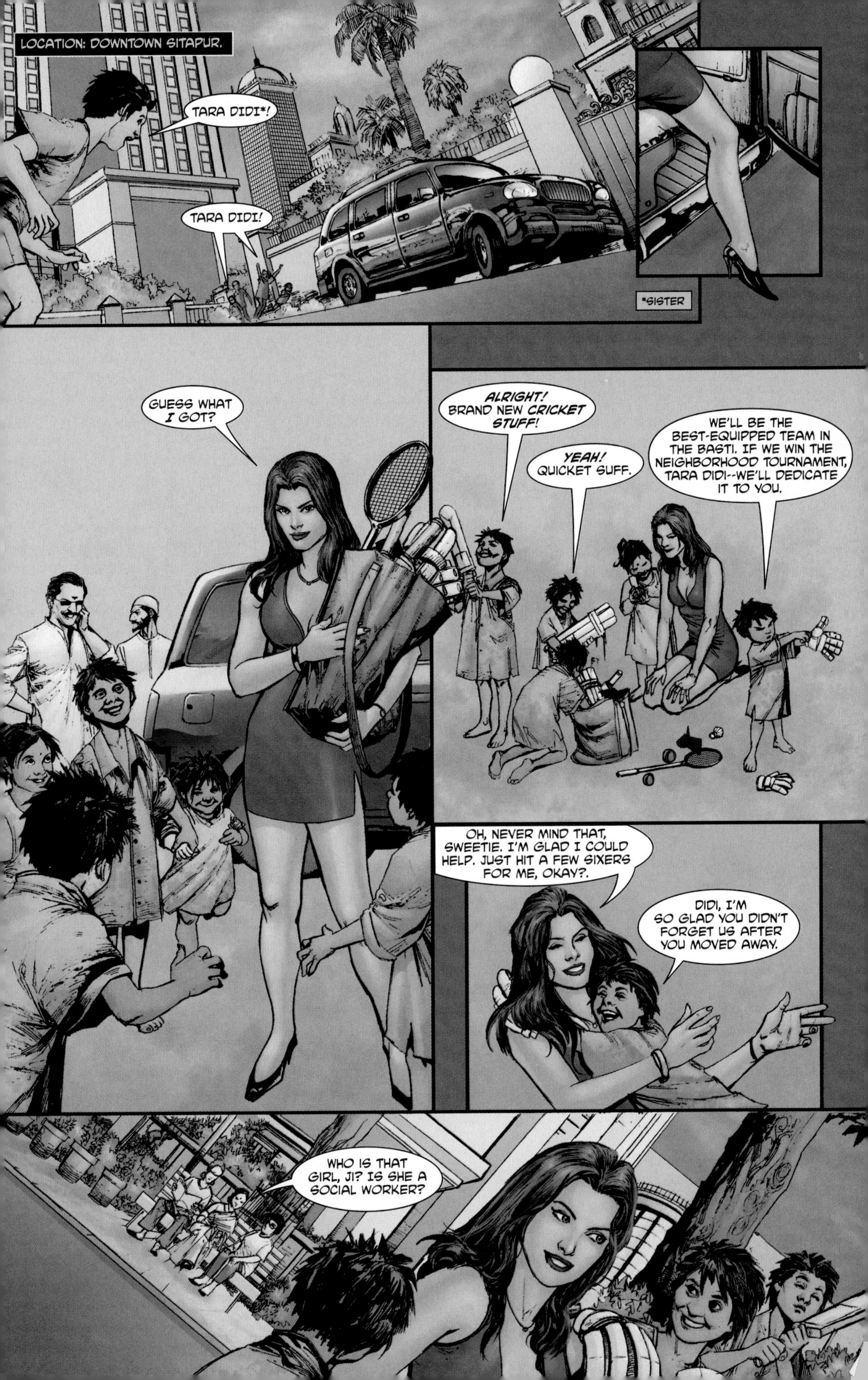
LOCATION: DOWNTOWN SITAPUR.
TARA DIDI*!
TARA DIDI!
*SISTER
GUESS WHAT I GOT?
ALRIGHT! BRAND NEW CRICKET STUFF!
YEAH! QUICKET SUFF.
WE'LL BE THE BEST-EQUIPPED TEAM IN THE BASTI. IF WE WIN THE NEIGHBORHOOD TOURNAMENT, TARA DIDI--WE'LL DEDICATE IT TO YOU.
OH, NEVER MIND THAT, SWEETIE. I'M GLAD I COULD HELP. JUST HIT A FEW SIXERS FOR ME, OKAY?.
DIDI, I'M SO GLAD YOU DIDN'T FORGET US AFTER YOU MOVED AWAY.
WHO IS THAT GIRL, JI? IS SHE A SOCIAL WORKER?

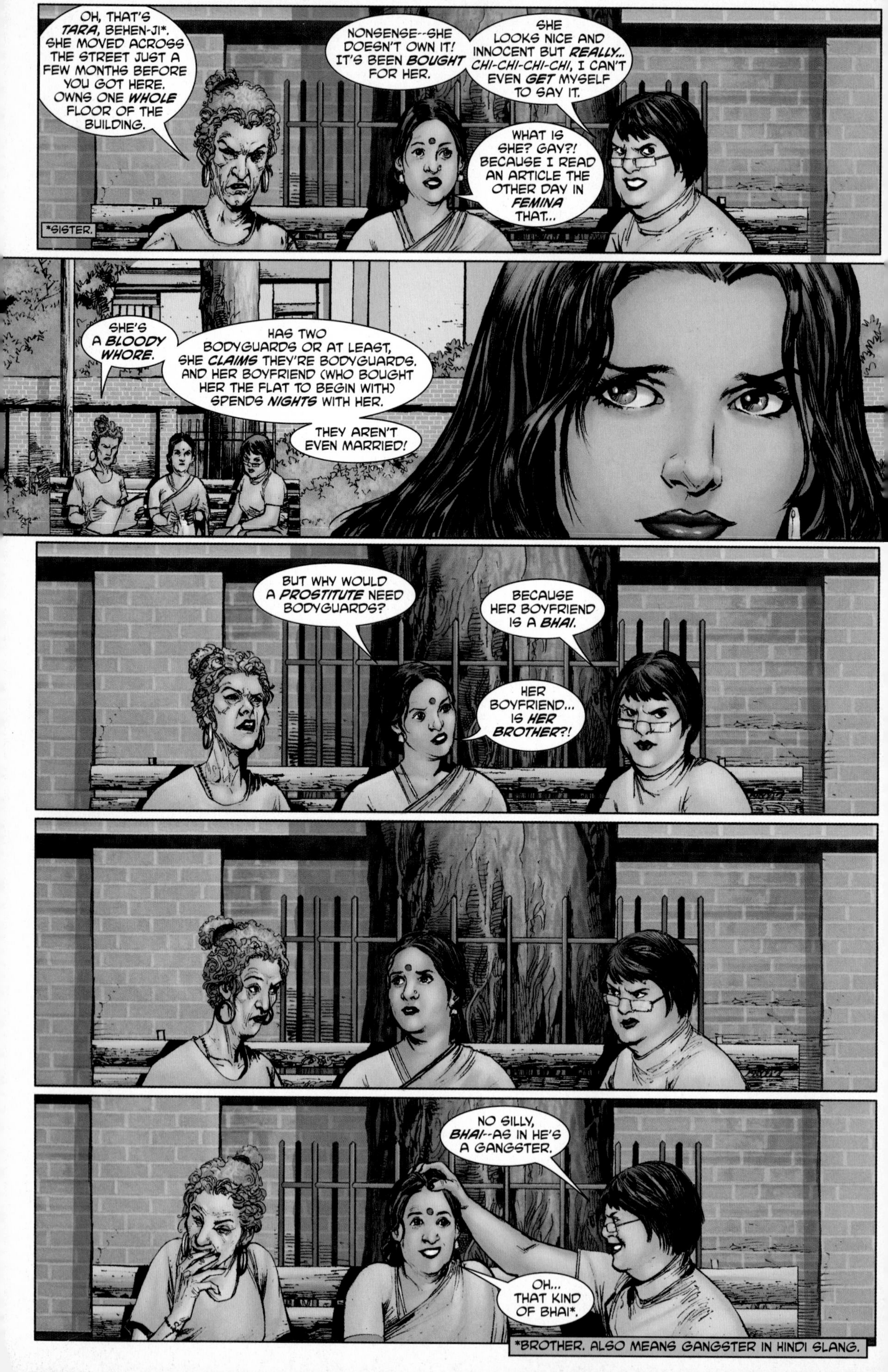
OH, THAT'S TARA, BEHEN-JI*. SHE MOVED ACROSS THE STREET JUST A FEW MONTHS BEFORE YOU GOT HERE. OWNS ONE WHOLE FLOOR OF THE BUILDING.
NONSENSE--SHE DOESN'T OWN IT! IT'S BEEN BOUGHT FOR HER.
SHE LOOKS NICE AND INNOCENT BUT REALLY... CHI-CHI-CHI-CHI, I CAN'T EVEN GET MYSELF TO SAY IT.
WHAT IS SHE? GAY?! BECAUSE I READ AN ARTICLE THE OTHER DAY IN FEMINA THAT...
*SISTER.
SHE'S A BLOODY WHORE.
HAS TWO BODYGUARDS OR AT LEAST, SHE CLAIMS THEY'RE BODYGUARDS. AND HER BOYFRIEND (WHO BOUGHT HER THE FLAT TO BEGIN WITH) SPENDS NIGHTS WITH HER.
THEY AREN'T EVEN MARRIED!
BUT WHY WOULD A PROSTITUTE NEED BODYGUARDS?
BECAUSE HER BOYFRIEND IS A BHAI.
HER BOYFRIEND... IS HER BROTHER?!
NO SILLY, BHAI--AS IN HE'S A GANGSTER.
OH... THAT KIND OF BHAI*.
*BROTHER. ALSO MEANS GANGSTER IN HINDI SLANG.

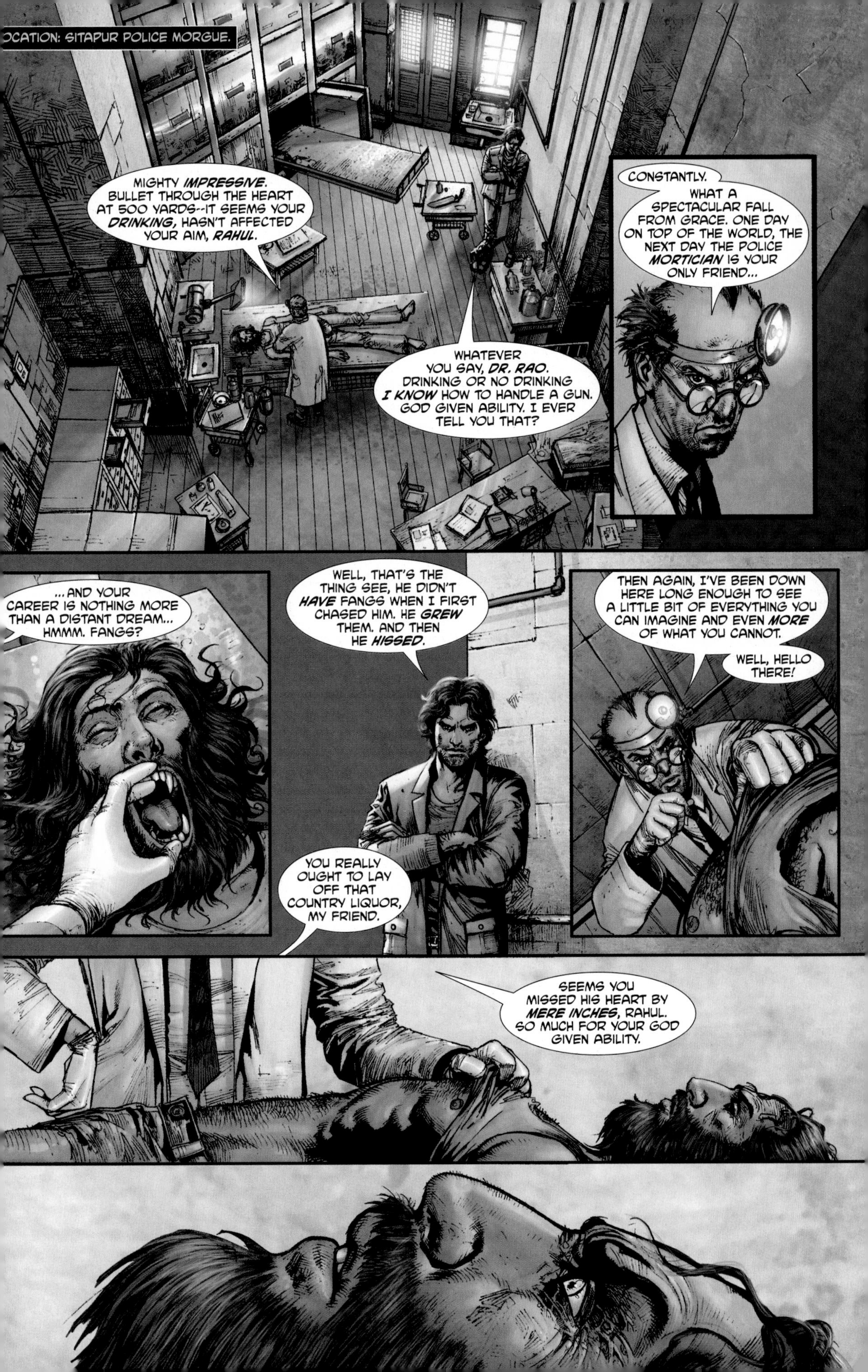
OCATION: SITAPUR POLICE MORGUE.
MIGHTY IMPRESSIVE. BULLET THROUGH THE HEART AT 500 YARDS--IT SEEMS YOUR DRINKING, HASN'T AFFECTED YOUR AIM, RAHUL.
WHATEVER YOU SAY, DR. RAO. DRINKING OR NO DRINKING I KNOW HOW TO HANDLE A GUN. GOD GIVEN ABILITY. I EVER TELL YOU THAT?
CONSTANTLY.
WHAT A SPECTACULAR FALL FROM GRACE. ONE DAY ON TOP OF THE WORLD, THE NEXT DAY THE POLICE MORTICIAN IS YOUR ONLY FRIEND...
...AND YOUR CAREER IS NOTHING MORE THAN A DISTANT DREAM... HMMM. FANGS?
WELL, THAT'S THE THING SEE, HE DIDN'T HAVE FANGS WHEN I FIRST CHASED HIM. HE GREW THEM. AND THEN HE HISSED.
YOU REALLY OUGHT TO LAY OFF THAT COUNTRY LIQUOR, MY FRIEND.
THEN AGAIN, I'VE BEEN DOWN HERE LONG ENOUGH TO SEE A LITTLE BIT OF EVERYTHING YOU CAN IMAGINE AND EVEN MORE OF WHAT YOU CANNOT.
WELL, HELLO THERE!
SEEMS YOU MISSED HIS HEART BY MERE INCHES, RAHUL. SO MUCH FOR YOUR GOD GIVEN ABILITY.

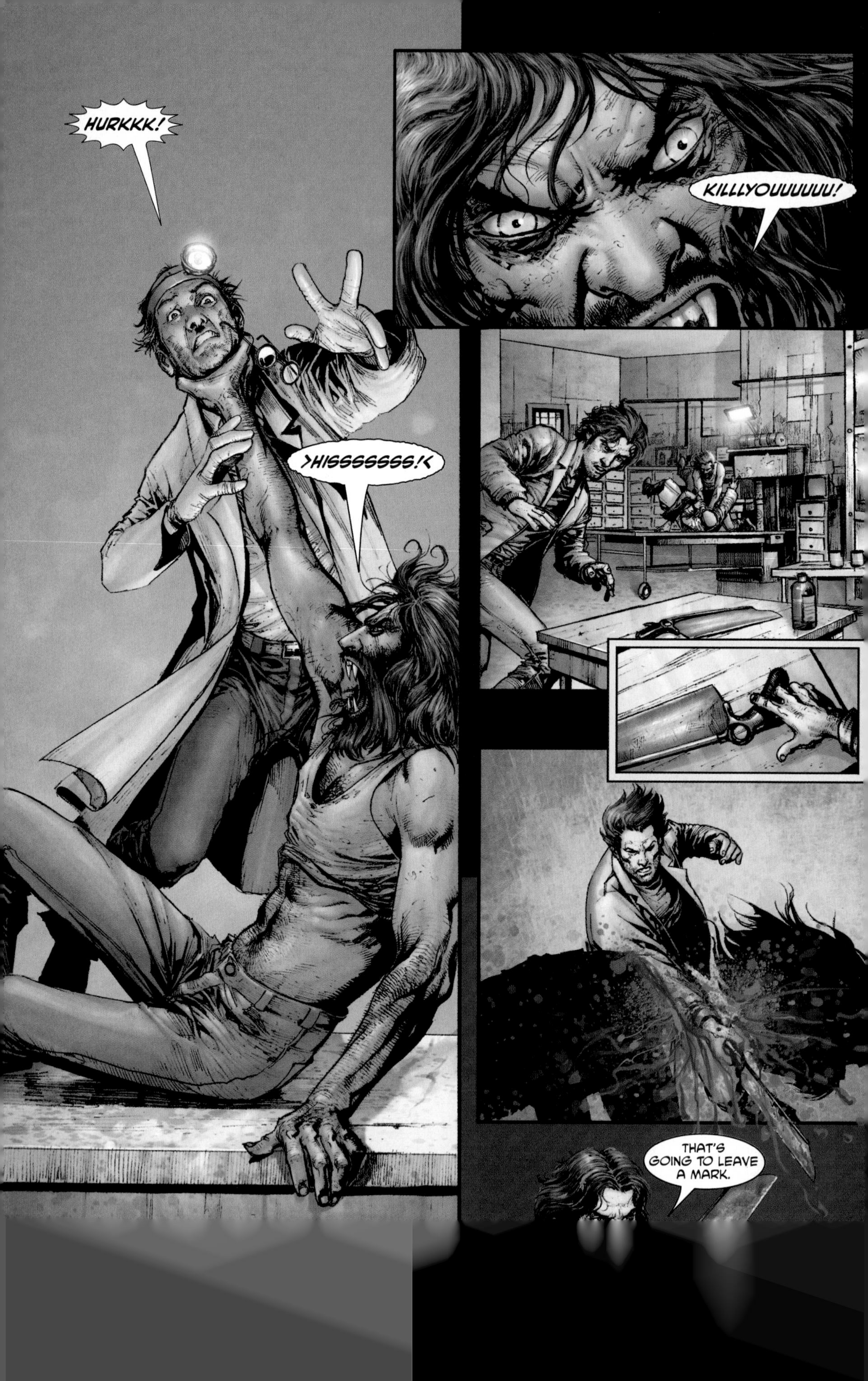
HURKKK!
KILLLYOUUUUUU!
>HISSSSSSS!<
THAT'S GOING TO LEAVE A MARK.

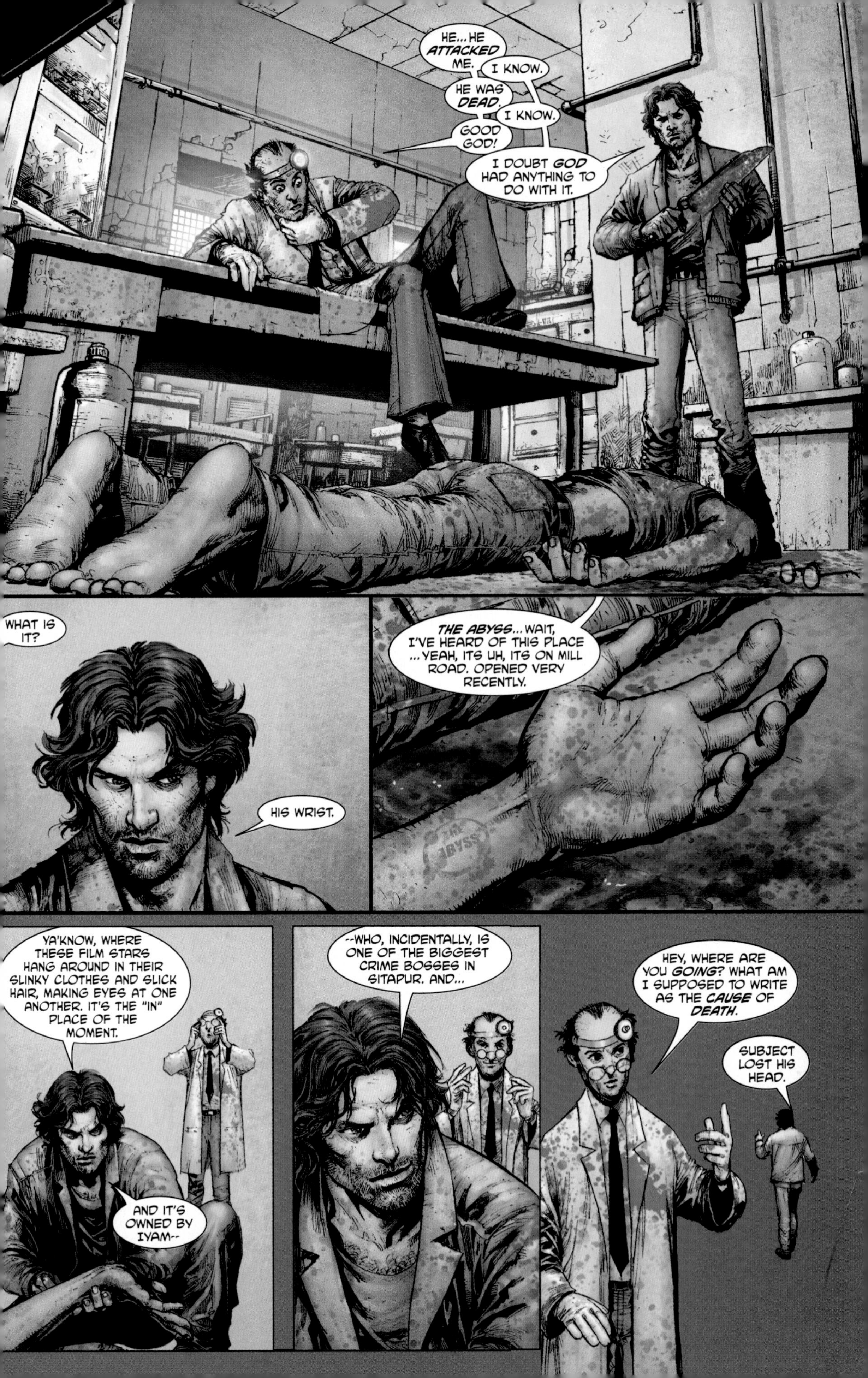
HE... HE ATTACKED ME.
I KNOW.
HE WAS DEAD.
I KNOW.
GOOD GOD!
I DOUBT GOD HAD ANYTHING TO DO WITH IT.
WHAT IS IT?
HIS WRIST.
THE ABYSS
THE ABYSS... WAIT, I'VE HEARD OF THIS PLACE ...YEAH, ITS UH, ITS ON MILL ROAD. OPENED VERY RECENTLY.
YA'KNOW, WHERE THESE FILM STARS HANG AROUND IN THEIR SLINKY CLOTHES AND SLICK HAIR, MAKING EYES AT ONE ANOTHER. IT'S THE "IN" PLACE OF THE MOMENT.
AND IT'S OWNED BY IYAM--
--WHO, INCIDENTALLY, IS ONE OF THE BIGGEST CRIME BOSSES IN SITAPUR. AND...
HEY, WHERE ARE YOU GOING? WHAT AM I SUPPOSED TO WRITE AS THE CAUSE OF DEATH.
SUBJECT LOST HIS HEAD.

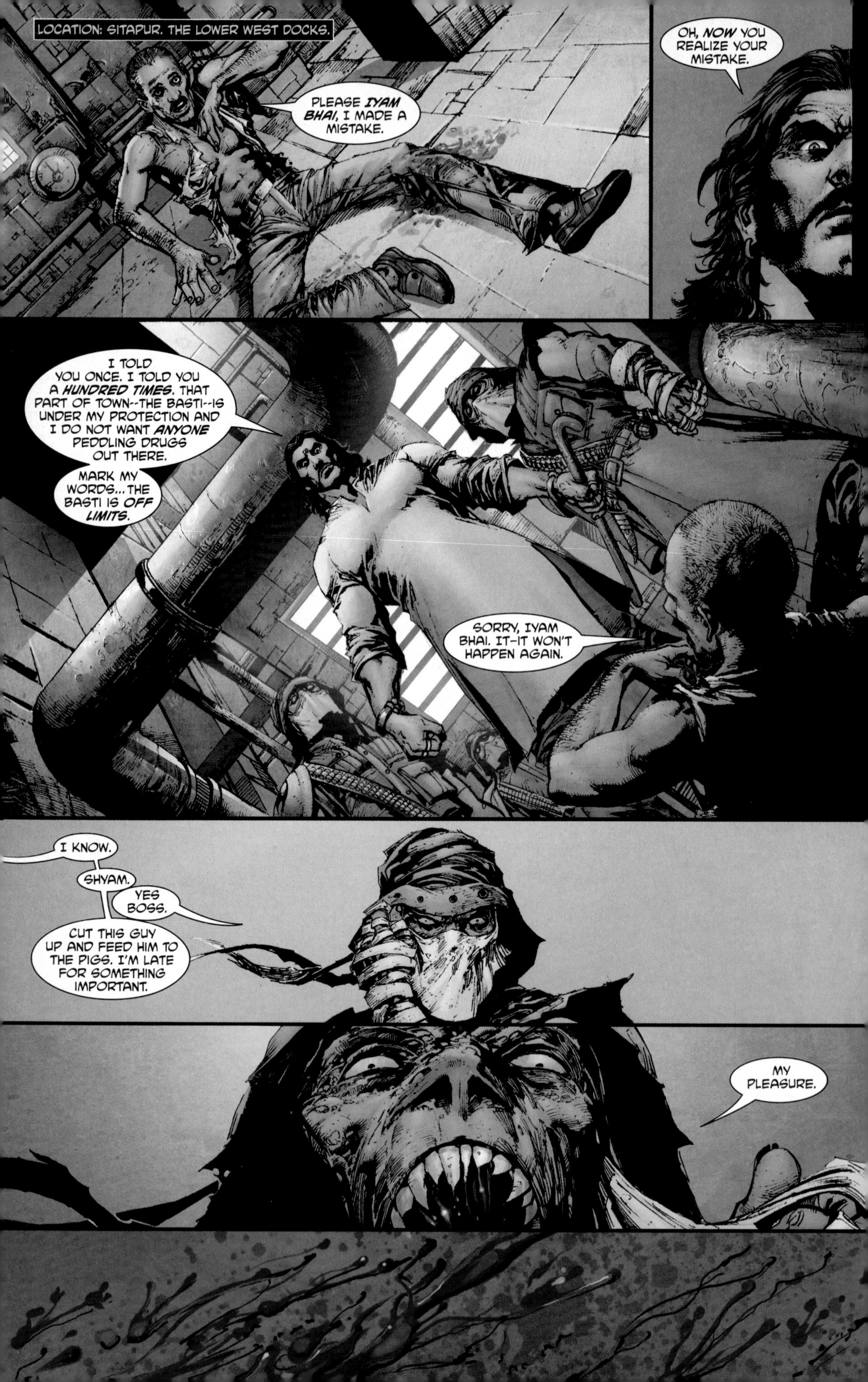
LOCATION: SITAPUR. THE LOWER WEST DOCKS.
PLEASE IYAM BHAI, I MADE A MISTAKE.
OH, NOW YOU REALIZE YOUR MISTAKE.
I TOLD YOU ONCE. I TOLD YOU A HUNDRED TIMES. THAT PART OF TOWN--THE BASTI--IS UNDER MY PROTECTION AND I DO NOT WANT ANYONE PEDDLING DRUGS OUT THERE.
MARK MY WORDS... THE BASTI IS OFF LIMITS.
SORRY, IYAM BHAI. IT-IT WON'T HAPPEN AGAIN.
I KNOW.
SHYAM.
YES BOSS.
CUT THIS GUY UP AND FEED HIM TO THE PIGS. I'M LATE FOR SOMETHING IMPORTANT.
MY PLEASURE.

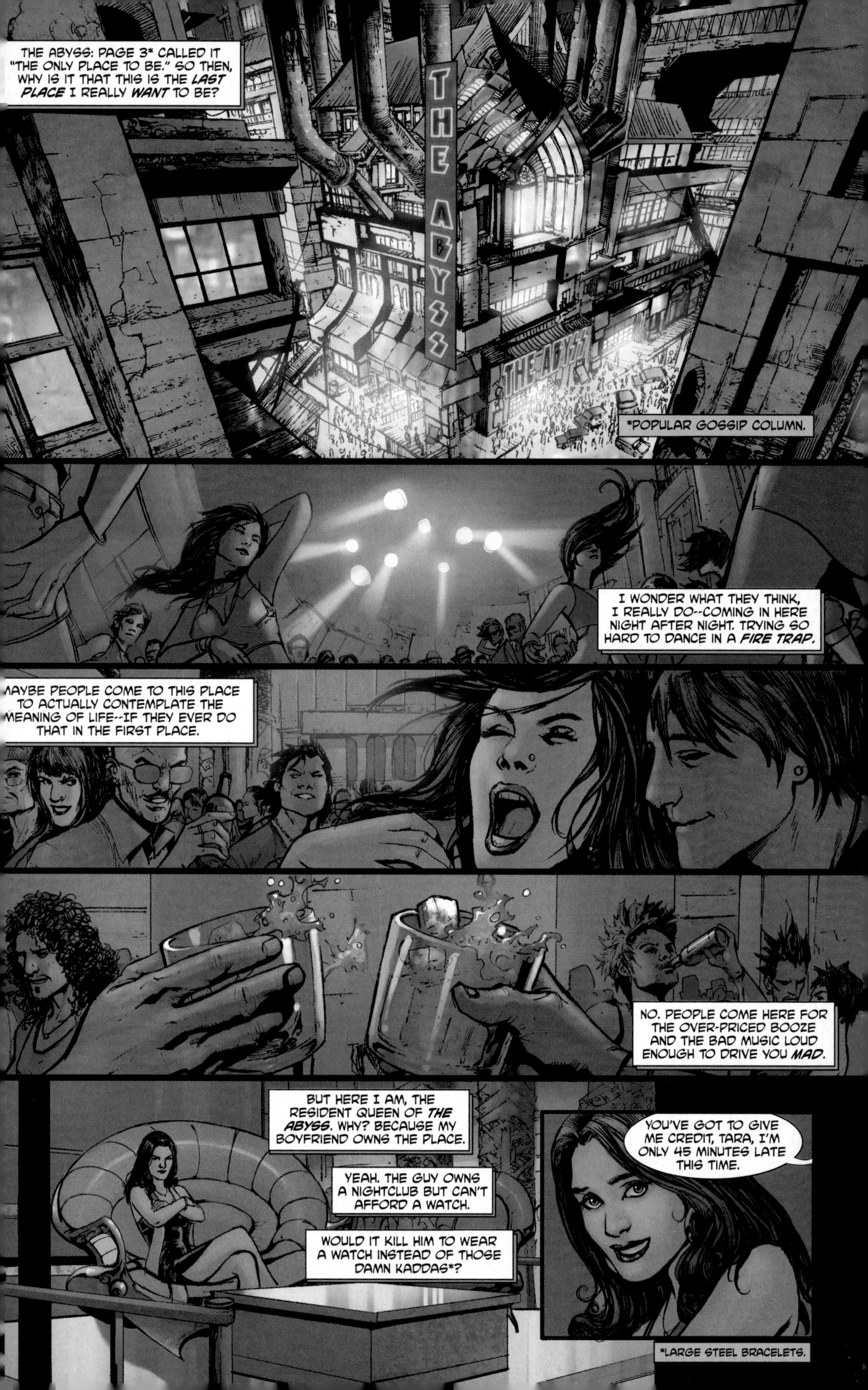
THE ABYSS: PAGE 3* CALLED IT "THE ONLY PLACE TO BE." SO THEN, WHY IS IT THAT THIS IS THE LAST PLACE I REALLY WANT TO BE?
THE ABYSS
THE ABYSS
*POPULAR GOSSIP COLUMN.
I WONDER WHAT THEY THINK, I REALLY DO--COMING IN HERE NIGHT AFTER NIGHT. TRYING SO HARD TO DANCE IN A FIRE TRAP.
MAYBE PEOPLE COME TO THIS PLACE TO ACTUALLY CONTEMPLATE THE MEANING OF LIFE--IF THEY EVER DO THAT IN THE FIRST PLACE.
NO. PEOPLE COME HERE FOR THE OVER-PRICED BOOZE AND THE BAD MUSIC LOUD ENOUGH TO DRIVE YOU MAD.
BUT HERE I AM, THE RESIDENT QUEEN OF THE ABYSS. WHY? BECAUSE MY BOYFRIEND OWNS THE PLACE.
YEAH. THE GUY OWNS A NIGHTCLUB BUT CAN'T AFFORD A WATCH.
WOULD IT KILL HIM TO WEAR A WATCH INSTEAD OF THOSE DAMN KADDAS*?
YOU'VE GOT TO GIVE ME CREDIT, TARA, I'M ONLY 45 MINUTES LATE THIS TIME.
*LARGE STEEL BRACELETS.

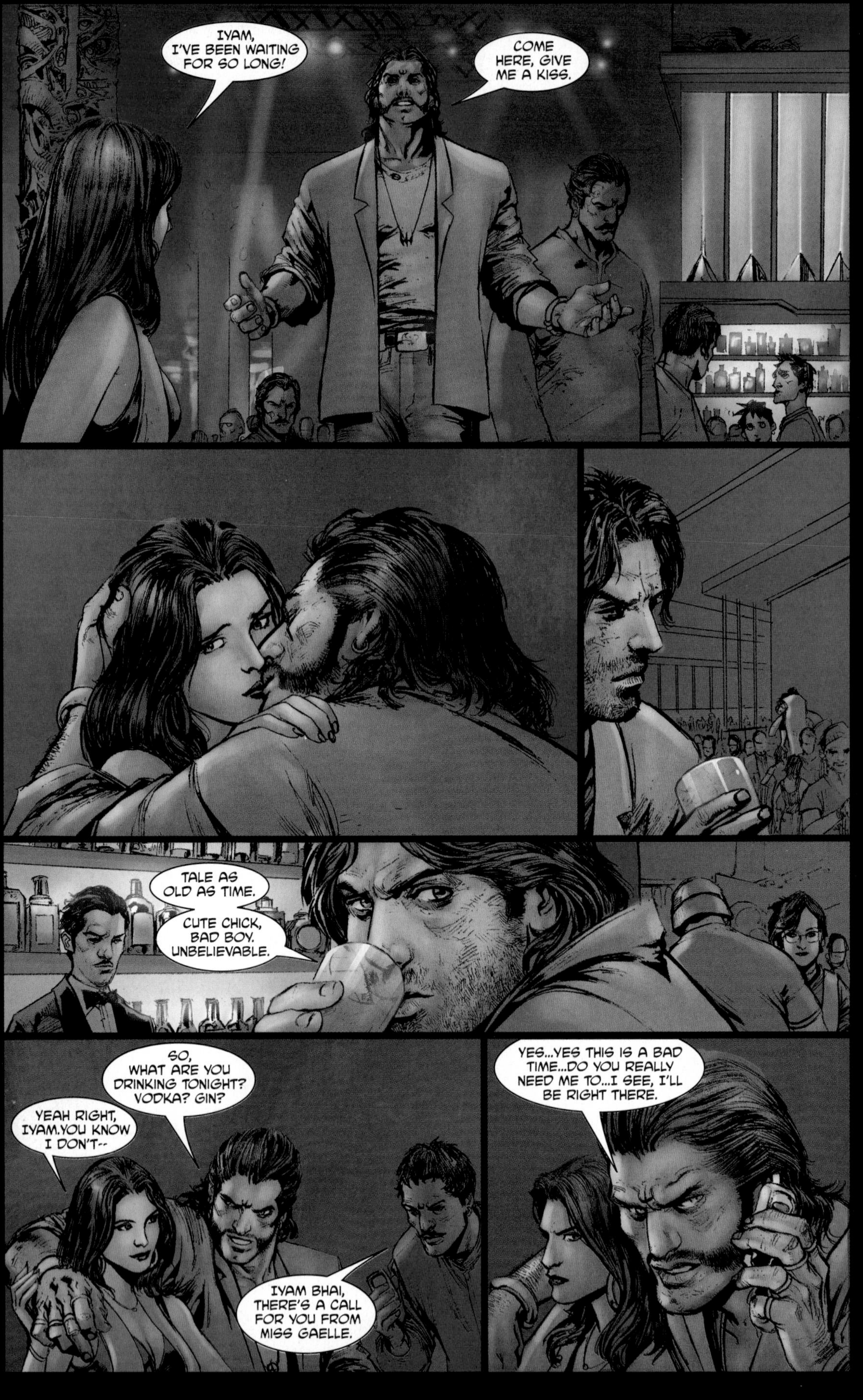
IYAM, I'VE BEEN WAITING FOR SO LONG!
COME HERE, GIVE ME A KISS.
TALE AS OLD AS TIME.
CUTE CHICK, BAD BOY. UNBELIEVABLE.
SO, WHAT ARE YOU DRINKING TONIGHT? VODKA? GIN?
YEAH RIGHT, IYAM.YOU KNOW I DON'T--
IYAM BHAI, THERE'S A CALL FOR YOU FROM MISS GAELLE.
YES...YES THIS IS A BAD TIME...DO YOU REALLY NEED ME TO...I SEE, I'LL BE RIGHT THERE.

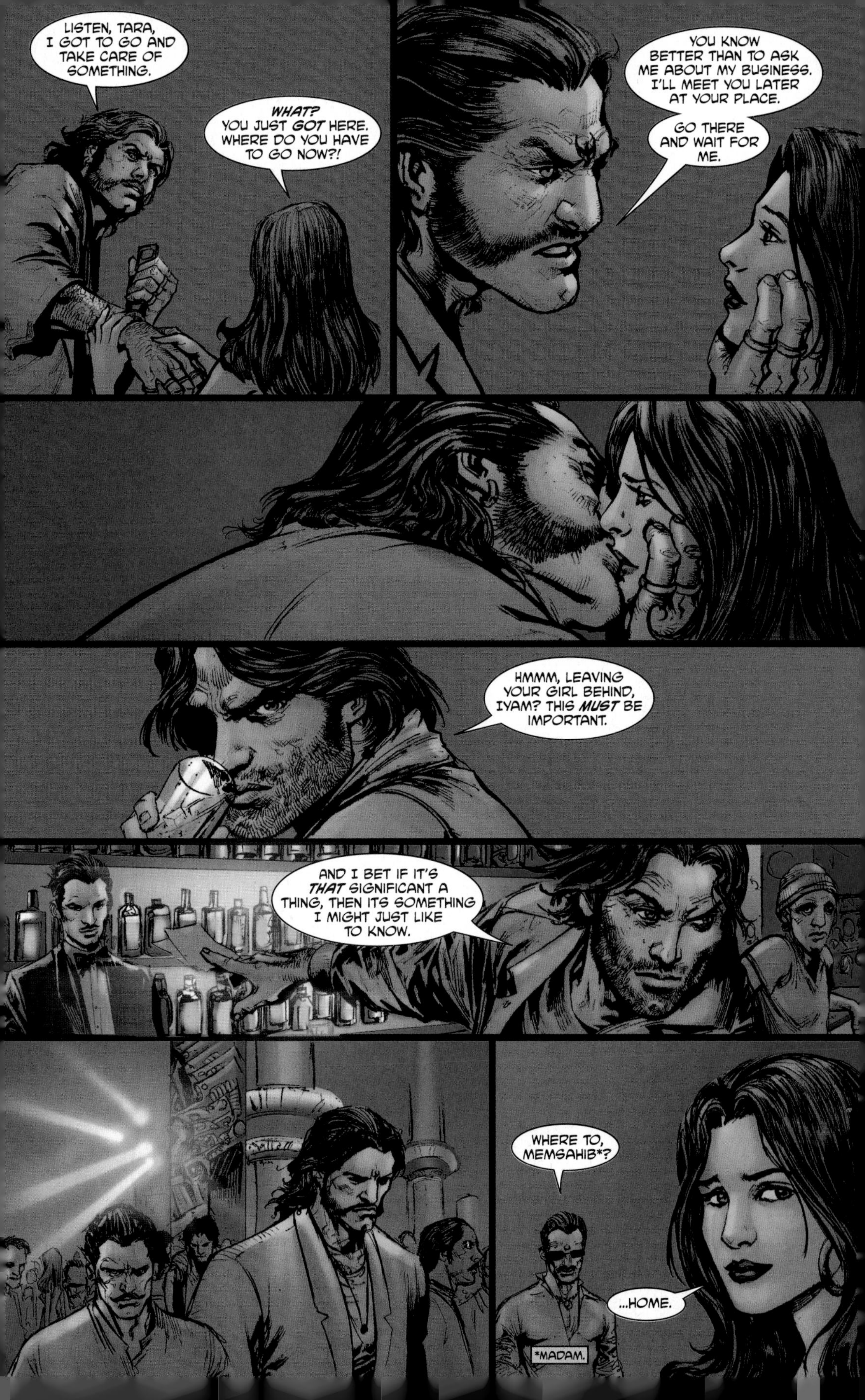
LISTEN, TARA, I GOT TO GO AND TAKE CARE OF SOMETHING.
WHAT? YOU JUST GOT HERE. WHERE DO YOU HAVE TO GO NOW?!
YOU KNOW BETTER THAN TO ASK ME ABOUT MY BUSINESS. I'LL MEET YOU LATER AT YOUR PLACE.
GO THERE AND WAIT FOR ME.
HMMM, LEAVING YOUR GIRL BEHIND, IYAM? THIS MUST BE IMPORTANT.
AND I BET IF IT'S THAT SIGNIFICANT A THING, THEN ITS SOMETHING I MIGHT JUST LIKE TO KNOW.
WHERE TO, MEMSAHIB*?
...HOME.
*MADAM.

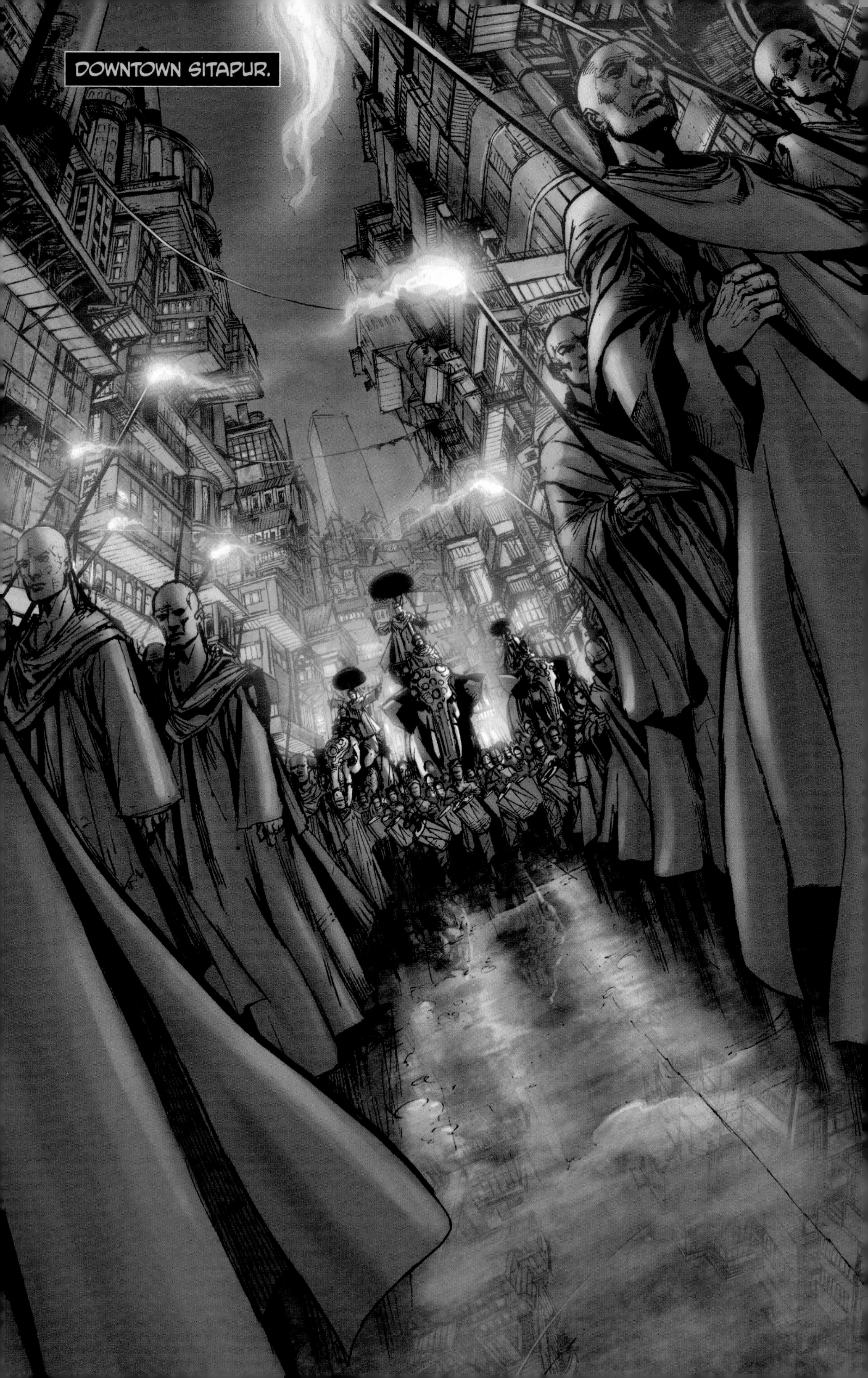
DOWNTOWN SITAPUR.

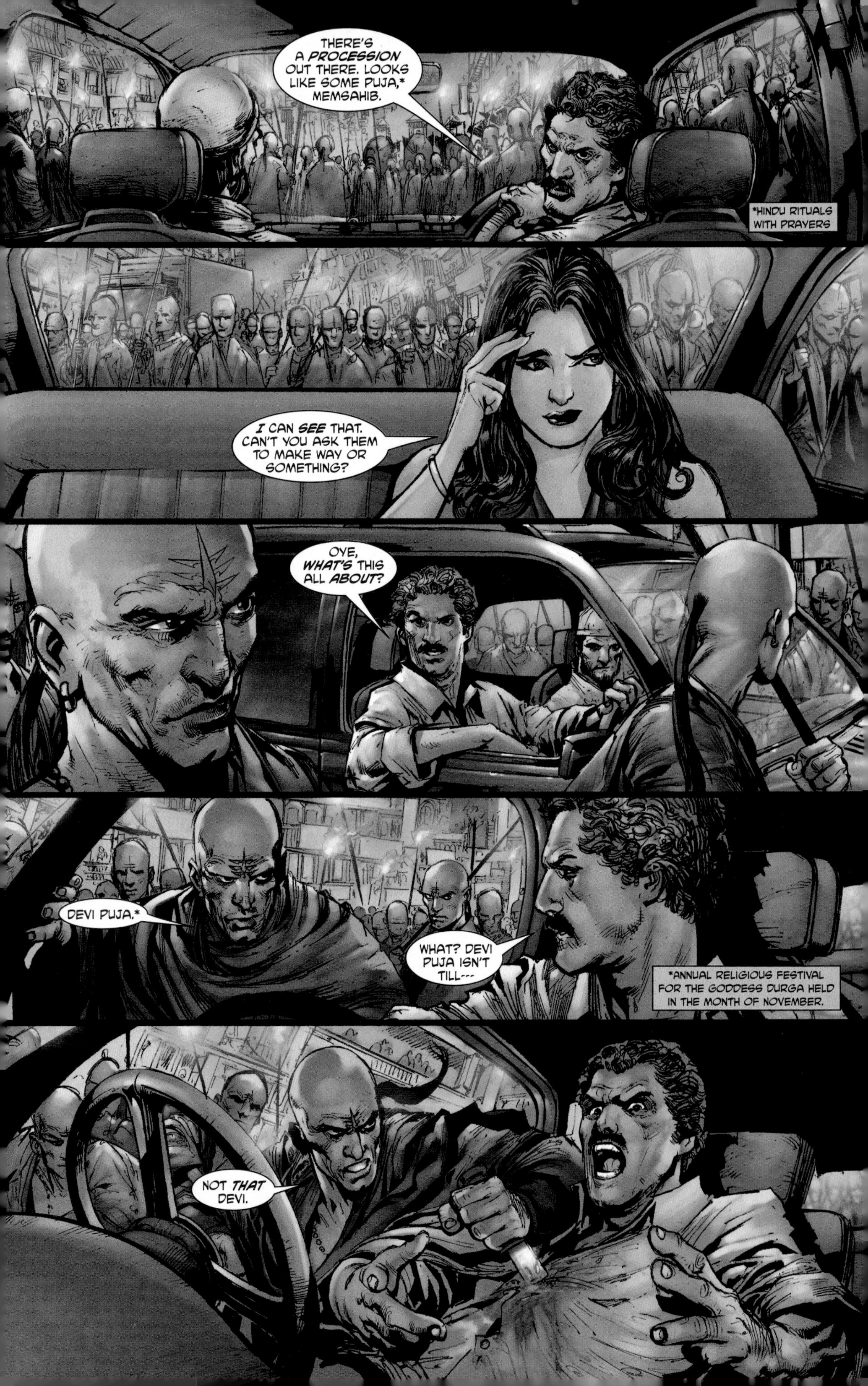
THERE'S A *PROCESSION* OUT THERE. LOOKS LIKE SOME PUJA,* MEMSAHIB.
*HINDU RITUALS WITH PRAYERS
I CAN SEE THAT. CAN'T YOU ASK THEM TO MAKE WAY OR SOMETHING?
OYE, *WHAT'S* THIS ALL *ABOUT*?
DEVI PUJA.*
WHAT? DEVI PUJA ISN'T TILL---
*ANNUAL RELIGIOUS FESTIVAL FOR THE GODDESS DURGA HELD IN THE MONTH OF NOVEMBER.
NOT *THAT* DEVI.

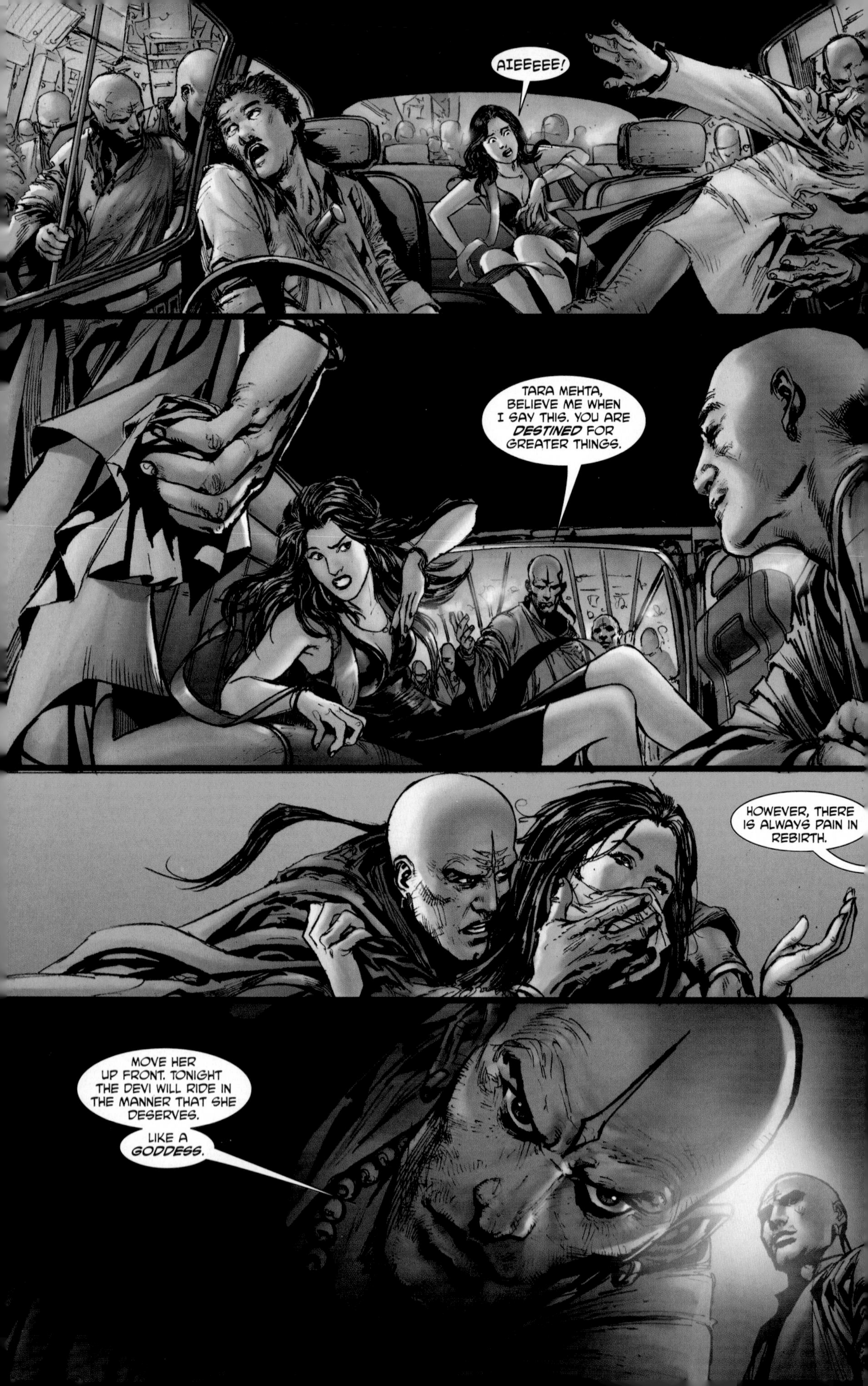
AIEEEEE!
TARA MEHTA, BELIEVE ME WHEN I SAY THIS. YOU ARE DESTINED FOR GREATER THINGS.
HOWEVER, THERE IS ALWAYS PAIN IN REBIRTH.
MOVE HER UP FRONT. TONIGHT THE DEVI WILL RIDE IN THE MANNER THAT SHE DESERVES.
LIKE A GODDESS.

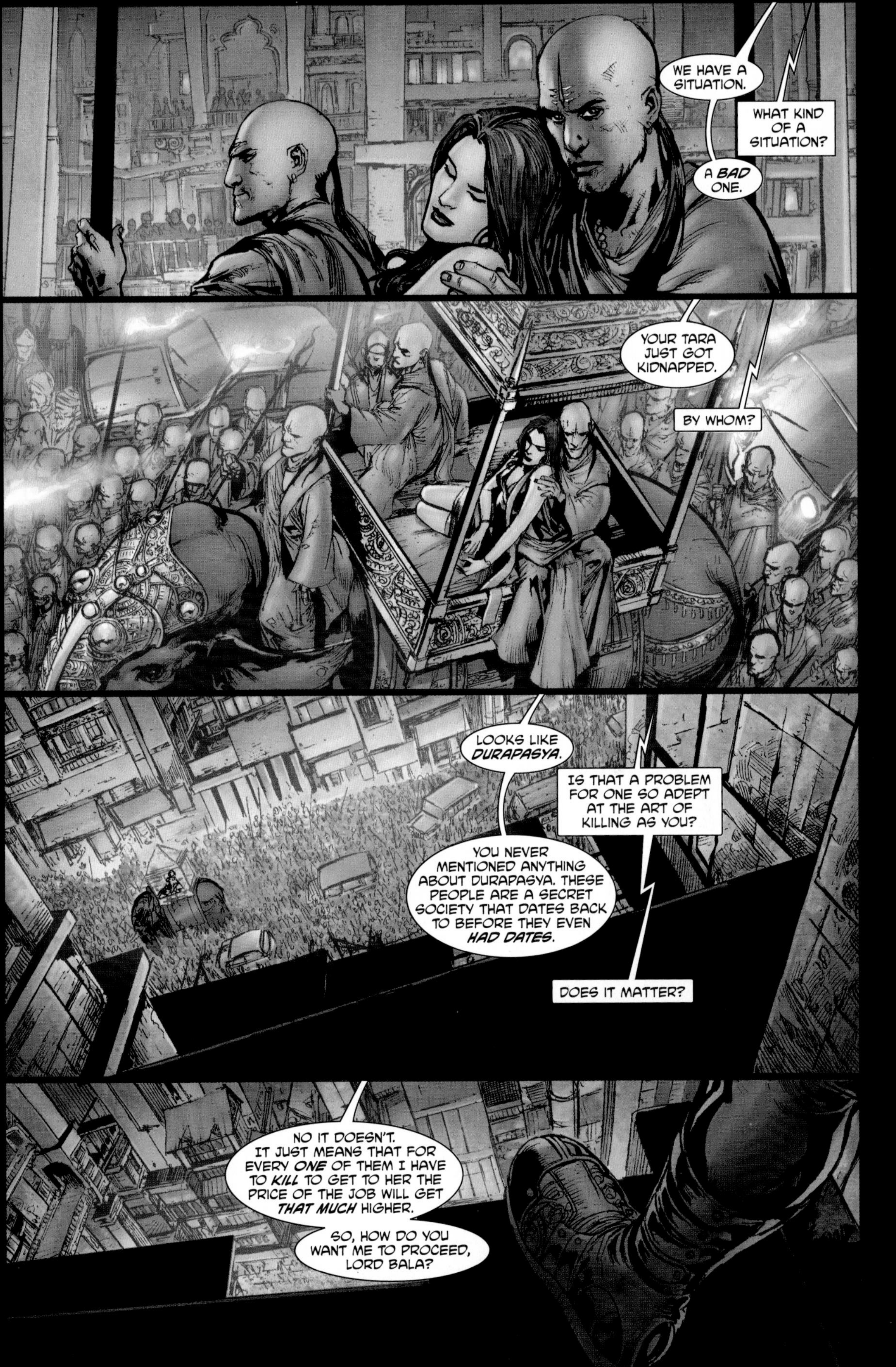
WE HAVE A SITUATION.
WHAT KIND OF A SITUATION?
A BAD ONE.
YOUR TARA JUST GOT KIDNAPPED.
BY WHOM?
LOOKS LIKE DURAPASYA.
IS THAT A PROBLEM FOR ONE SO ADEPT AT THE ART OF KILLING AS YOU?
YOU NEVER MENTIONED ANYTHING ABOUT DURAPASYA. THESE PEOPLE ARE A SECRET SOCIETY THAT DATES BACK TO BEFORE THEY EVEN HAD DATES.
DOES IT MATTER?
NO IT DOESN'T. IT JUST MEANS THAT FOR EVERY ONE OF THEM I HAVE TO KILL TO GET TO HER THE PRICE OF THE JOB WILL GET THAT MUCH HIGHER.
SO, HOW DO YOU WANT ME TO PROCEED, LORD BALA?

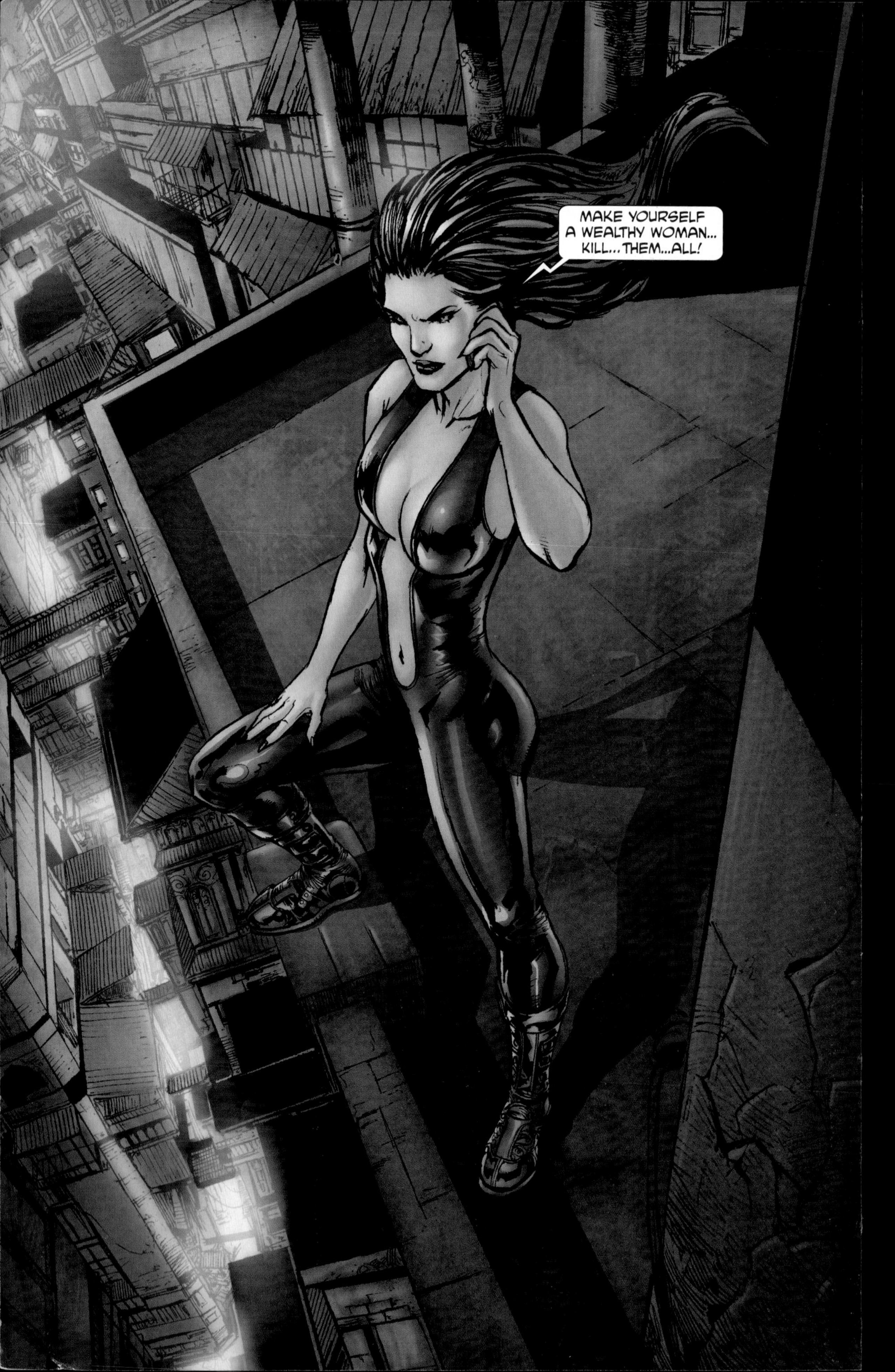
MAKE YOURSELF A WEALTHY WOMAN... KILL...THEM...ALL!

Part Three
Namaha

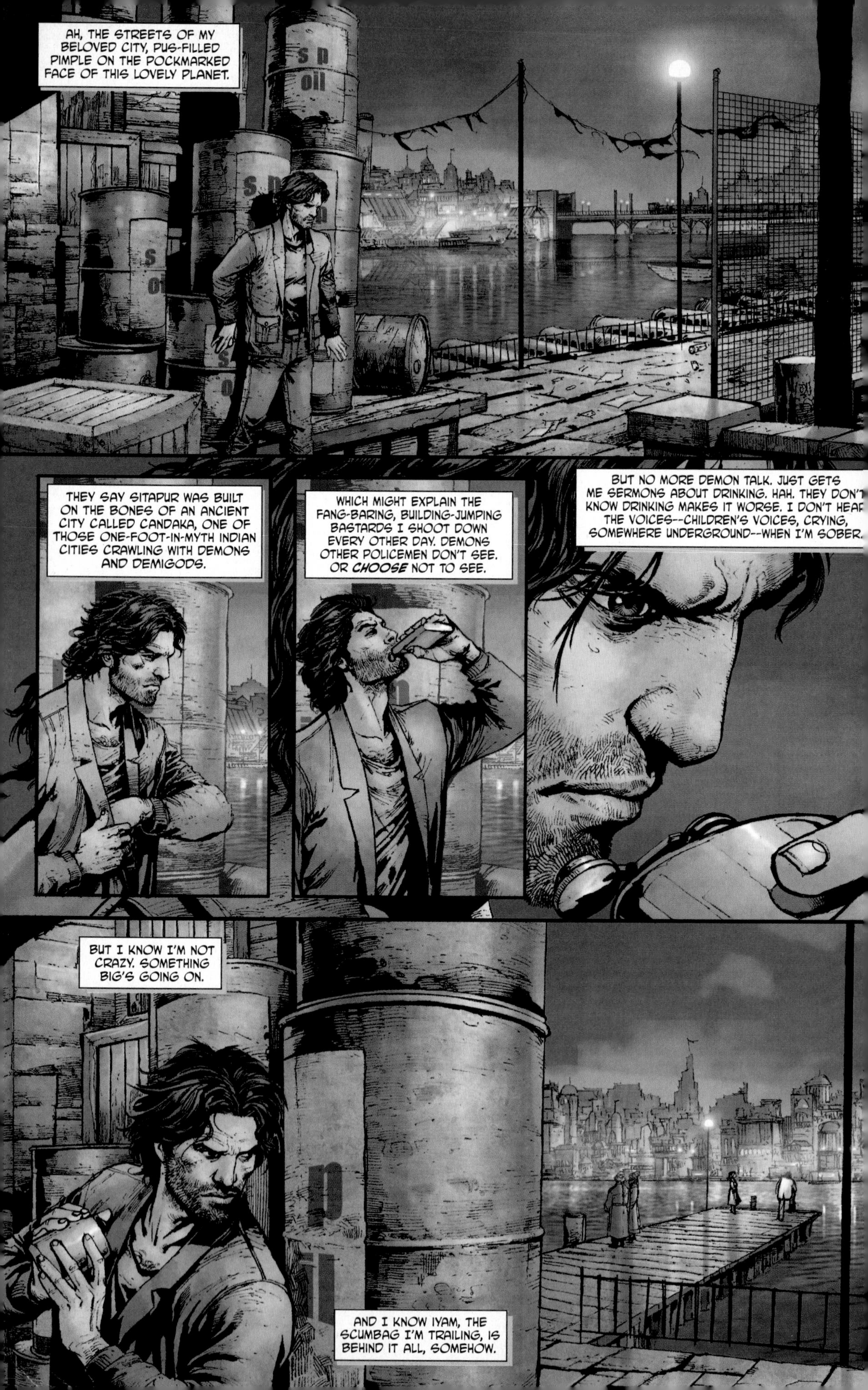
AH, THE STREETS OF MY BELOVED CITY, PUS-FILLED PIMPLE ON THE POCKMARKED FACE OF THIS LOVELY PLANET.
THEY SAY SITAPUR WAS BUILT ON THE BONES OF AN ANCIENT CITY CALLED CANDAKA, ONE OF THOSE ONE-FOOT-IN-MYTH INDIAN CITIES CRAWLING WITH DEMONS AND DEMIGODS.
WHICH MIGHT EXPLAIN THE FANG-BARING, BUILDING-JUMPING BASTARDS I SHOOT DOWN EVERY OTHER DAY. DEMONS OTHER POLICEMEN DON'T SEE. OR *CHOOSE* NOT TO SEE.
BUT NO MORE DEMON TALK. JUST GETS ME SERMONS ABOUT DRINKING. HAH. THEY DON'T KNOW DRINKING MAKES IT WORSE. I DON'T HEAR THE VOICES--CHILDREN'S VOICES, CRYING, SOMEWHERE UNDERGROUND--WHEN I'M SOBER.
BUT I KNOW I'M NOT CRAZY. SOMETHING BIG'S GOING ON.
AND I KNOW IYAM, THE SCUMBAG I'M TRAILING, IS BEHIND IT ALL, SOMEHOW.

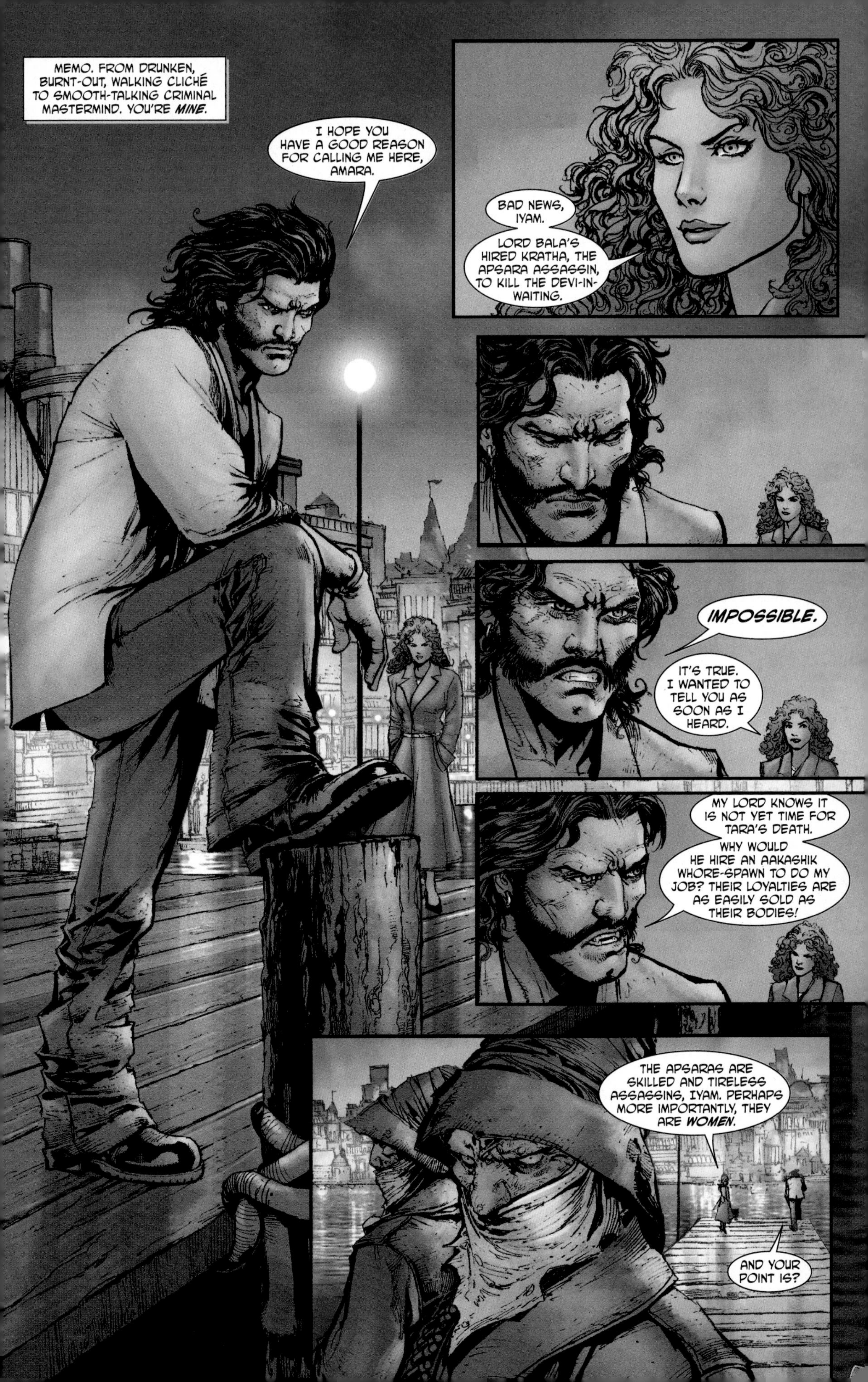

MEMO. FROM DRUNKEN, BURNT-OUT, WALKING CLICHÉ TO SMOOTH-TALKING CRIMINAL MASTERMIND. YOU'RE *MINE*.
I HOPE YOU HAVE A GOOD REASON FOR CALLING ME HERE, AMARA.
BAD NEWS, IYAM.
LORD BALA'S HIRED KRATHA, THE APSARA ASSASSIN, TO KILL THE DEVI-IN-WAITING.
IMPOSSIBLE.
IT'S TRUE. I WANTED TO TELL YOU AS SOON AS I HEARD.
MY LORD KNOWS IT IS NOT YET TIME FOR TARA'S DEATH.
WHY WOULD HE HIRE AN AAKASHIK WHORE-SPAWN TO DO MY JOB? THEIR LOYALTIES ARE AS EASILY SOLD AS THEIR BODIES!
THE APSARAS ARE SKILLED AND TIRELESS ASSASSINS, IYAM. PERHAPS MORE IMPORTANTLY, THEY ARE *WOMEN*.
AND YOUR POINT IS?

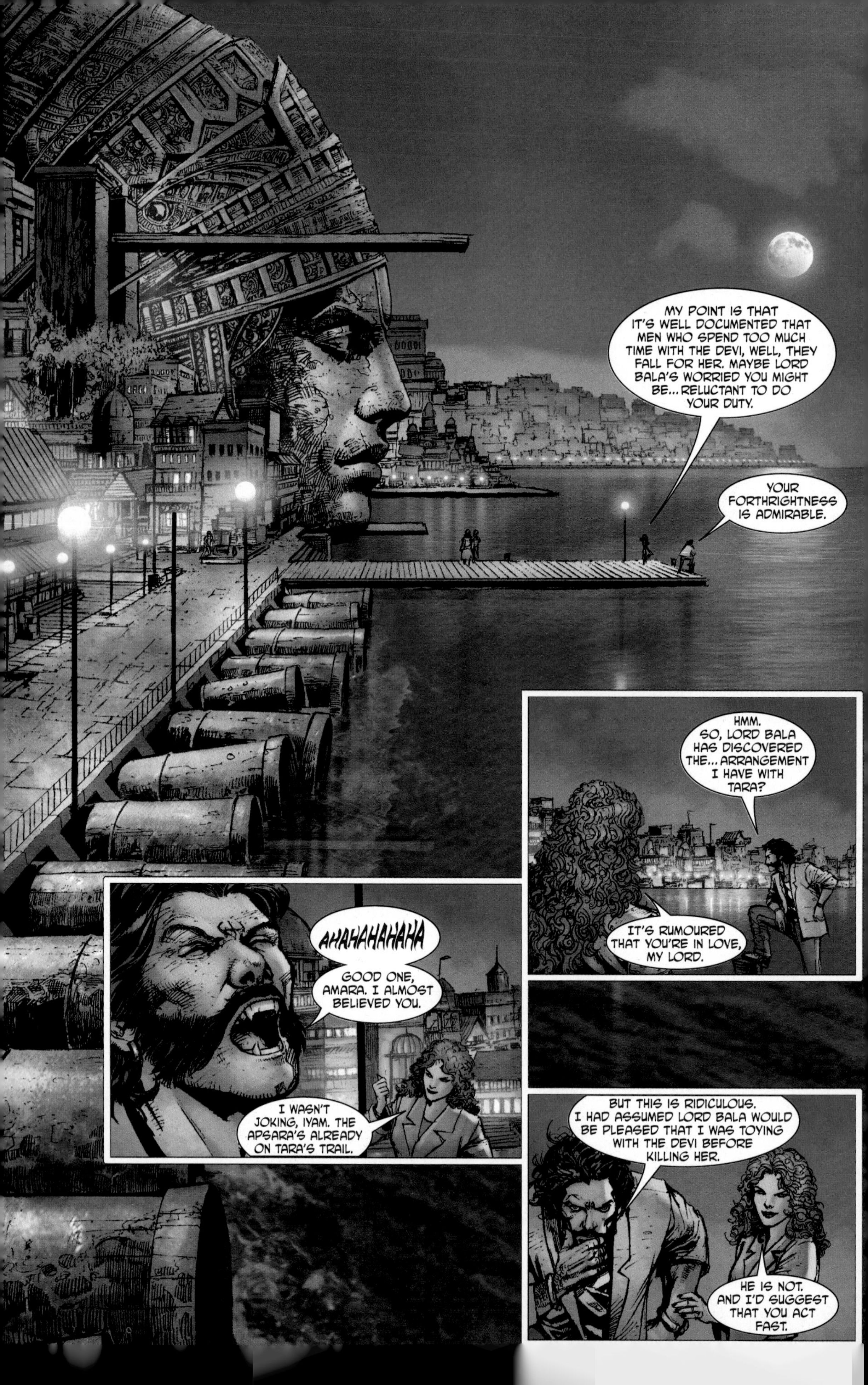
MY POINT IS THAT IT'S WELL DOCUMENTED THAT MEN WHO SPEND TOO MUCH TIME WITH THE DEVI, WELL, THEY FALL FOR HER. MAYBE LORD BALA'S WORRIED YOU MIGHT BE... RELUCTANT TO DO YOUR DUTY.
YOUR FORTHRIGHTNESS IS ADMIRABLE.
HMM. SO, LORD BALA HAS DISCOVERED THE... ARRANGEMENT I HAVE WITH TARA?
IT'S RUMOURED THAT YOU'RE IN LOVE, MY LORD.
AHAHAHAHAHA
GOOD ONE, AMARA. I ALMOST BELIEVED YOU.
I WASN'T JOKING, IYAM. THE APSARA'S ALREADY ON TARA'S TRAIL.
BUT THIS IS RIDICULOUS. I HAD ASSUMED LORD BALA WOULD BE PLEASED THAT I WAS TOYING WITH THE DEVI BEFORE KILLING HER.
HE IS NOT. AND I'D SUGGEST THAT YOU ACT FAST.

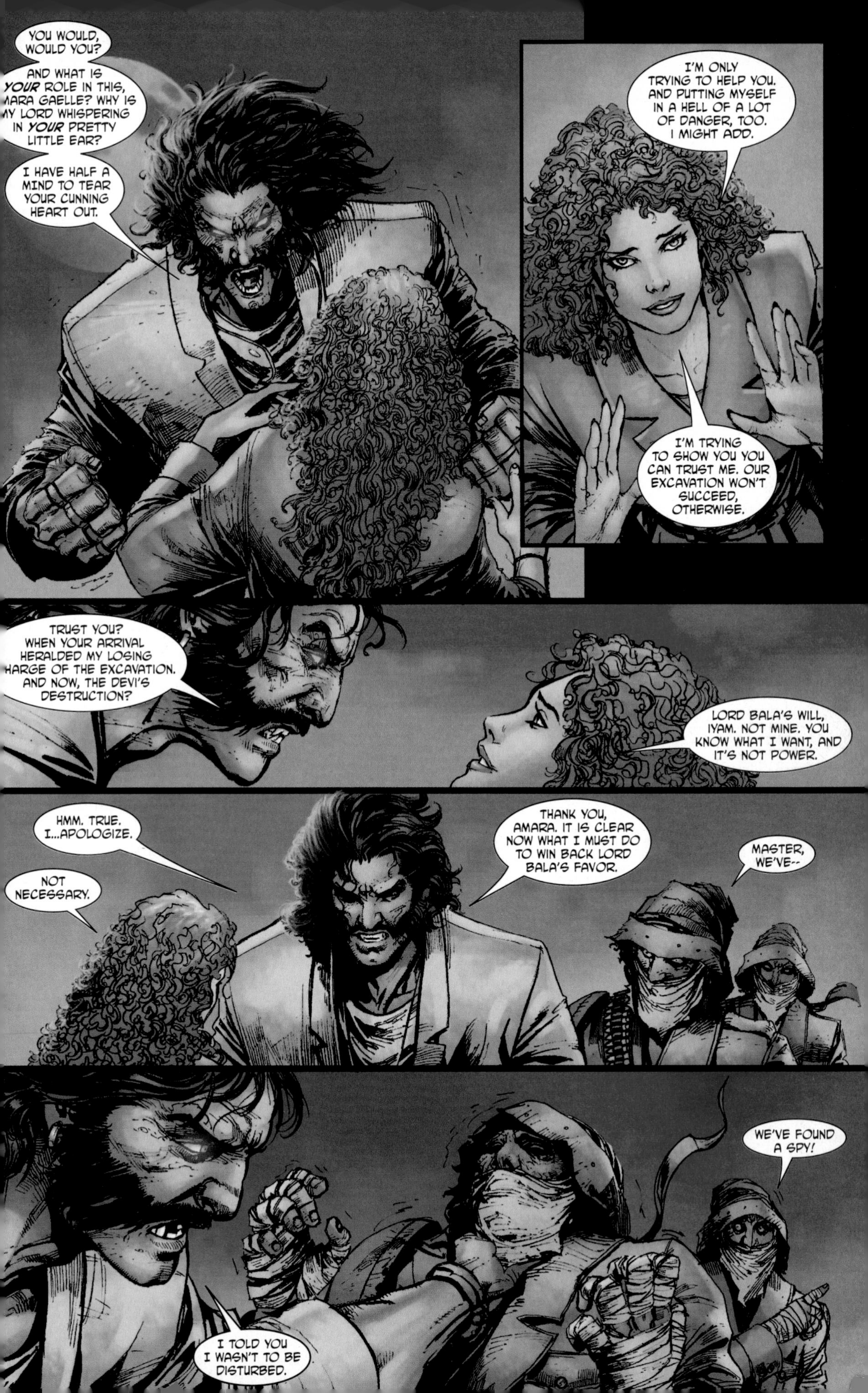
YOU WOULD, WOULD YOU?
AND WHAT IS *YOUR* ROLE IN THIS, AMARA GAELLE? WHY IS MY LORD WHISPERING IN *YOUR* PRETTY LITTLE EAR?
I HAVE HALF A MIND TO TEAR YOUR CUNNING HEART OUT.
I'M ONLY TRYING TO HELP YOU. AND PUTTING MYSELF IN A HELL OF A LOT OF DANGER, TOO. I MIGHT ADD.
I'M TRYING TO SHOW YOU YOU CAN TRUST ME. OUR EXCAVATION WON'T SUCCEED, OTHERWISE.
TRUST YOU? WHEN YOUR ARRIVAL HERALDED MY LOSING CHARGE OF THE EXCAVATION. AND NOW, THE DEVI'S DESTRUCTION?
LORD BALA'S WILL, IYAM. NOT MINE. YOU KNOW WHAT I WANT, AND IT'S NOT POWER.
HMM. TRUE. I...APOLOGIZE.
NOT NECESSARY.
THANK YOU, AMARA. IT IS CLEAR NOW WHAT I MUST DO TO WIN BACK LORD BALA'S FAVOR.
MASTER, WE'VE--
WE'VE FOUND A SPY!
I TOLD YOU I WASN'T TO BE DISTURBED.

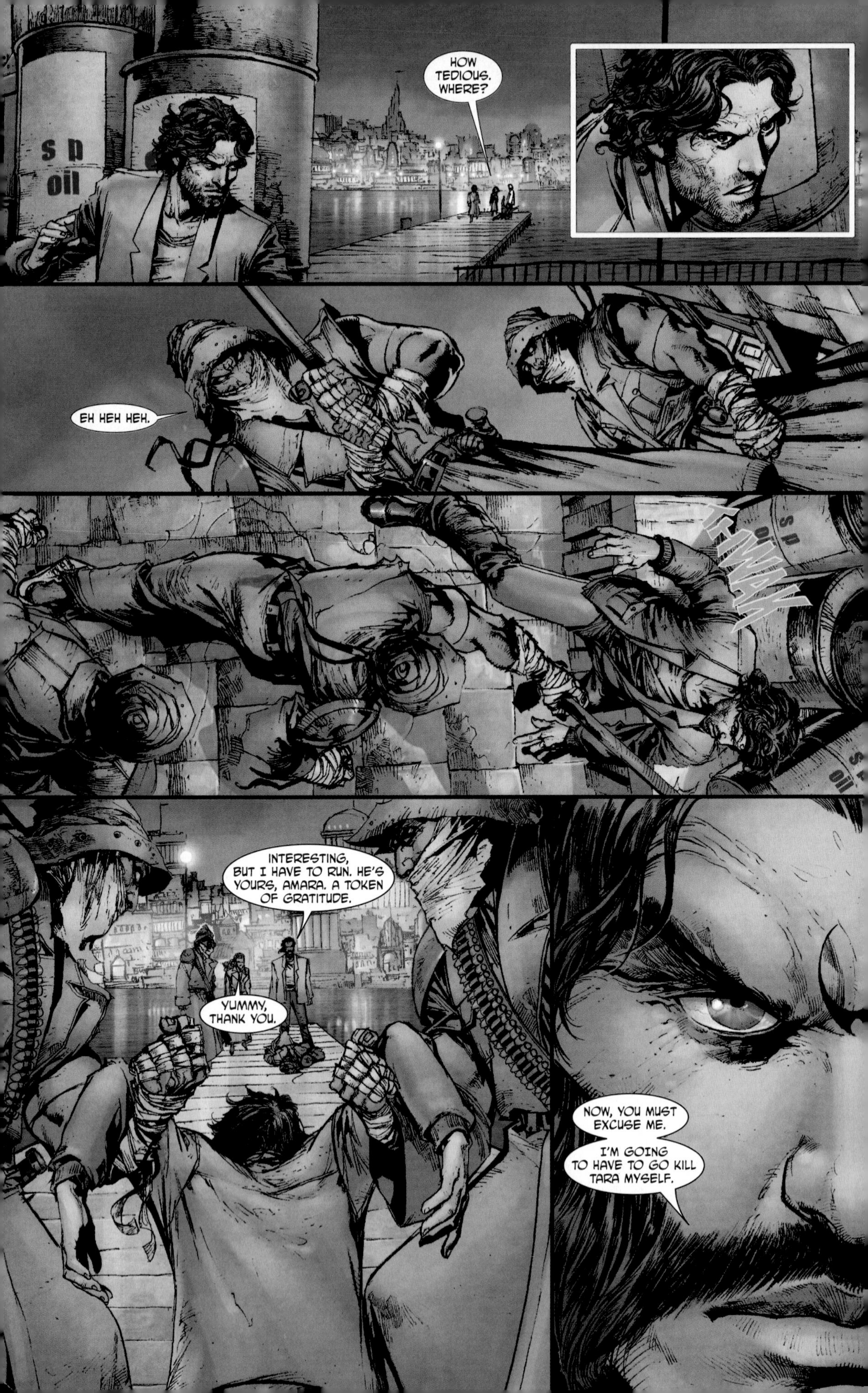
s p
oil
HOW TEDIOUS. WHERE?
EH HEH HEH.
INTERESTING, BUT I HAVE TO RUN. HE'S YOURS, AMARA. A TOKEN OF GRATITUDE.
YUMMY, THANK YOU.
NOW, YOU MUST EXCUSE ME.
I'M GOING TO HAVE TO GO KILL TARA MYSELF.

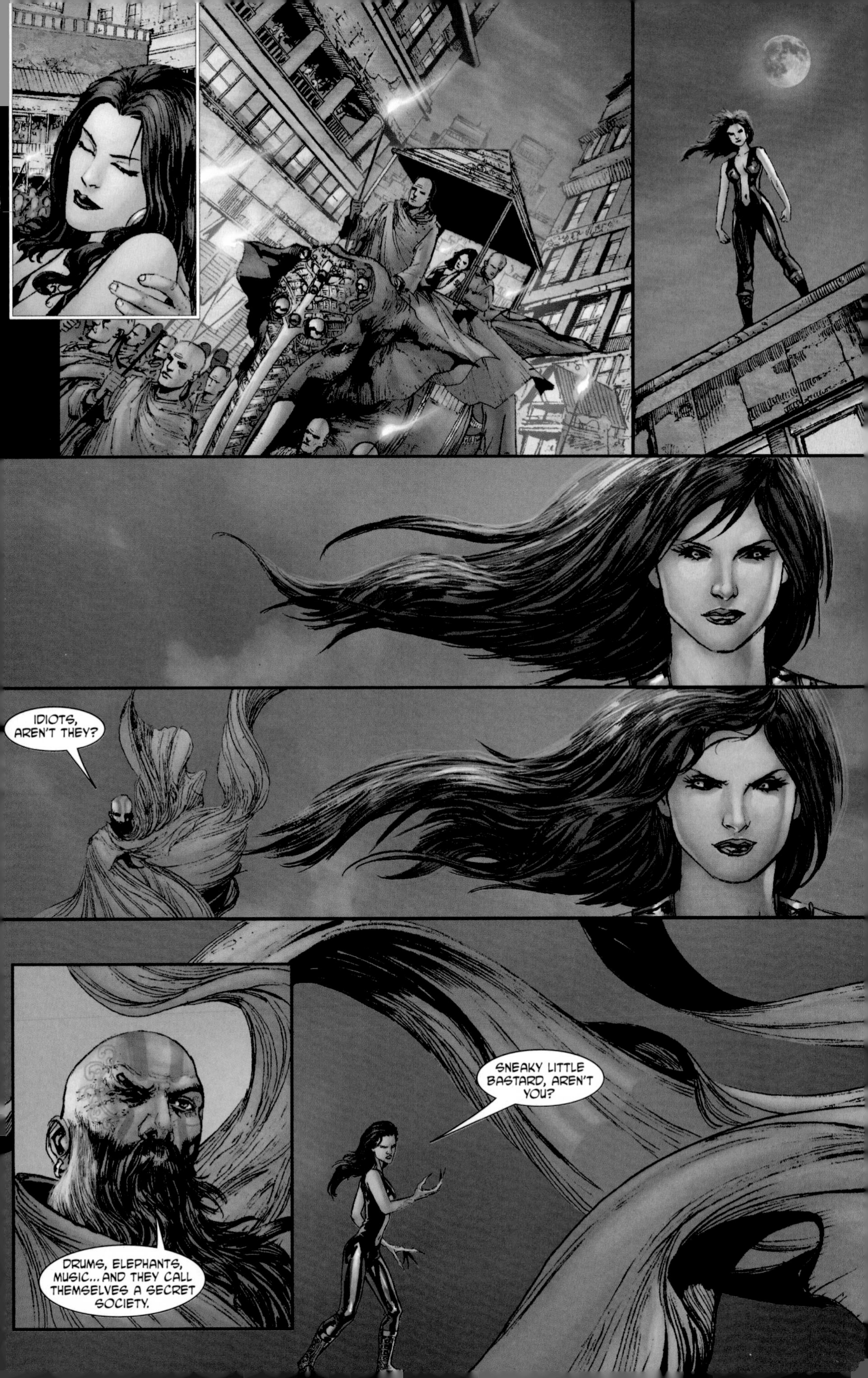
IDIOTS, AREN'T THEY?
SNEAKY LITTLE BASTARD, AREN'T YOU?
DRUMS, ELEPHANTS, MUSIC... AND THEY CALL THEMSELVES A SECRET SOCIETY.

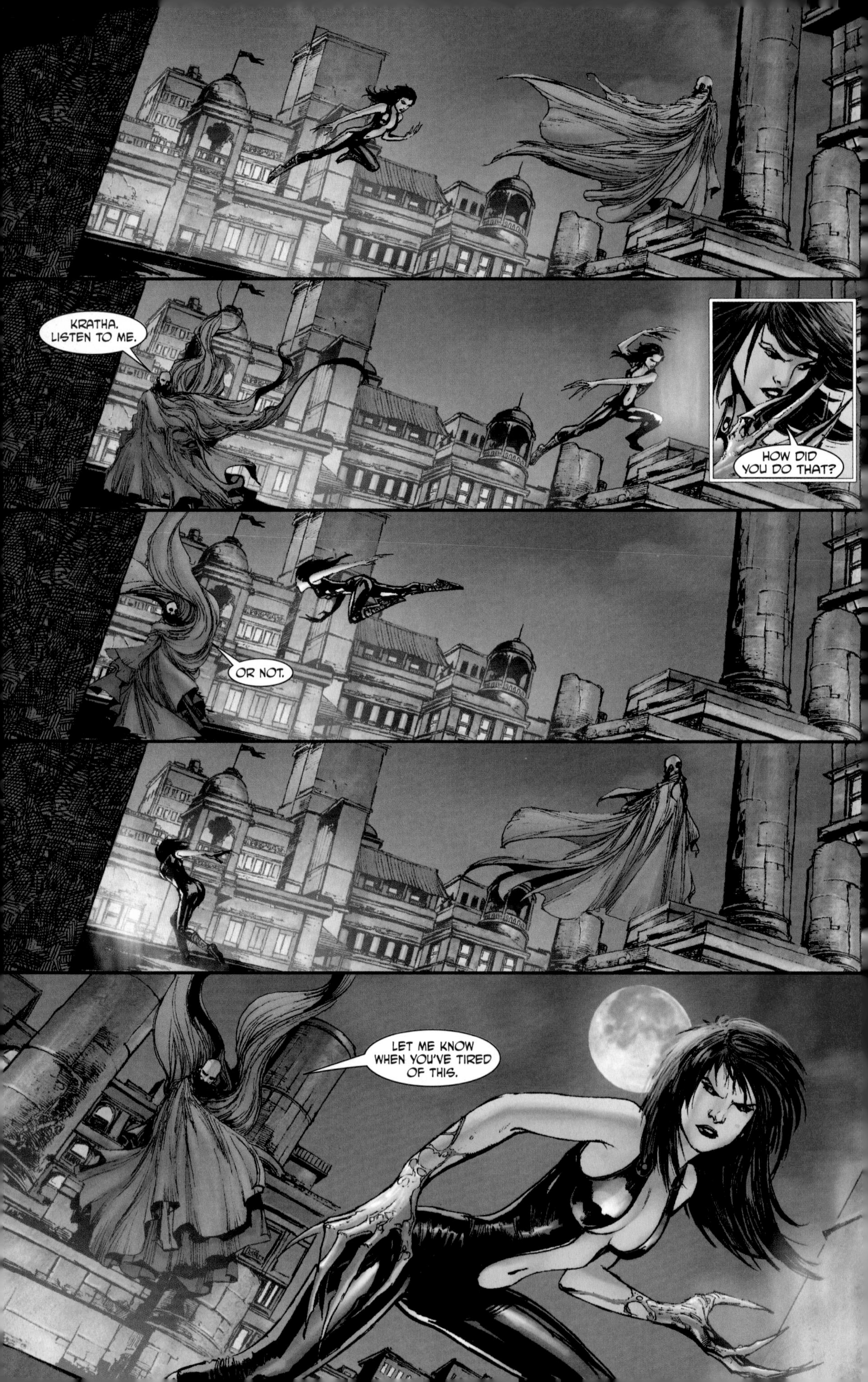
KRATHA. LISTEN TO ME.
HOW DID YOU DO THAT?
OR NOT.
LET ME KNOW WHEN YOU'VE TIRED OF THIS.

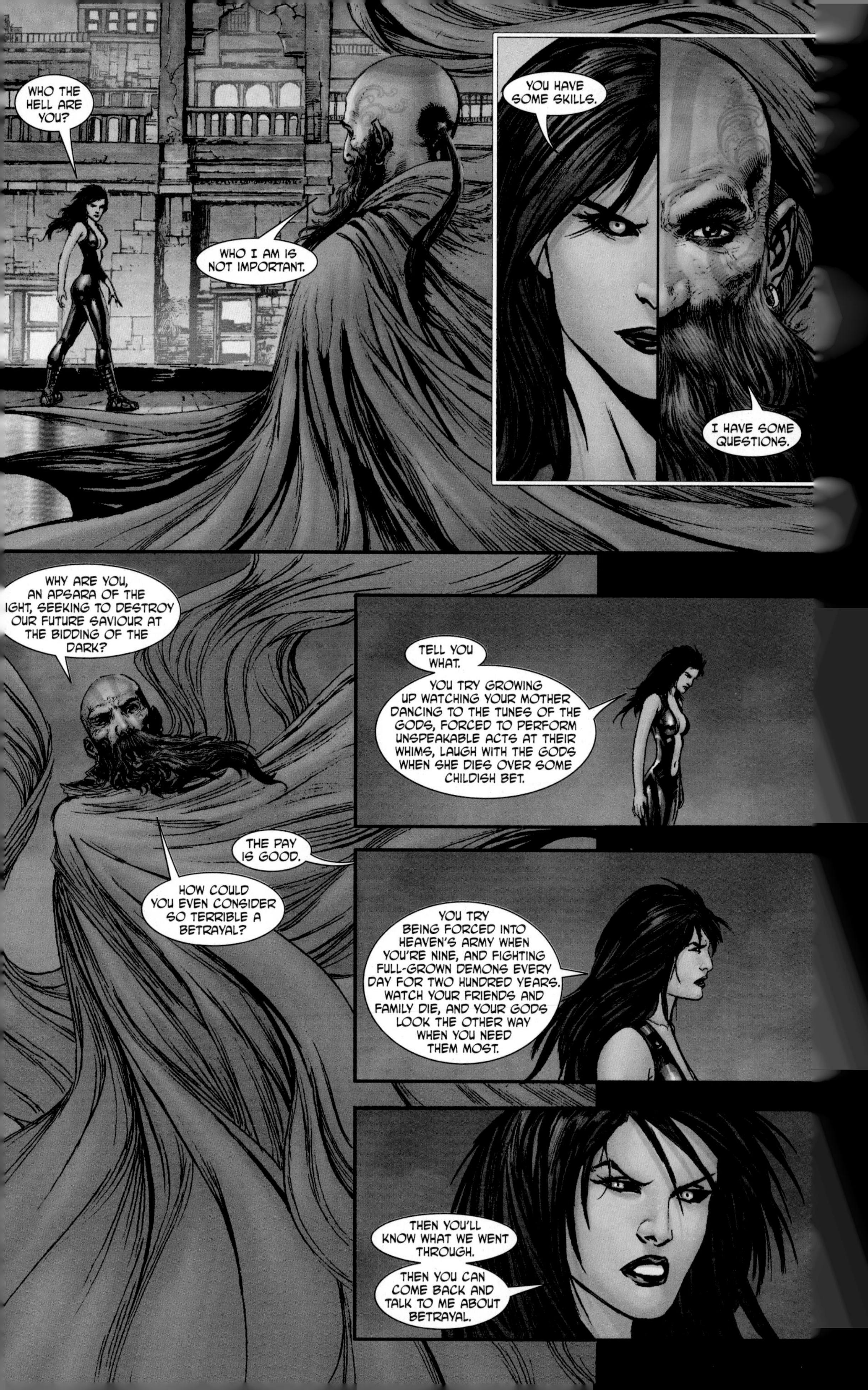
WHO THE HELL ARE YOU?
WHO I AM IS NOT IMPORTANT.
YOU HAVE SOME SKILLS.
I HAVE SOME QUESTIONS.
WHY ARE YOU, AN APSARA OF THE LIGHT, SEEKING TO DESTROY OUR FUTURE SAVIOUR AT THE BIDDING OF THE DARK?
THE PAY IS GOOD.
HOW COULD YOU EVEN CONSIDER SO TERRIBLE A BETRAYAL?
TELL YOU WHAT.
YOU TRY GROWING UP WATCHING YOUR MOTHER DANCING TO THE TUNES OF THE GODS, FORCED TO PERFORM UNSPEAKABLE ACTS AT THEIR WHIMS, LAUGH WITH THE GODS WHEN SHE DIES OVER SOME CHILDISH BET.
YOU TRY BEING FORCED INTO HEAVEN'S ARMY WHEN YOU'RE NINE, AND FIGHTING FULL-GROWN DEMONS EVERY DAY FOR TWO HUNDRED YEARS. WATCH YOUR FRIENDS AND FAMILY DIE, AND YOUR GODS LOOK THE OTHER WAY WHEN YOU NEED THEM MOST.
THEN YOU'LL KNOW WHAT WE WENT THROUGH.
THEN YOU CAN COME BACK AND TALK TO ME ABOUT BETRAYAL.

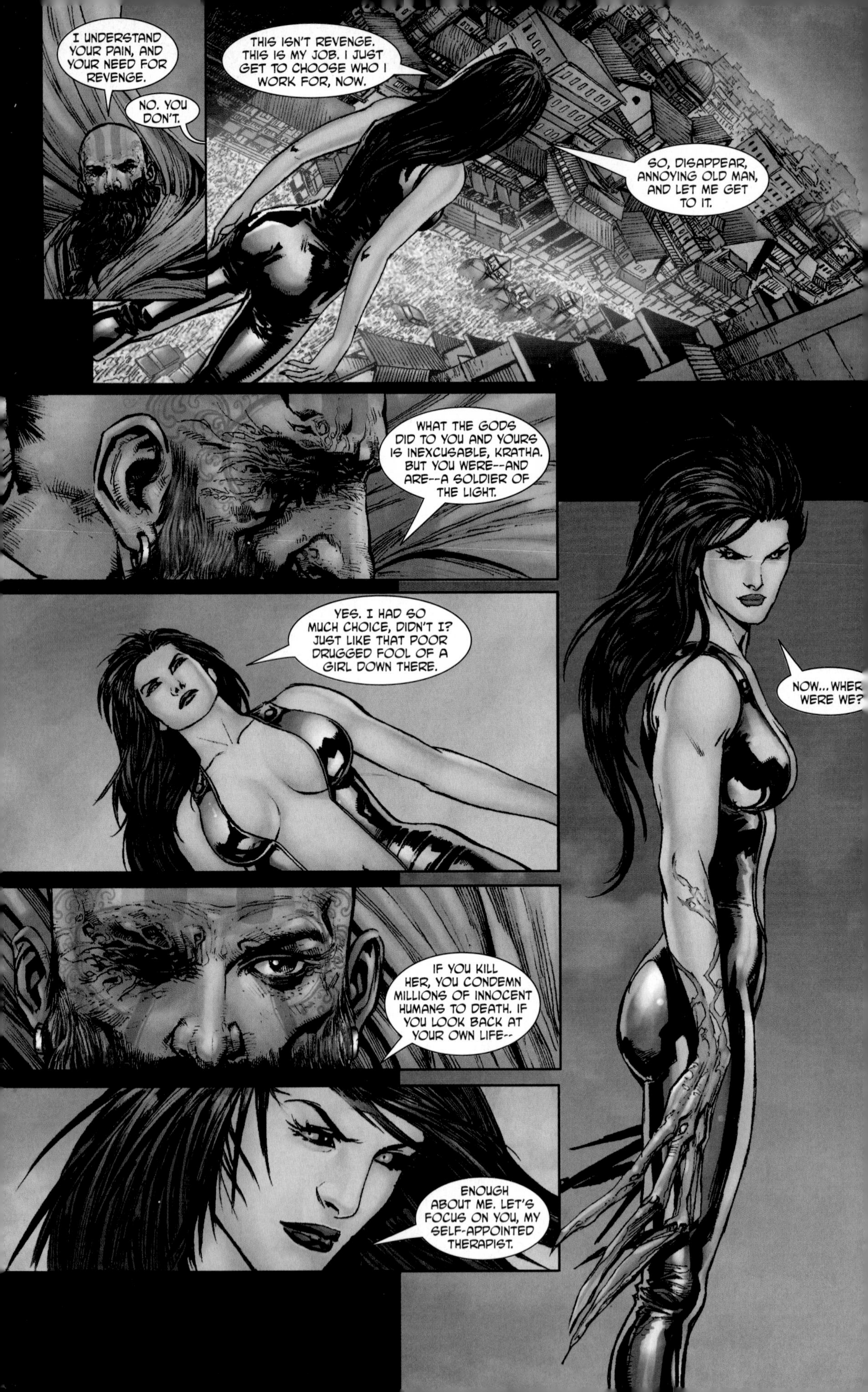
I UNDERSTAND YOUR PAIN, AND YOUR NEED FOR REVENGE.
NO. YOU DON'T.
THIS ISN'T REVENGE. THIS IS MY JOB. I JUST GET TO CHOOSE WHO I WORK FOR, NOW.
SO, DISAPPEAR, ANNOYING OLD MAN, AND LET ME GET TO IT.
WHAT THE GODS DID TO YOU AND YOURS IS INEXCUSABLE, KRATHA. BUT YOU WERE--AND ARE--A SOLDIER OF THE LIGHT.
YES. I HAD SO MUCH CHOICE, DIDN'T I? JUST LIKE THAT POOR DRUGGED FOOL OF A GIRL DOWN THERE.
IF YOU KILL HER, YOU CONDEMN MILLIONS OF INNOCENT HUMANS TO DEATH. IF YOU LOOK BACK AT YOUR OWN LIFE--
ENOUGH ABOUT ME. LET'S FOCUS ON YOU, MY SELF-APPOINTED THERAPIST.
NOW... WHER WERE WE?

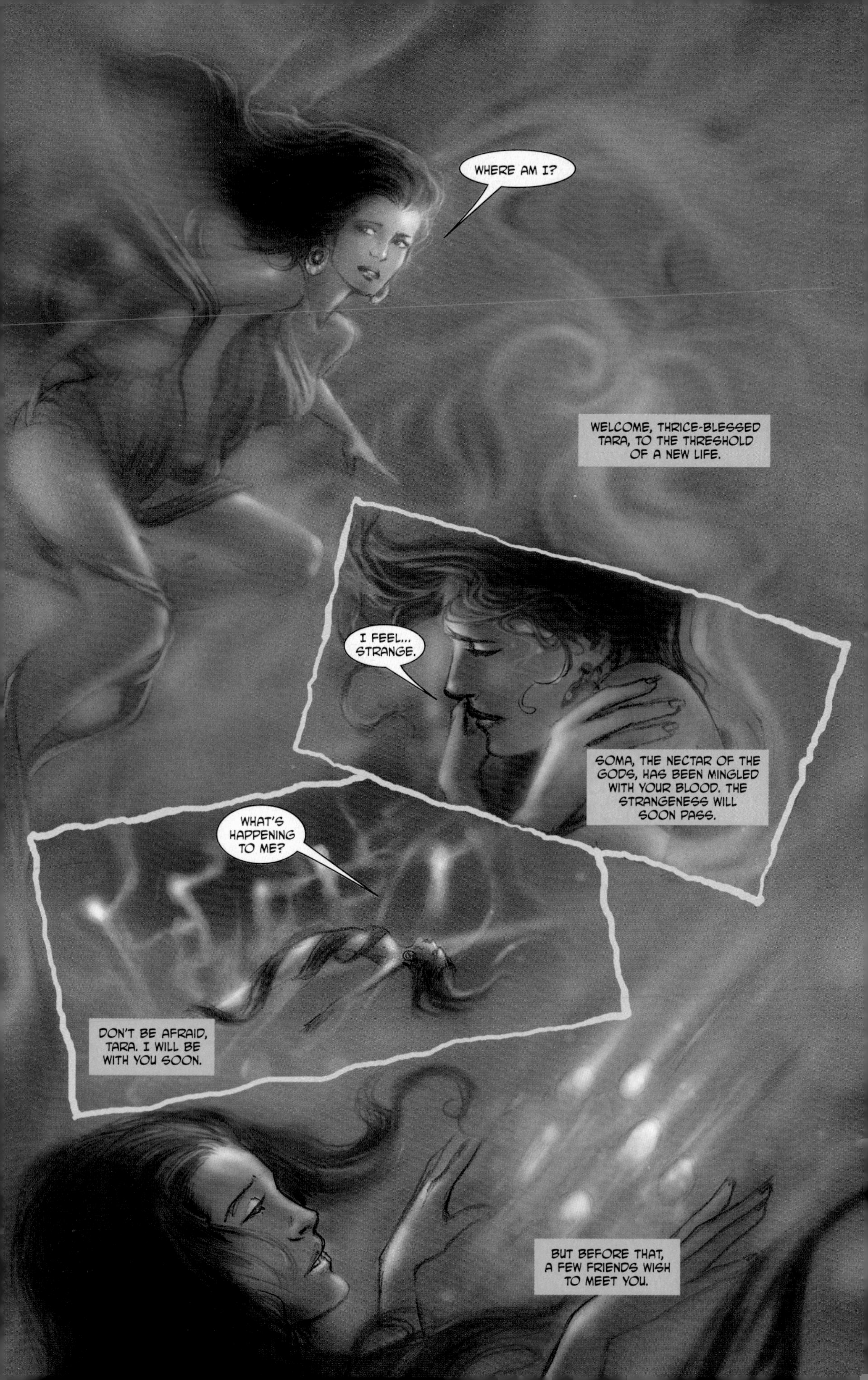
WHERE AM I?
WELCOME, THRICE-BLESSED TARA, TO THE THRESHOLD OF A NEW LIFE.
I FEEL... STRANGE.
SOMA, THE NECTAR OF THE GODS, HAS BEEN MINGLED WITH YOUR BLOOD. THE STRANGENESS WILL SOON PASS.
WHAT'S HAPPENING TO ME?
DON'T BE AFRAID, TARA. I WILL BE WITH YOU SOON.
BUT BEFORE THAT, A FEW FRIENDS WISH TO MEET YOU.

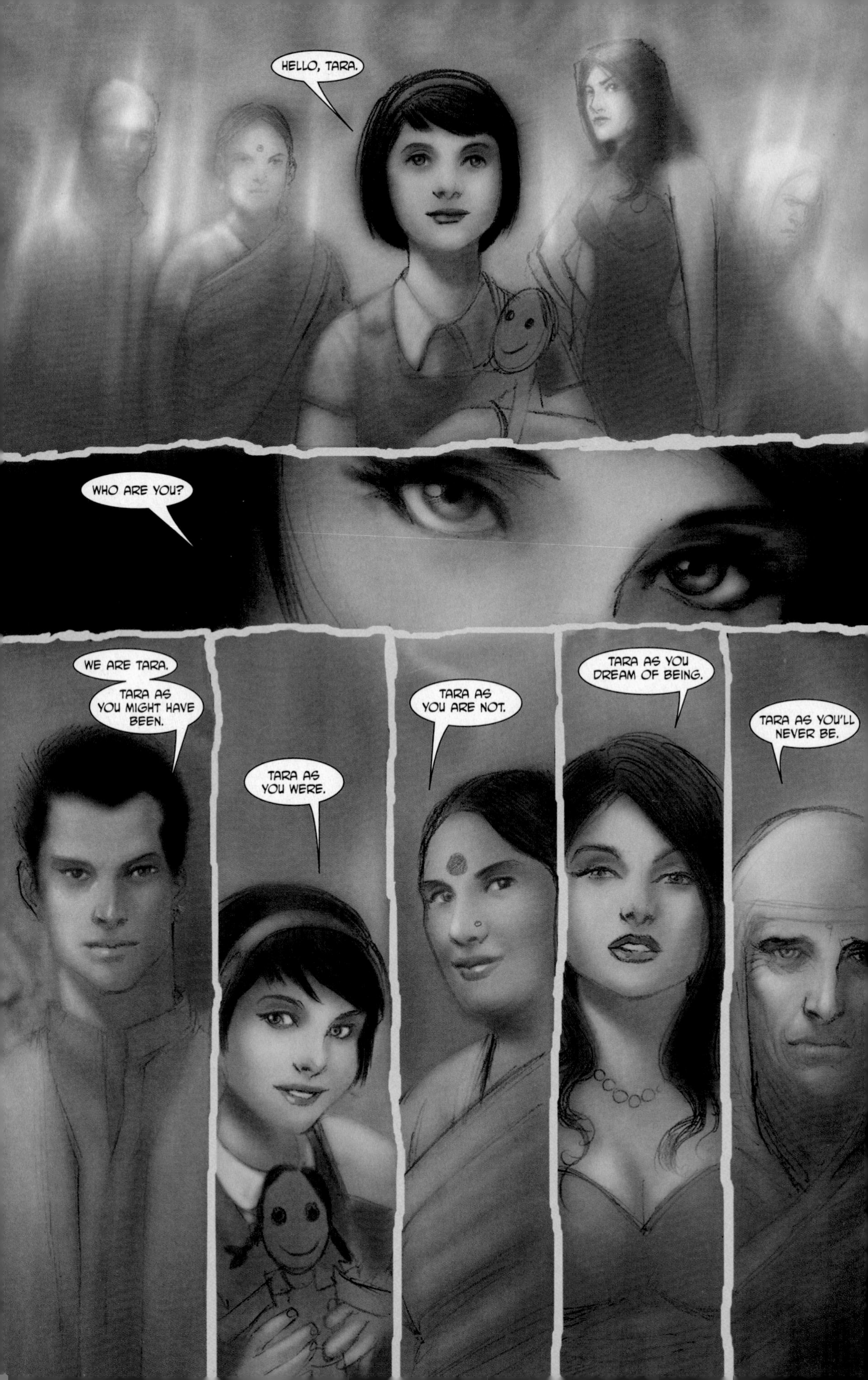
HELLO, TARA.
WHO ARE YOU?
WE ARE TARA.
TARA AS YOU MIGHT HAVE BEEN.
TARA AS YOU WERE.
TARA AS YOU ARE NOT.
TARA AS YOU DREAM OF BEING.
TARA AS YOU'LL NEVER BE.

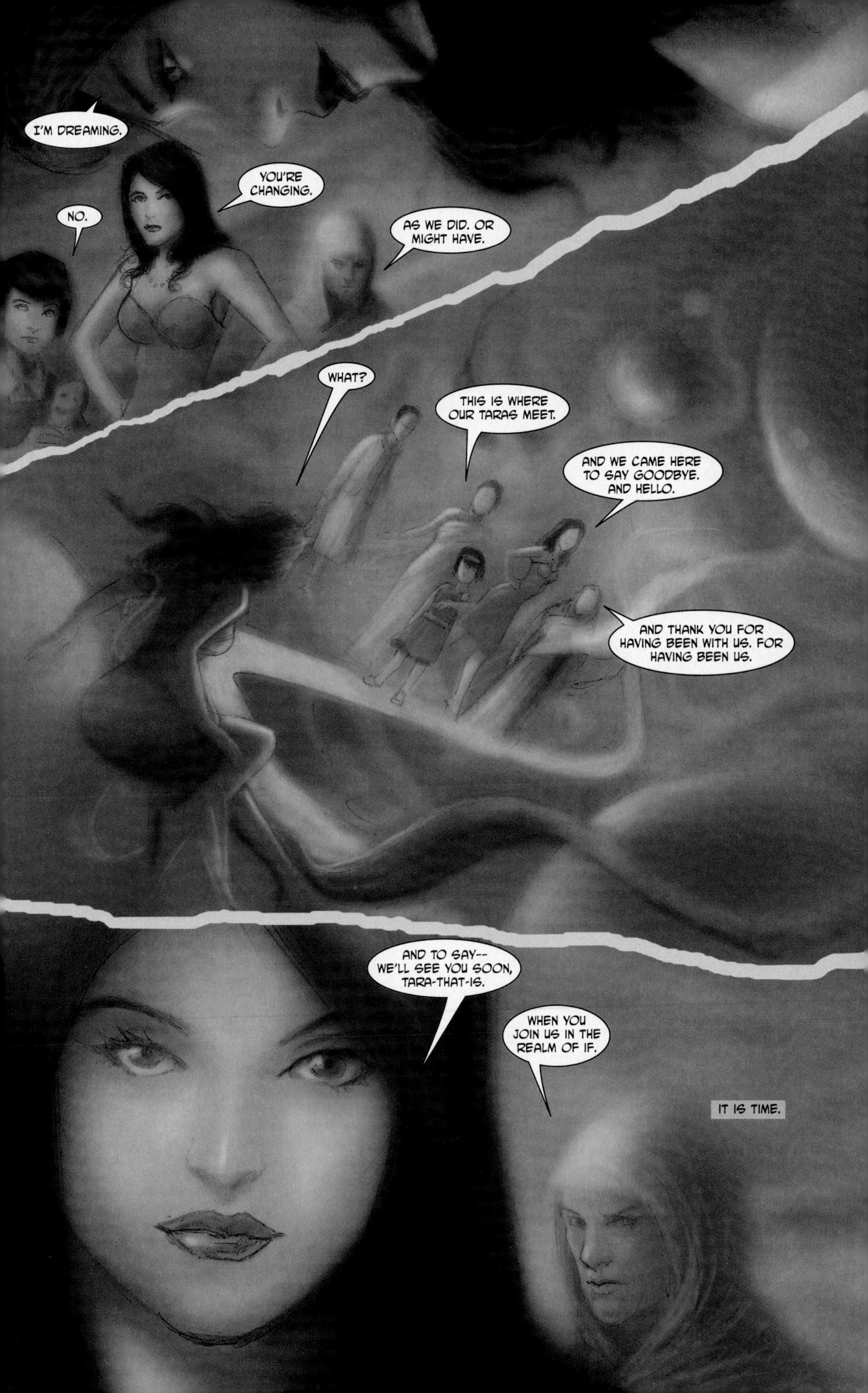
I'M DREAMING.
YOU'RE CHANGING.
NO.
AS WE DID. OR MIGHT HAVE.
WHAT?
THIS IS WHERE OUR TARAS MEET.
AND WE CAME HERE TO SAY GOODBYE. AND HELLO.
AND THANK YOU FOR HAVING BEEN WITH US. FOR HAVING BEEN US.
AND TO SAY-- WE'LL SEE YOU SOON, TARA-THAT-IS.
WHEN YOU JOIN US IN THE REALM OF IF.
IT IS TIME.

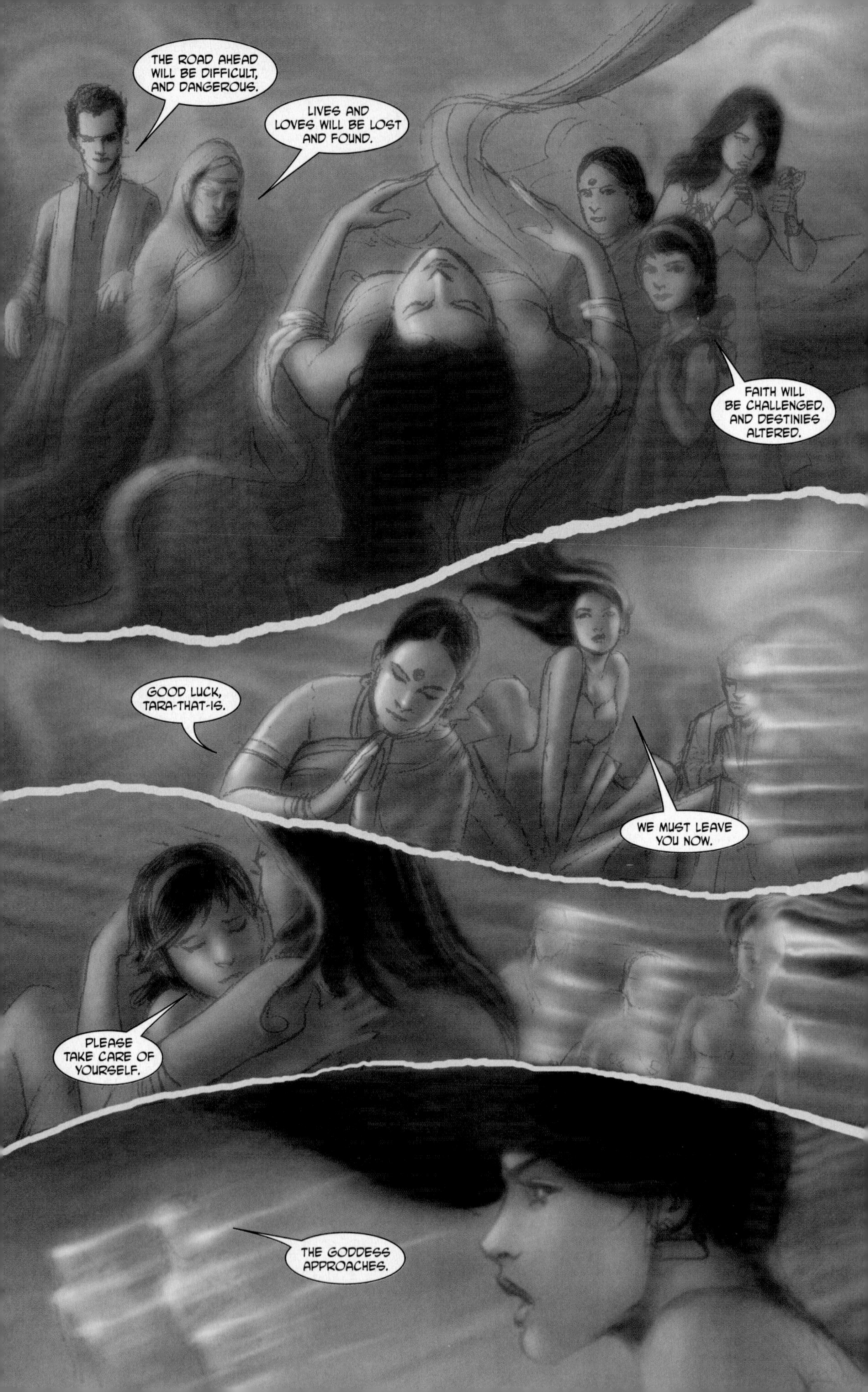
THE ROAD AHEAD WILL BE DIFFICULT, AND DANGEROUS.
LIVES AND LOVES WILL BE LOST AND FOUND.
FAITH WILL BE CHALLENGED, AND DESTINIES ALTERED.
GOOD LUCK, TARA-THAT-IS.
WE MUST LEAVE YOU NOW.
PLEASE TAKE CARE OF YOURSELF.
THE GODDESS APPROACHES.

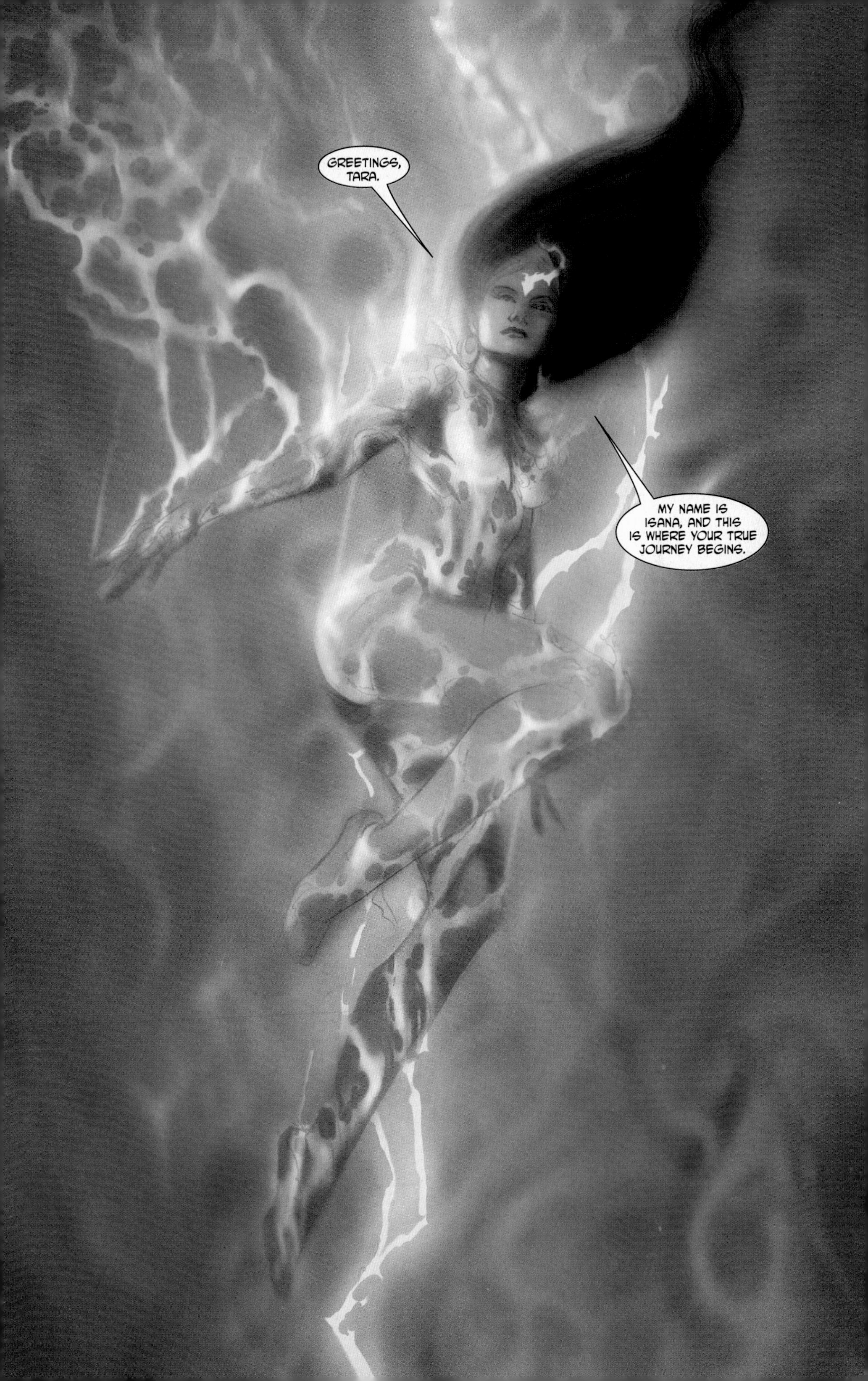
GREETINGS, TARA.
MY NAME IS ISANA, AND THIS IS WHERE YOUR TRUE JOURNEY BEGINS.

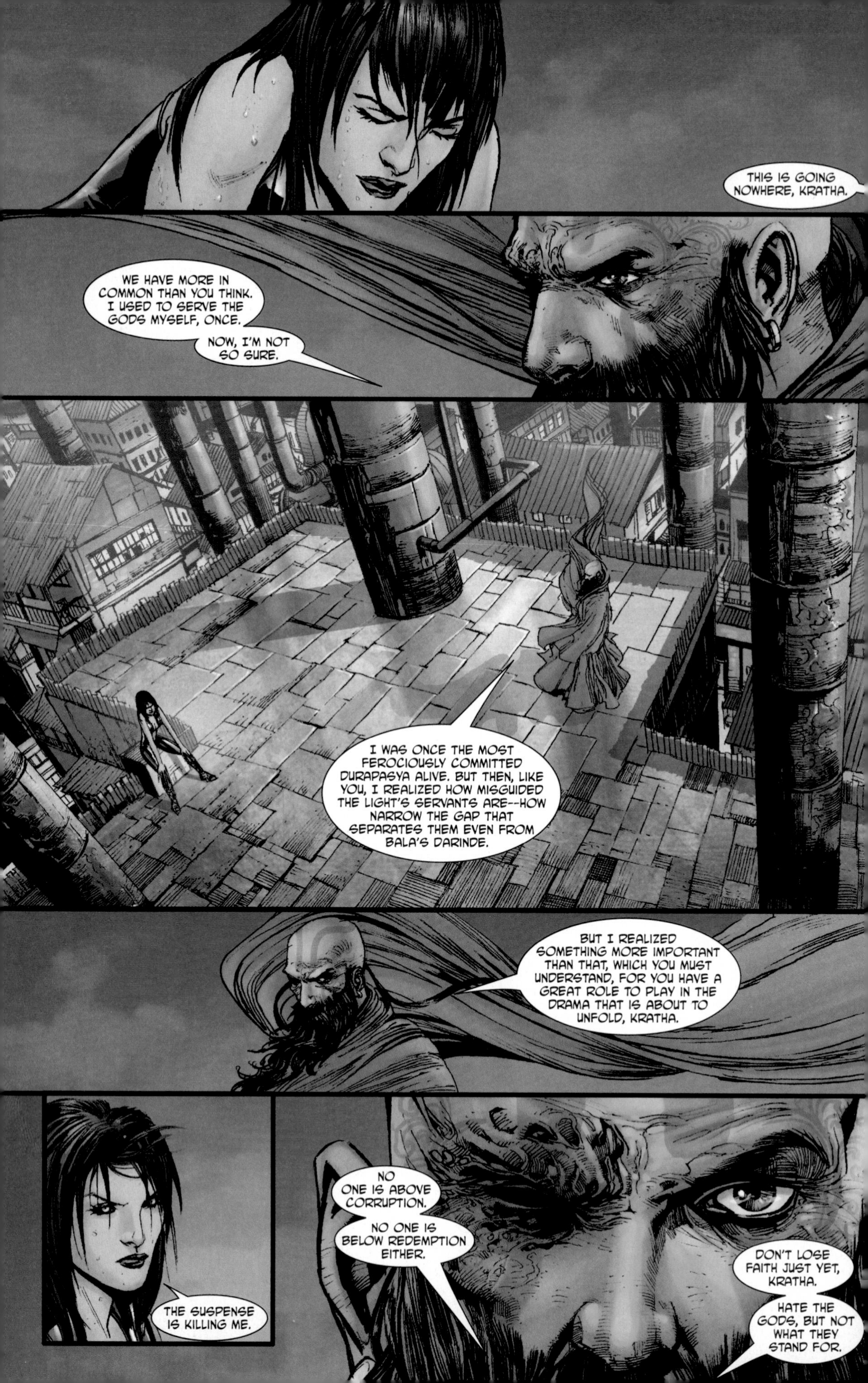

THIS IS GOING NOWHERE, KRATHA.
WE HAVE MORE IN COMMON THAN YOU THINK. I USED TO SERVE THE GODS MYSELF, ONCE.
NOW, I'M NOT SO SURE.
I WAS ONCE THE MOST FEROCIOUSLY COMMITTED DURAPASYA ALIVE. BUT THEN, LIKE YOU, I REALIZED HOW MISGUIDED THE LIGHT'S SERVANTS ARE--HOW NARROW THE GAP THAT SEPARATES THEM EVEN FROM BALA'S DARINDE.
BUT I REALIZED SOMETHING MORE IMPORTANT THAN THAT, WHICH YOU MUST UNDERSTAND, FOR YOU HAVE A GREAT ROLE TO PLAY IN THE DRAMA THAT IS ABOUT TO UNFOLD, KRATHA.
THE SUSPENSE IS KILLING ME.
NO ONE IS ABOVE CORRUPTION.
NO ONE IS BELOW REDEMPTION EITHER.
DON'T LOSE FAITH JUST YET, KRATHA.
HATE THE GODS, BUT NOT WHAT THEY STAND FOR.

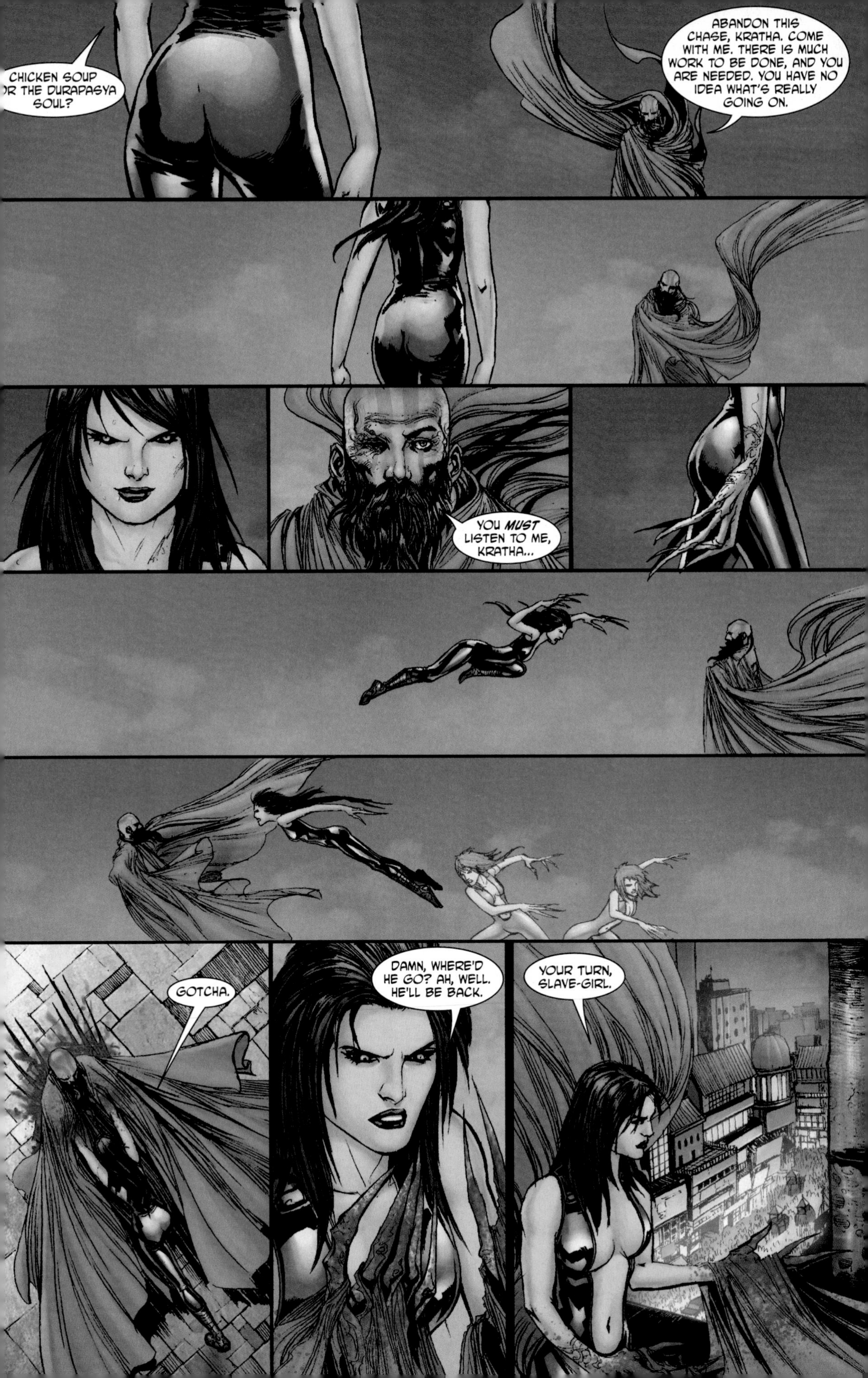
CHICKEN SOUP FOR THE DURAPASYA SOUL?
ABANDON THIS CHASE, KRATHA. COME WITH ME. THERE IS MUCH WORK TO BE DONE, AND YOU ARE NEEDED. YOU HAVE NO IDEA WHAT'S REALLY GOING ON.
YOU MUST LISTEN TO ME, KRATHA...
GOTCHA.
DAMN, WHERE'D HE GO? AH, WELL. HE'LL BE BACK.
YOUR TURN, SLAVE-GIRL.

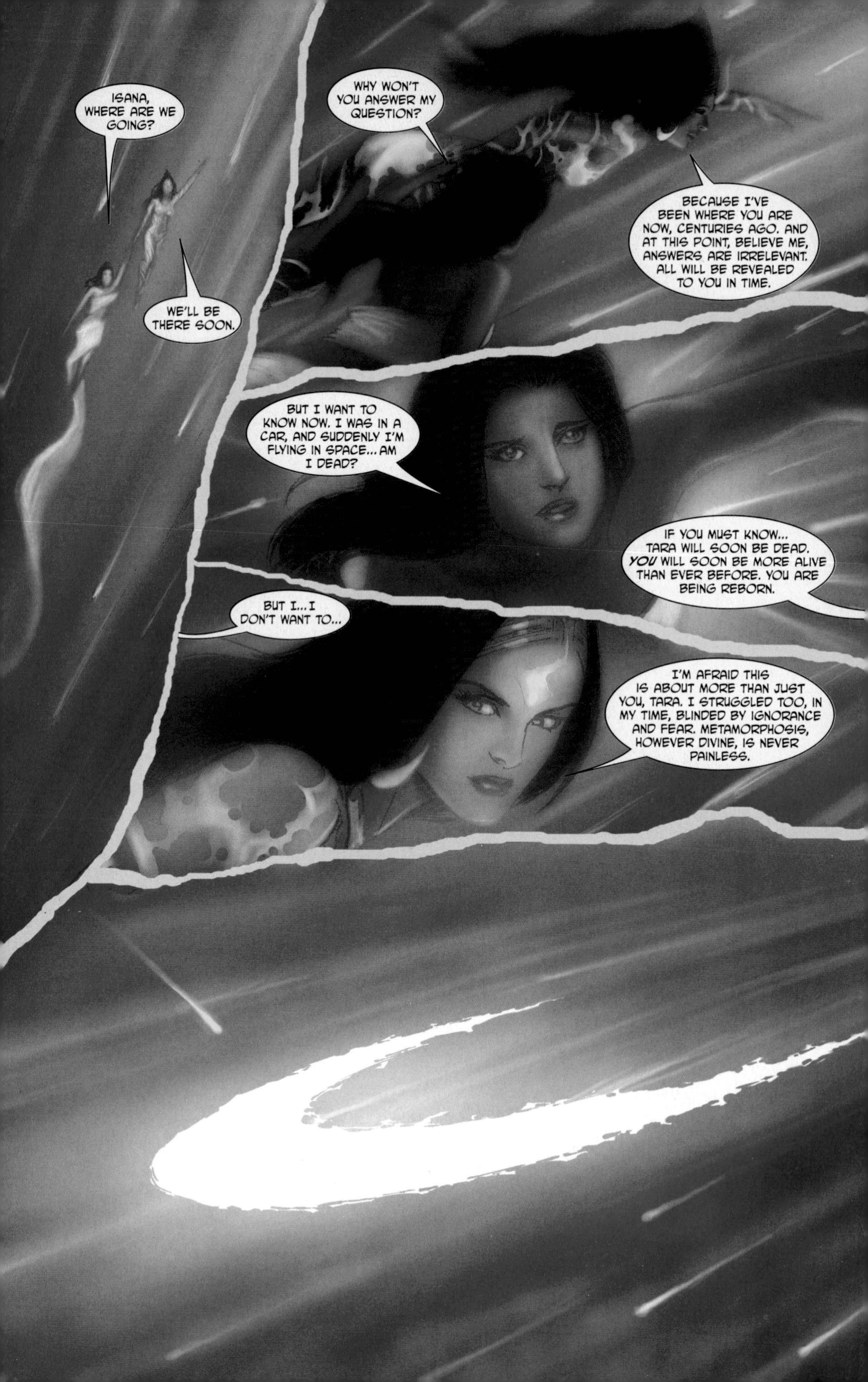
ISANA, WHERE ARE WE GOING?
WE'LL BE THERE SOON.
WHY WON'T YOU ANSWER MY QUESTION?
BECAUSE I'VE BEEN WHERE YOU ARE NOW, CENTURIES AGO. AND AT THIS POINT, BELIEVE ME, ANSWERS ARE IRRELEVANT. ALL WILL BE REVEALED TO YOU IN TIME.
BUT I WANT TO KNOW NOW. I WAS IN A CAR, AND SUDDENLY I'M FLYING IN SPACE... AM I DEAD?
IF YOU MUST KNOW... TARA WILL SOON BE DEAD. ***YOU*** WILL SOON BE MORE ALIVE THAN EVER BEFORE. YOU ARE BEING REBORN.
BUT I... I DON'T WANT TO...
I'M AFRAID THIS IS ABOUT MORE THAN JUST YOU, TARA. I STRUGGLED TOO, IN MY TIME, BLINDED BY IGNORANCE AND FEAR. METAMORPHOSIS, HOWEVER DIVINE, IS NEVER PAINLESS.

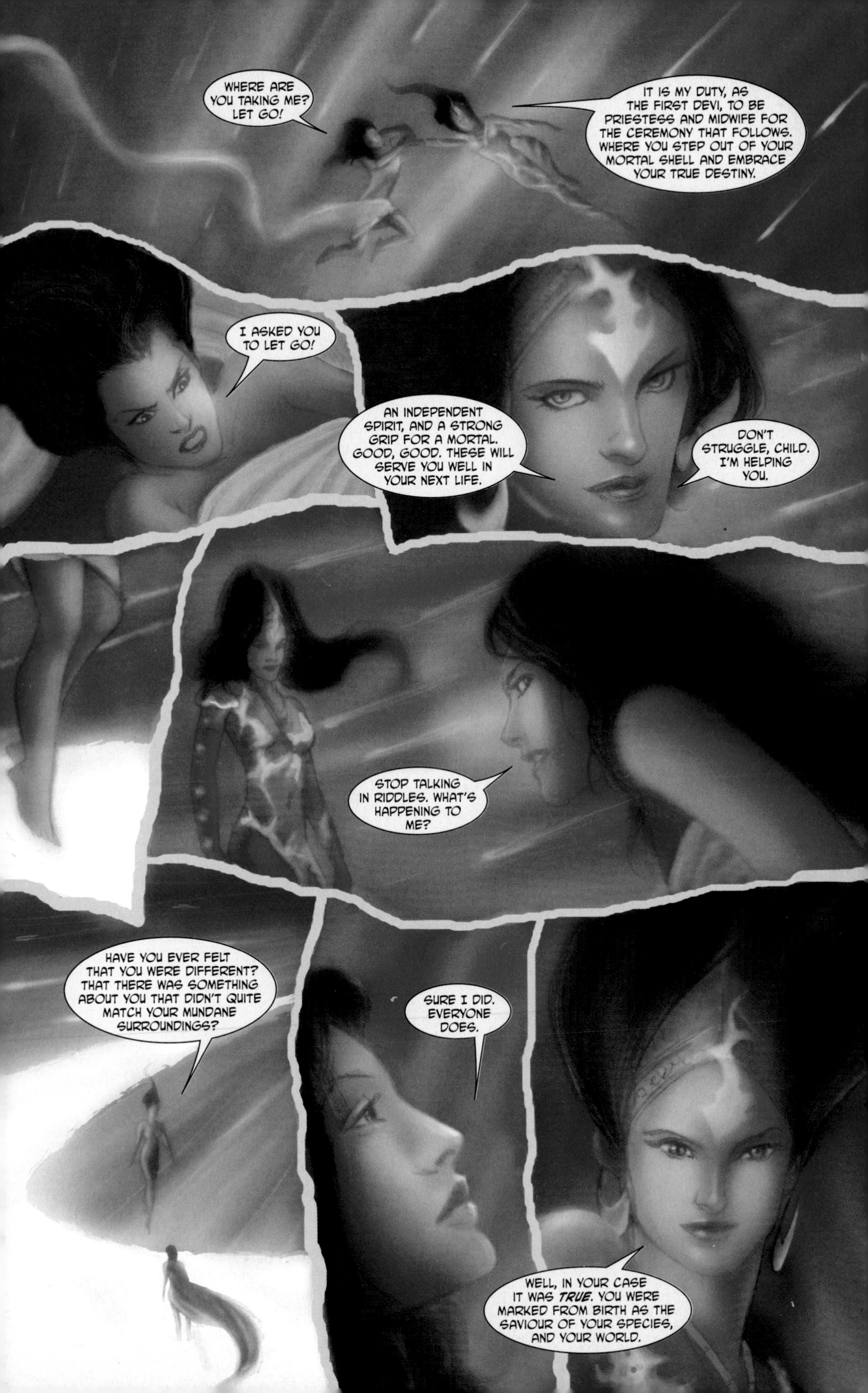
WHERE ARE YOU TAKING ME? LET GO!
IT IS MY DUTY, AS THE FIRST DEVI, TO BE PRIESTESS AND MIDWIFE FOR THE CEREMONY THAT FOLLOWS. WHERE YOU STEP OUT OF YOUR MORTAL SHELL AND EMBRACE YOUR TRUE DESTINY.
I ASKED YOU TO LET GO!
AN INDEPENDENT SPIRIT, AND A STRONG GRIP FOR A MORTAL. GOOD, GOOD. THESE WILL SERVE YOU WELL IN YOUR NEXT LIFE.
DON'T STRUGGLE, CHILD. I'M HELPING YOU.
STOP TALKING IN RIDDLES. WHAT'S HAPPENING TO ME?
HAVE YOU EVER FELT THAT YOU WERE DIFFERENT? THAT THERE WAS SOMETHING ABOUT YOU THAT DIDN'T QUITE MATCH YOUR MUNDANE SURROUNDINGS?
SURE I DID. EVERYONE DOES.
WELL, IN YOUR CASE IT WAS *TRUE*. YOU WERE MARKED FROM BIRTH AS THE SAVIOUR OF YOUR SPECIES, AND YOUR WORLD.

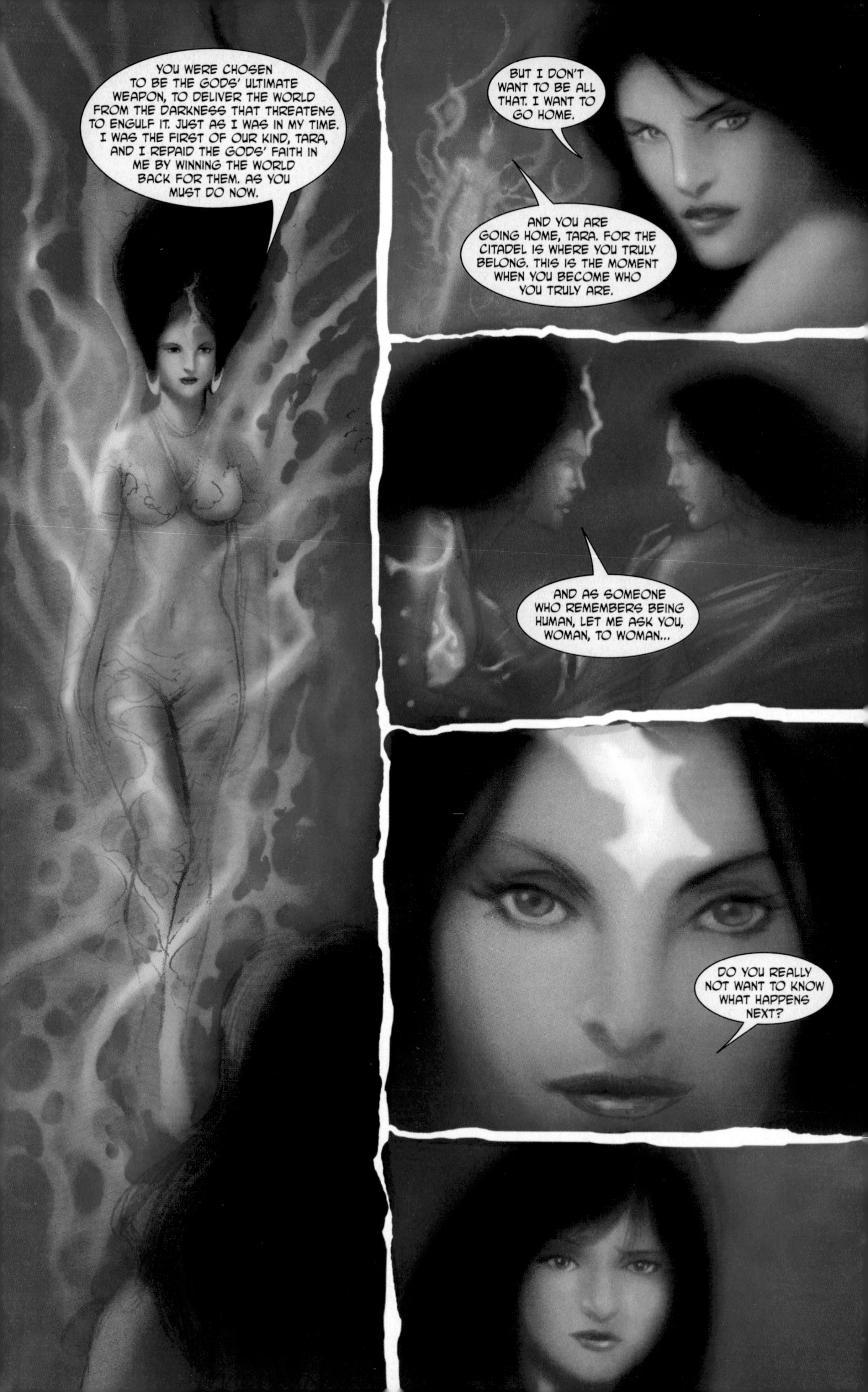
YOU WERE CHOSEN TO BE THE GODS' ULTIMATE WEAPON, TO DELIVER THE WORLD FROM THE DARKNESS THAT THREATENS TO ENGULF IT. JUST AS I WAS IN MY TIME. I WAS THE FIRST OF OUR KIND, TARA, AND I REPAID THE GODS' FAITH IN ME BY WINNING THE WORLD BACK FOR THEM. AS YOU MUST DO NOW.
BUT I DON'T WANT TO BE ALL THAT. I WANT TO GO HOME.
AND YOU ARE GOING HOME, TARA. FOR THE CITADEL IS WHERE YOU TRULY BELONG. THIS IS THE MOMENT WHEN YOU BECOME WHO YOU TRULY ARE.
AND AS SOMEONE WHO REMEMBERS BEING HUMAN, LET ME ASK YOU, WOMAN, TO WOMAN...
DO YOU REALLY NOT WANT TO KNOW WHAT HAPPENS NEXT?

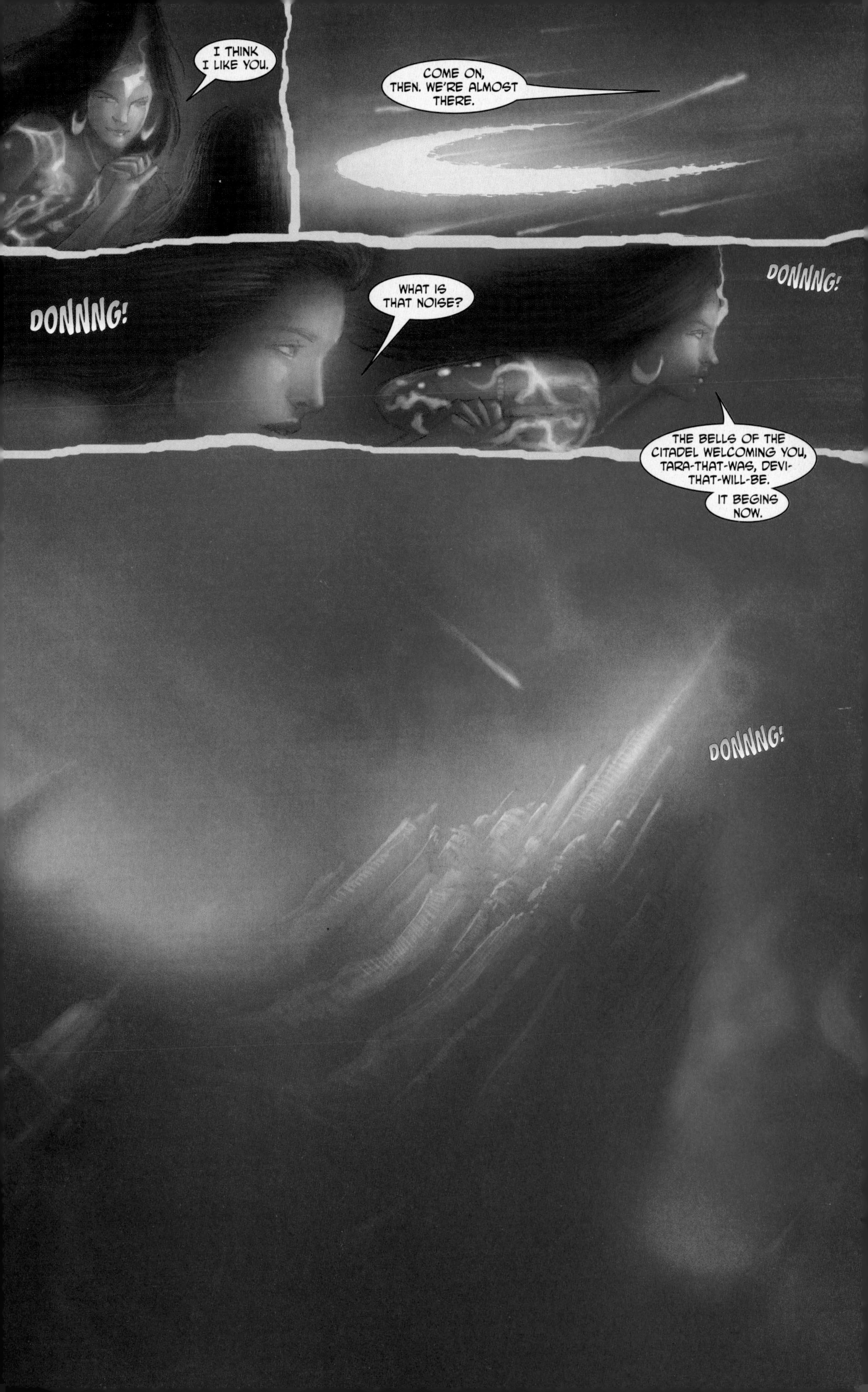
I THINK I LIKE YOU.
COME ON, THEN. WE'RE ALMOST THERE.
DONNNG!
WHAT IS THAT NOISE?
DONNNG!
THE BELLS OF THE CITADEL WELCOMING YOU, TARA-THAT-WAS, DEVI-THAT-WILL-BE.
IT BEGINS NOW.
DONNNG!

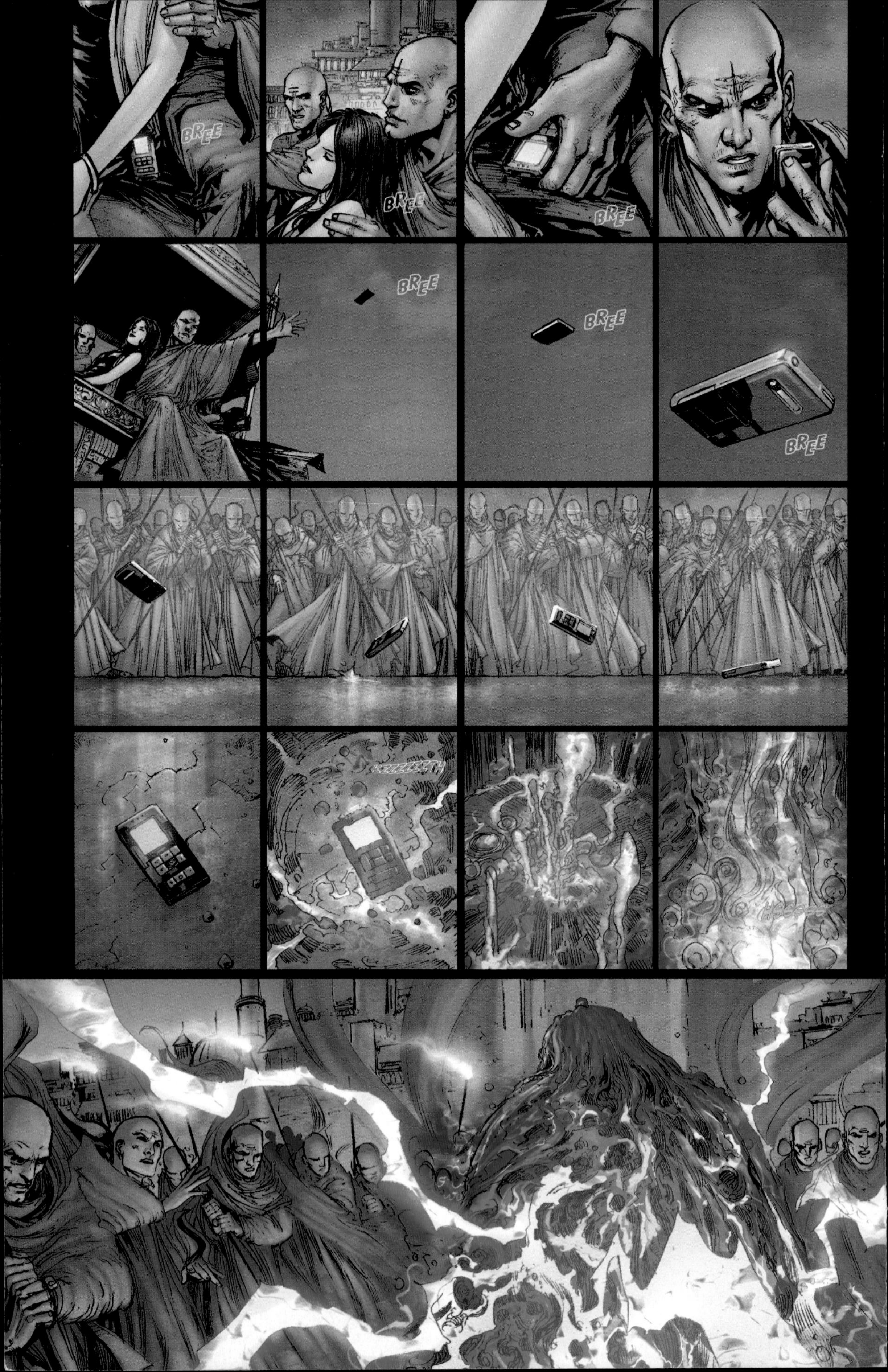
BREE
BREE
BREE
BREE
BREE
BREE
BREE

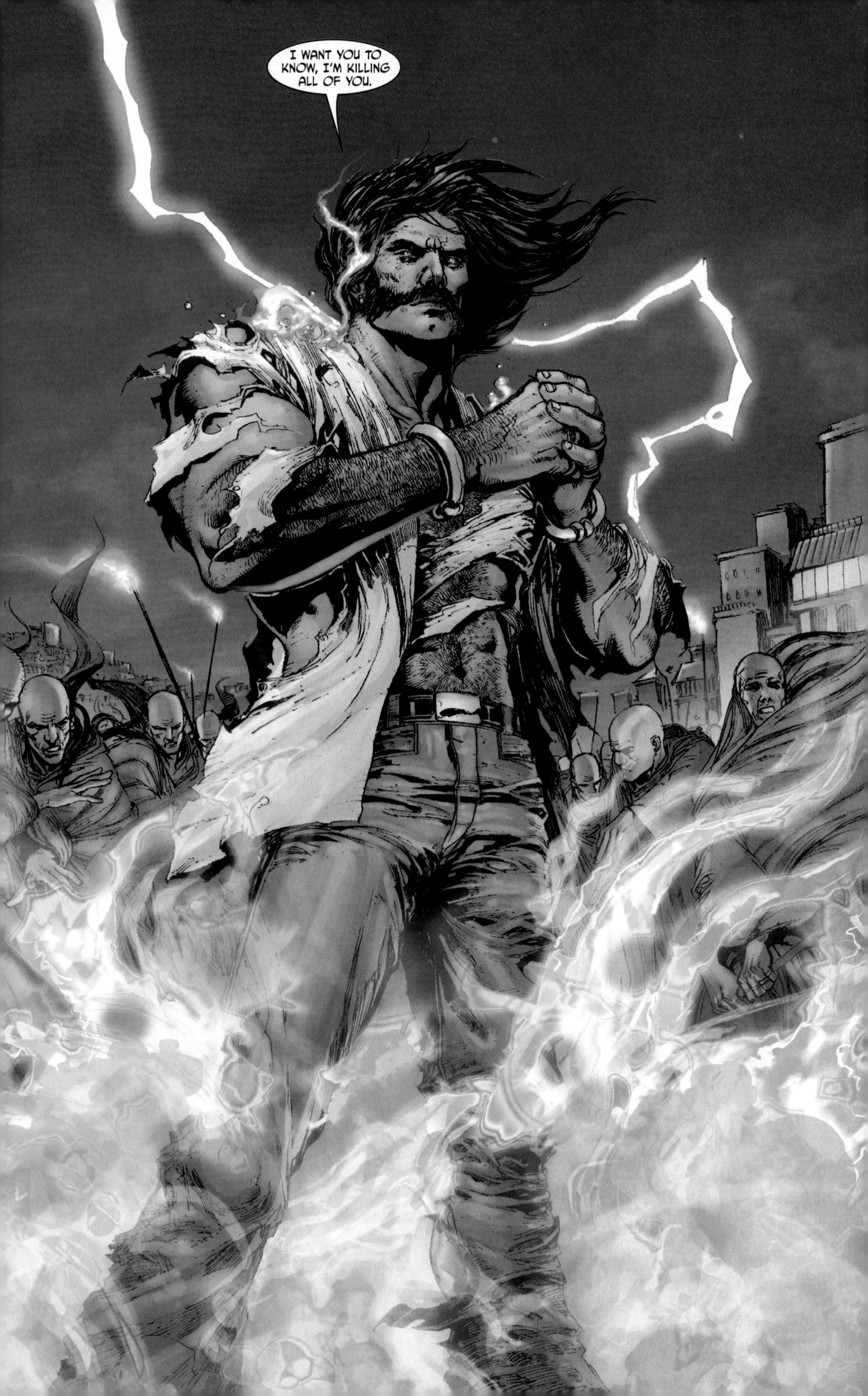
I WANT YOU TO KNOW, I'M KILLING ALL OF YOU.

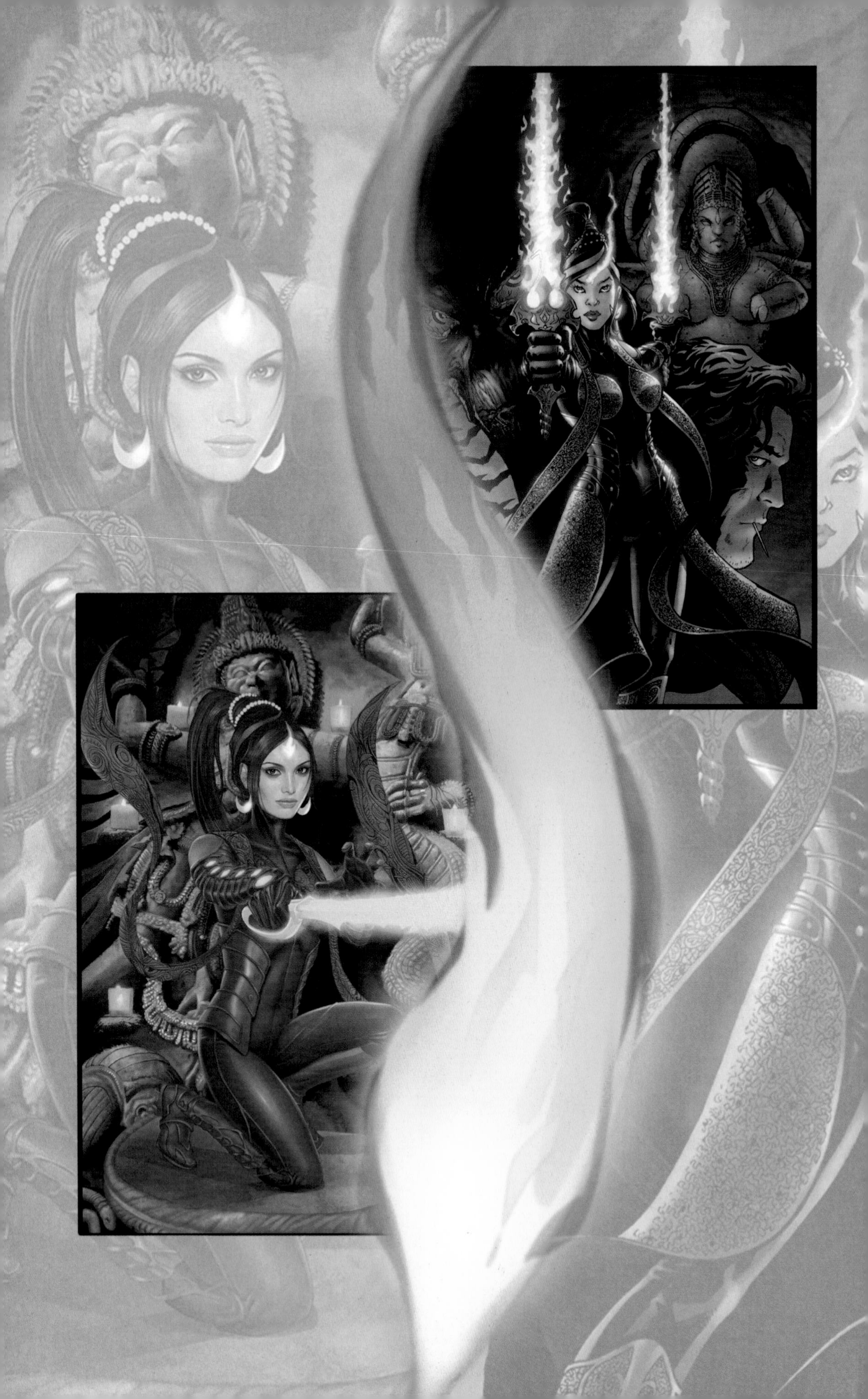

Part Four
PRARAMBH

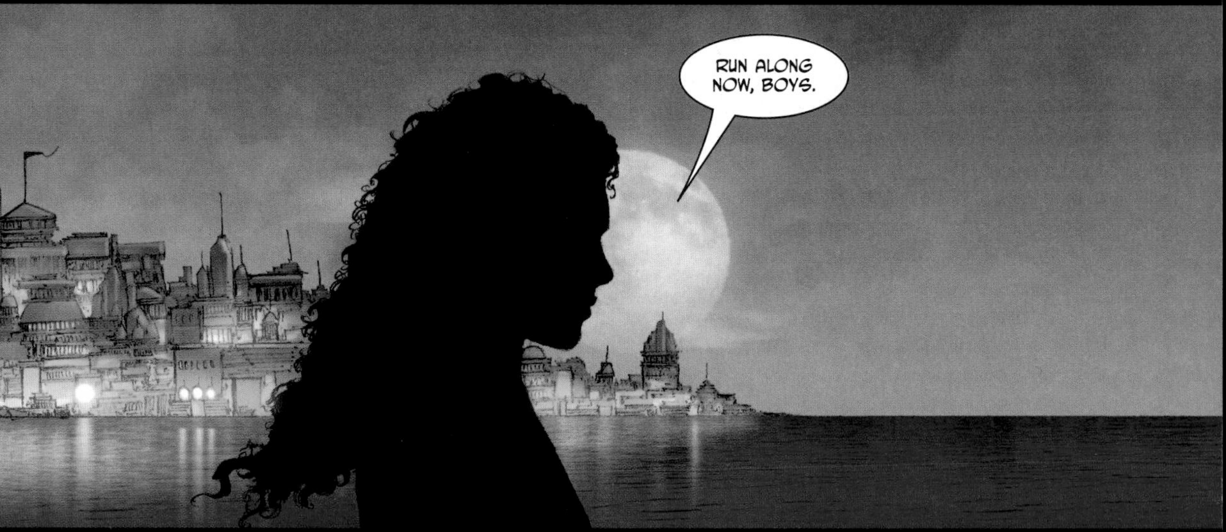
RUN ALONG NOW, BOYS.

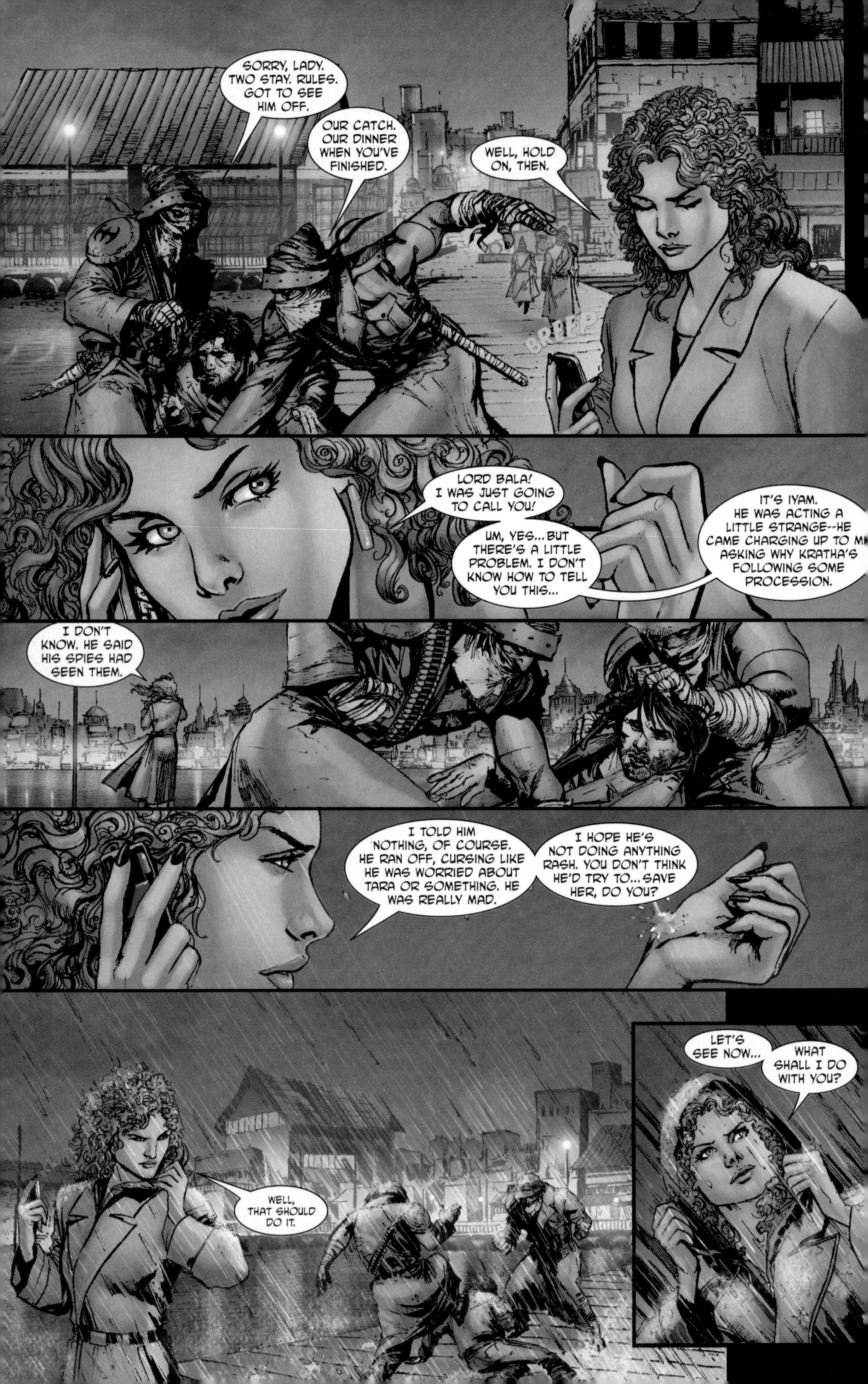
SORRY, LADY. TWO STAY. RULES. GOT TO SEE HIM OFF.
OUR CATCH. OUR DINNER WHEN YOU'VE FINISHED.
WELL, HOLD ON, THEN.
BREEP
LORD BALA! I WAS JUST GOING TO CALL YOU!
UM, YES... BUT THERE'S A LITTLE PROBLEM. I DON'T KNOW HOW TO TELL YOU THIS...
IT'S IYAM. HE WAS ACTING A LITTLE STRANGE--HE CAME CHARGING UP TO M ASKING WHY KRATHA'S FOLLOWING SOME PROCESSION.
I DON'T KNOW. HE SAID HIS SPIES HAD SEEN THEM.
I TOLD HIM NOTHING, OF COURSE. HE RAN OFF, CURSING LIKE HE WAS WORRIED ABOUT TARA OR SOMETHING. HE WAS REALLY MAD.
I HOPE HE'S NOT DOING ANYTHING RASH. YOU DON'T THINK HE'D TRY TO... SAVE HER, DO YOU?
WELL, THAT SHOULD DO IT.
LET'S SEE NOW...
WHAT SHALL I DO WITH YOU?

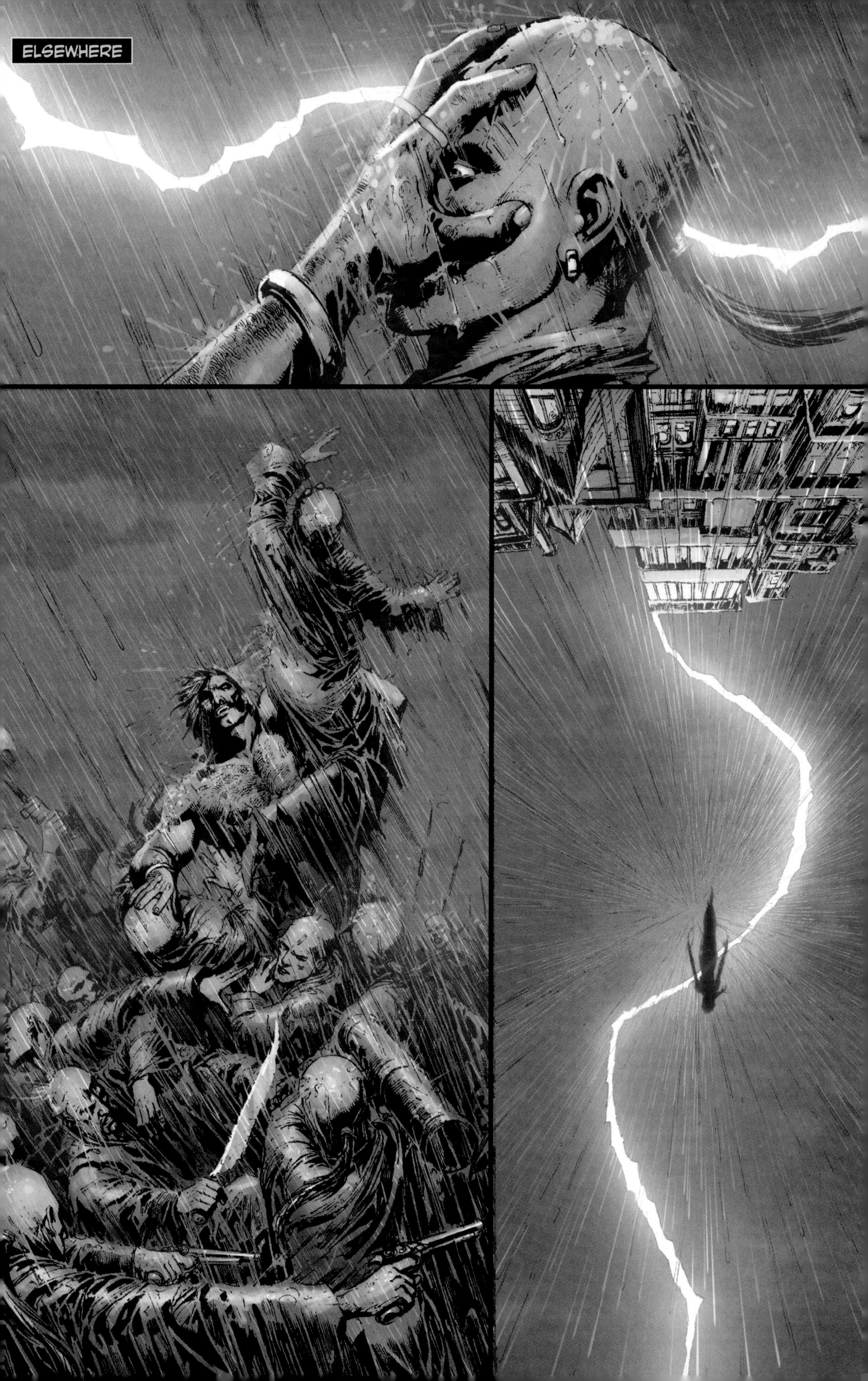
ELSEWHERE

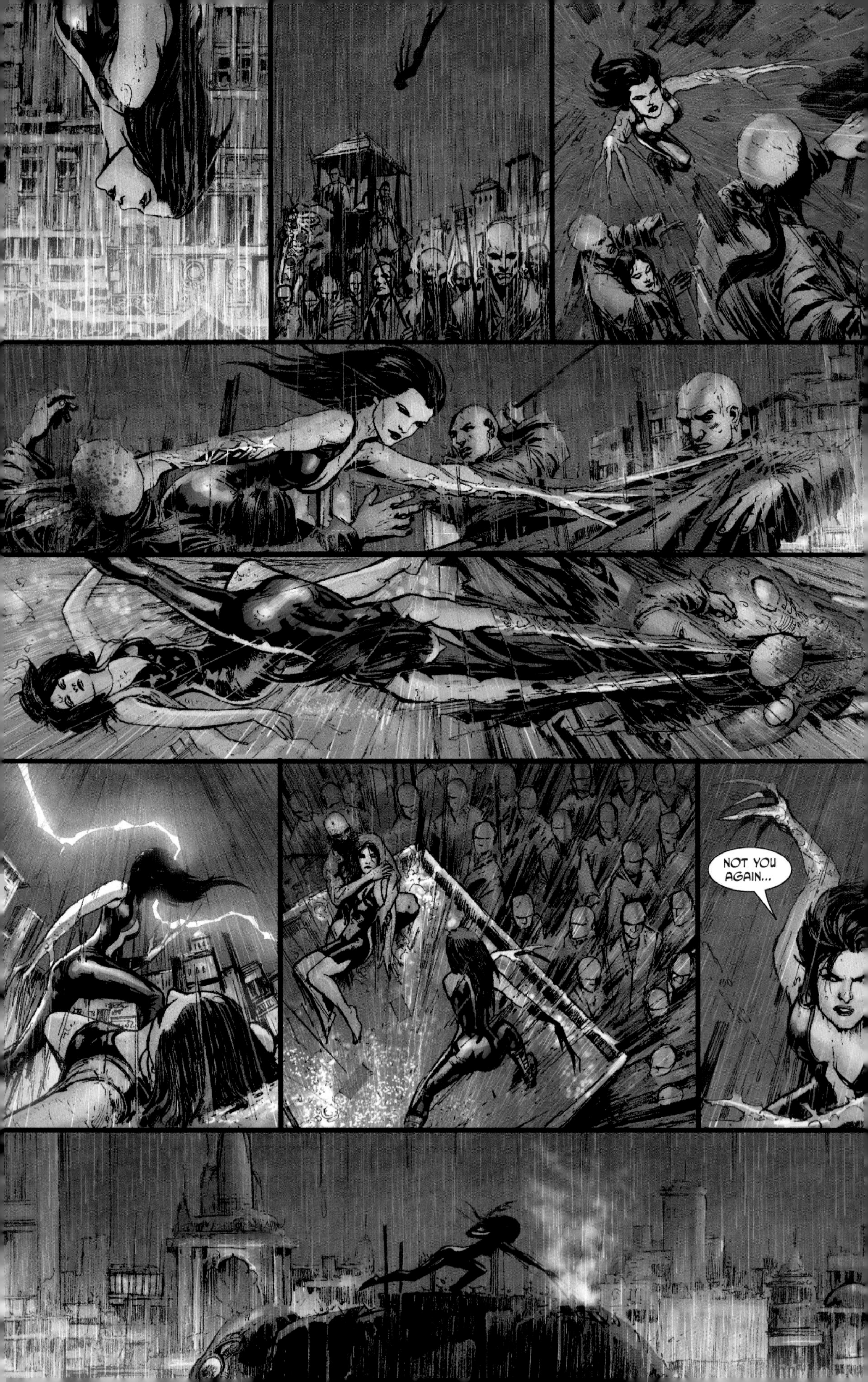
NOT YOU AGAIN...

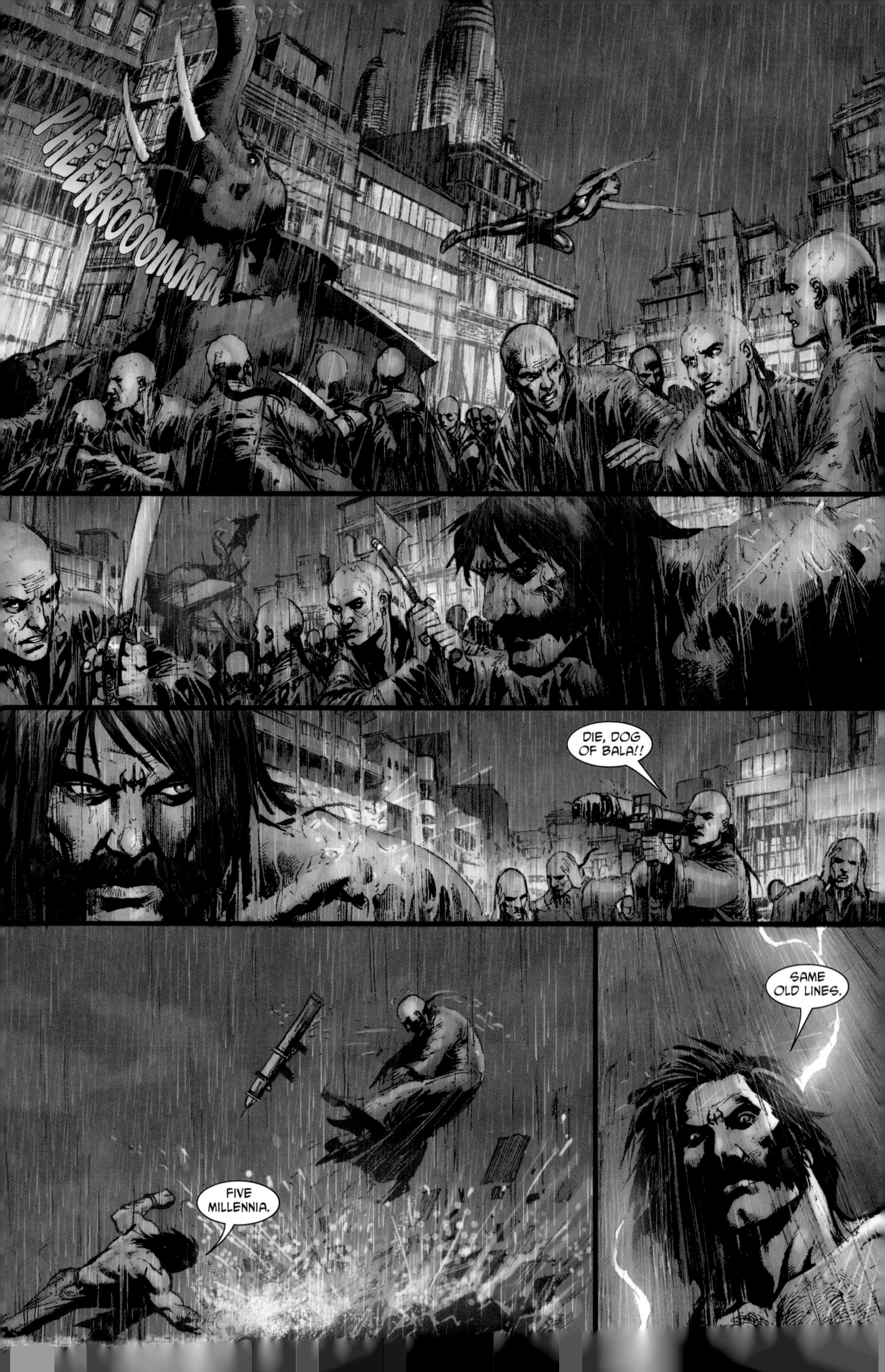
PHEERROOOMMM
DIE, DOG OF BALA!!
FIVE MILLENNIA.
SAME OLD LINES.

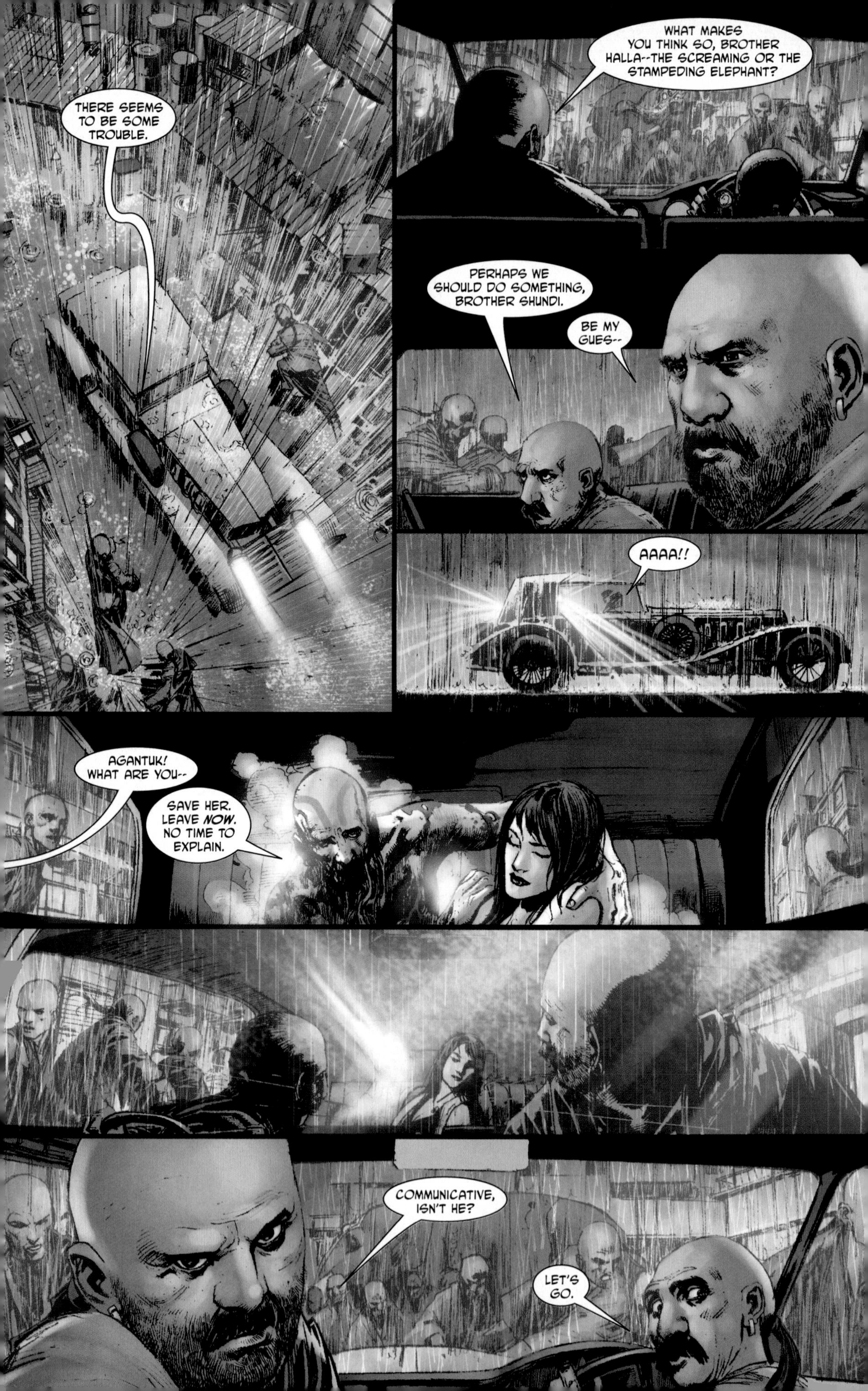

THERE SEEMS TO BE SOME TROUBLE.
WHAT MAKES YOU THINK SO, BROTHER HALLA--THE SCREAMING OR THE STAMPEDING ELEPHANT?
PERHAPS WE SHOULD DO SOMETHING, BROTHER SHUNDI.
BE MY GUES--
AAAA!!
AGANTUK! WHAT ARE YOU--
SAVE HER. LEAVE *NOW*. NO TIME TO EXPLAIN.
COMMUNICATIVE, ISN'T HE?
LET'S GO.

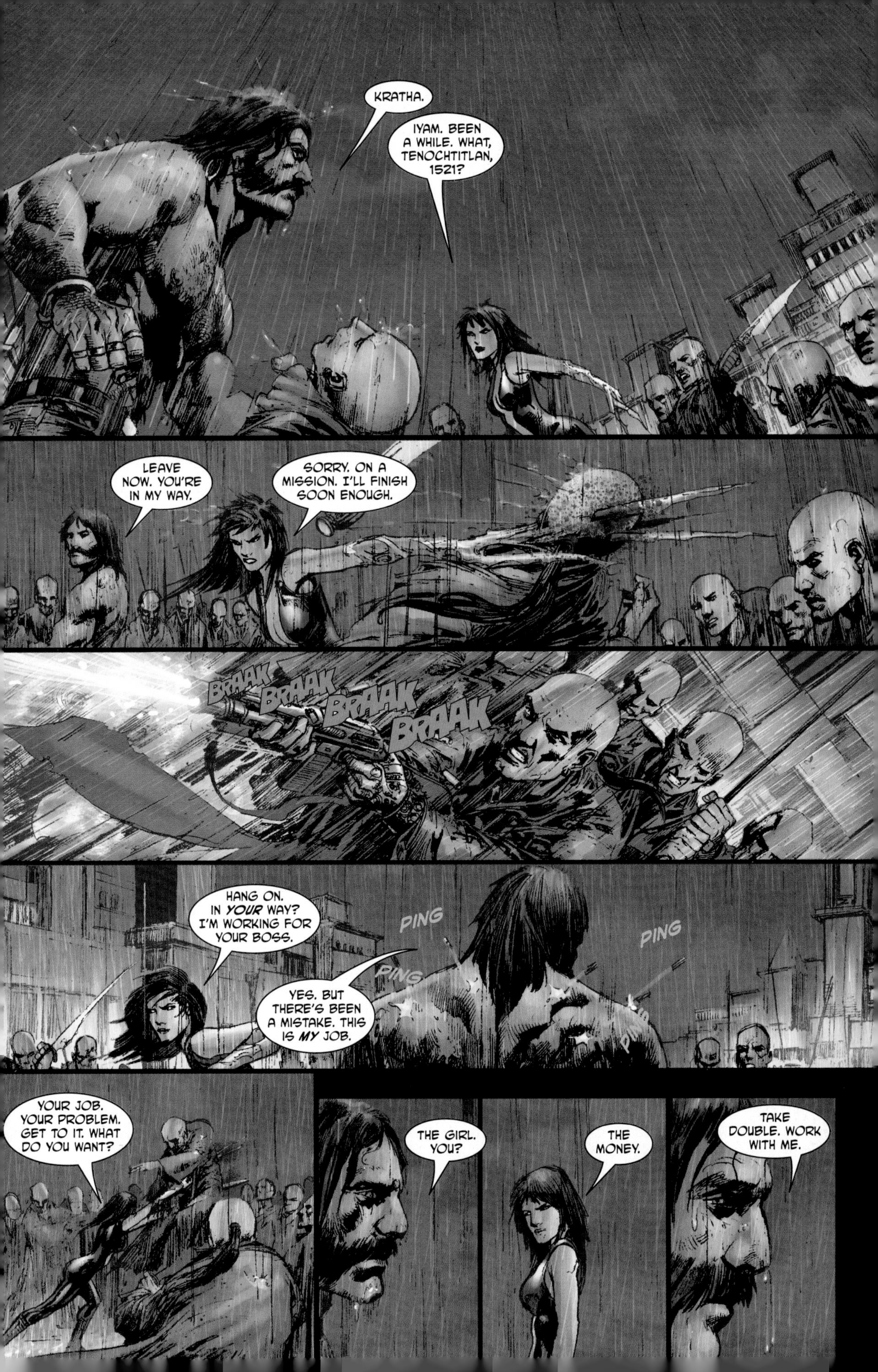
KRATHA.
IYAM. BEEN A WHILE. WHAT, TENOCHTITLAN, 1521?
LEAVE NOW. YOU'RE IN MY WAY.
SORRY. ON A MISSION. I'LL FINISH SOON ENOUGH.
BRAAK BRAAK BRAAK BRAAK
HANG ON. IN YOUR WAY? I'M WORKING FOR YOUR BOSS.
PING
PING
PING
YES. BUT THERE'S BEEN A MISTAKE. THIS IS MY JOB.
YOUR JOB. YOUR PROBLEM. GET TO IT. WHAT DO YOU WANT?
THE GIRL. YOU?
THE MONEY.
TAKE DOUBLE. WORK WITH ME.

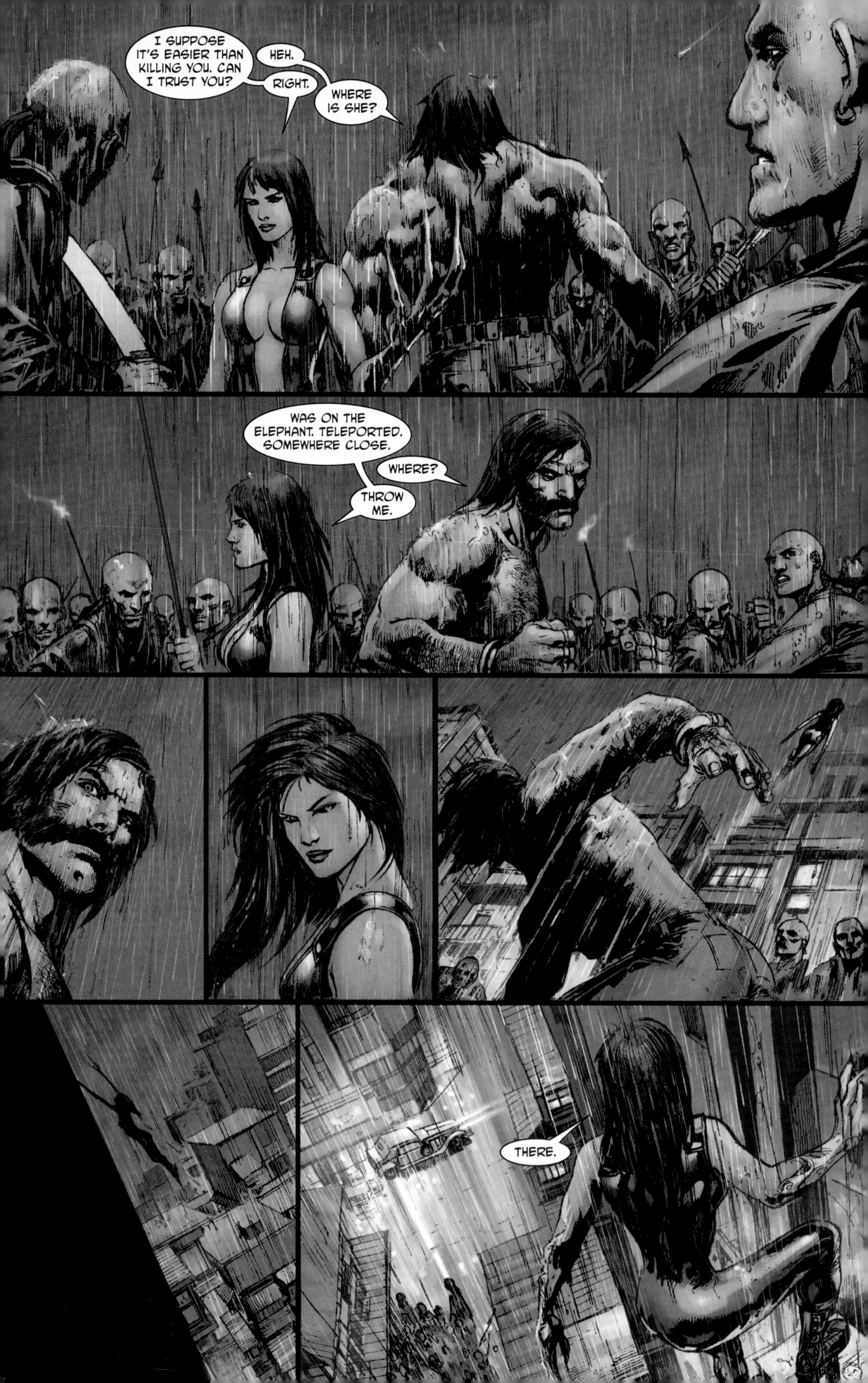
I SUPPOSE IT'S EASIER THAN KILLING YOU. CAN I TRUST YOU?
HEH.
RIGHT.
WHERE IS SHE?
WAS ON THE ELEPHANT. TELEPORTED. SOMEWHERE CLOSE.
WHERE?
THROW ME.
THERE.

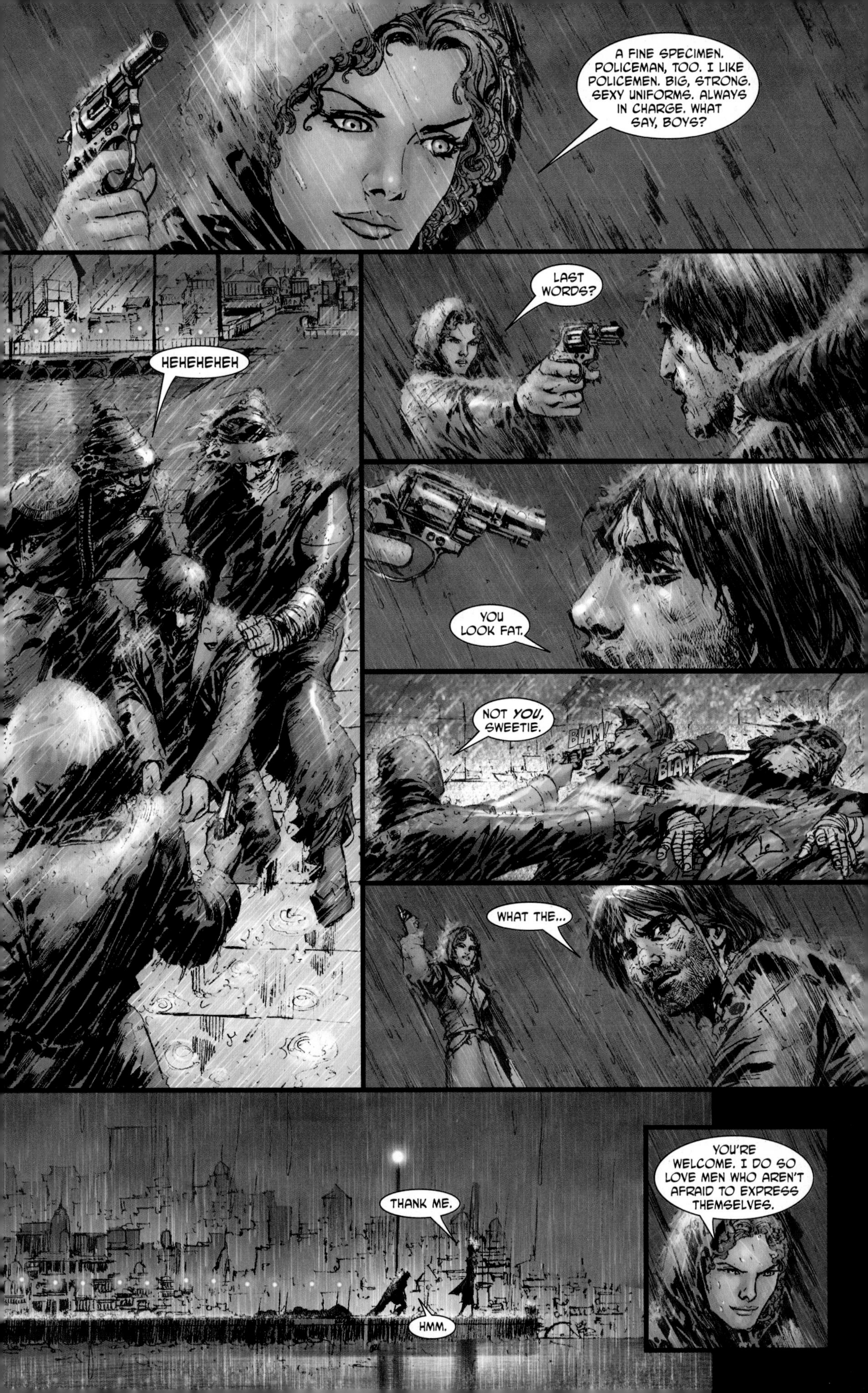
A FINE SPECIMEN. POLICEMAN, TOO. I LIKE POLICEMEN. BIG, STRONG. SEXY UNIFORMS. ALWAYS IN CHARGE. WHAT SAY, BOYS?
HEHEHEHEH
LAST WORDS?
YOU LOOK FAT.
NOT YOU, SWEETIE.
BLAM!
BLAM!
WHAT THE...
THANK ME.
HMM.
YOU'RE WELCOME. I DO SO LOVE MEN WHO AREN'T AFRAID TO EXPRESS THEMSELVES.

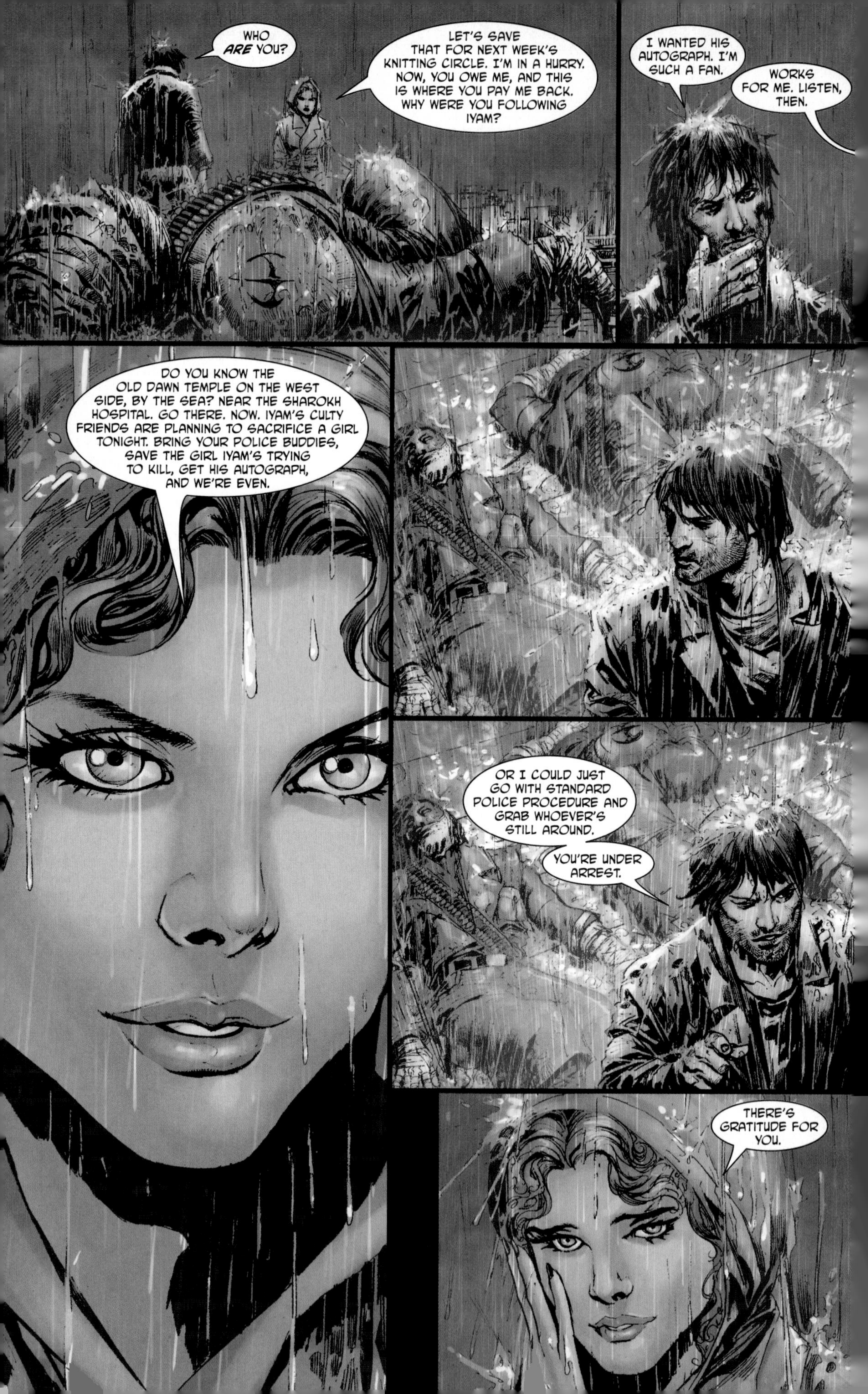
WHO *ARE* YOU?
LET'S SAVE THAT FOR NEXT WEEK'S KNITTING CIRCLE. I'M IN A HURRY. NOW, YOU OWE ME, AND THIS IS WHERE YOU PAY ME BACK. WHY WERE YOU FOLLOWING IYAM?
I WANTED HIS AUTOGRAPH. I'M SUCH A FAN.
WORKS FOR ME. LISTEN, THEN.
DO YOU KNOW THE OLD DAWN TEMPLE ON THE WEST SIDE, BY THE SEA? NEAR THE SHAROKH HOSPITAL. GO THERE. NOW. IYAM'S CULTY FRIENDS ARE PLANNING TO SACRIFICE A GIRL TONIGHT. BRING YOUR POLICE BUDDIES, SAVE THE GIRL IYAM'S TRYING TO KILL, GET HIS AUTOGRAPH, AND WE'RE EVEN.
OR I COULD JUST GO WITH STANDARD POLICE PROCEDURE AND GRAB WHOEVER'S STILL AROUND.
YOU'RE UNDER ARREST.
THERE'S GRATITUDE FOR YOU.

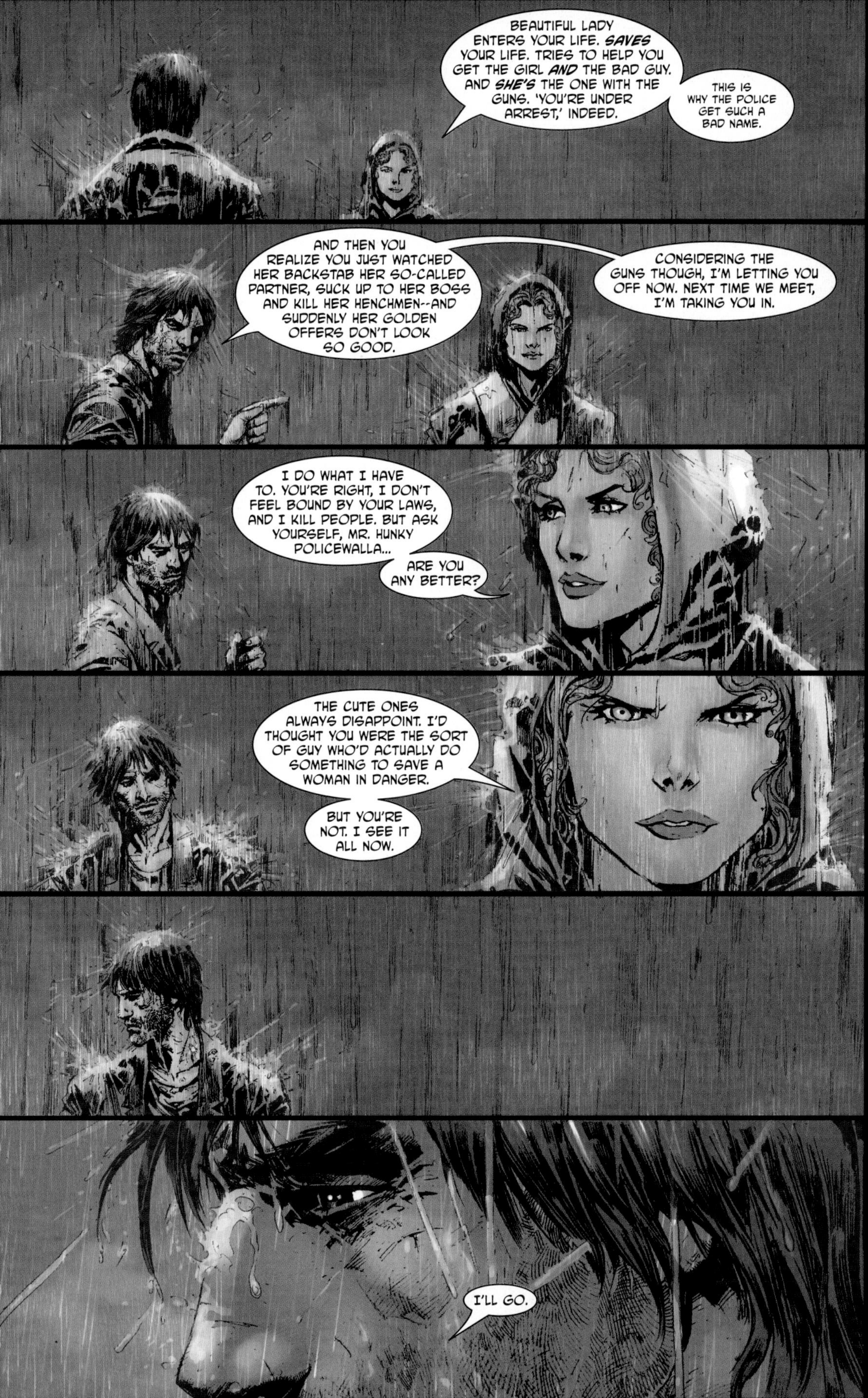
BEAUTIFUL LADY ENTERS YOUR LIFE. ***SAVES*** YOUR LIFE. TRIES TO HELP YOU GET THE GIRL ***AND*** THE BAD GUY. AND ***SHE'S*** THE ONE WITH THE GUNS. 'YOU'RE UNDER ARREST,' INDEED.
THIS IS WHY THE POLICE GET SUCH A BAD NAME.
AND THEN YOU REALIZE YOU JUST WATCHED HER BACKSTAB HER SO-CALLED PARTNER, SUCK UP TO HER BOSS AND KILL HER HENCHMEN--AND SUDDENLY HER GOLDEN OFFERS DON'T LOOK SO GOOD.
CONSIDERING THE GUNS THOUGH, I'M LETTING YOU OFF NOW. NEXT TIME WE MEET, I'M TAKING YOU IN.
I DO WHAT I HAVE TO. YOU'RE RIGHT, I DON'T FEEL BOUND BY YOUR LAWS, AND I KILL PEOPLE. BUT ASK YOURSELF, MR. HUNKY POLICEWALLA...
ARE YOU ANY BETTER?
THE CUTE ONES ALWAYS DISAPPOINT. I'D THOUGHT YOU WERE THE SORT OF GUY WHO'D ACTUALLY DO SOMETHING TO SAVE A WOMAN IN DANGER.
BUT YOU'RE NOT. I SEE IT ALL NOW.
I'LL GO.

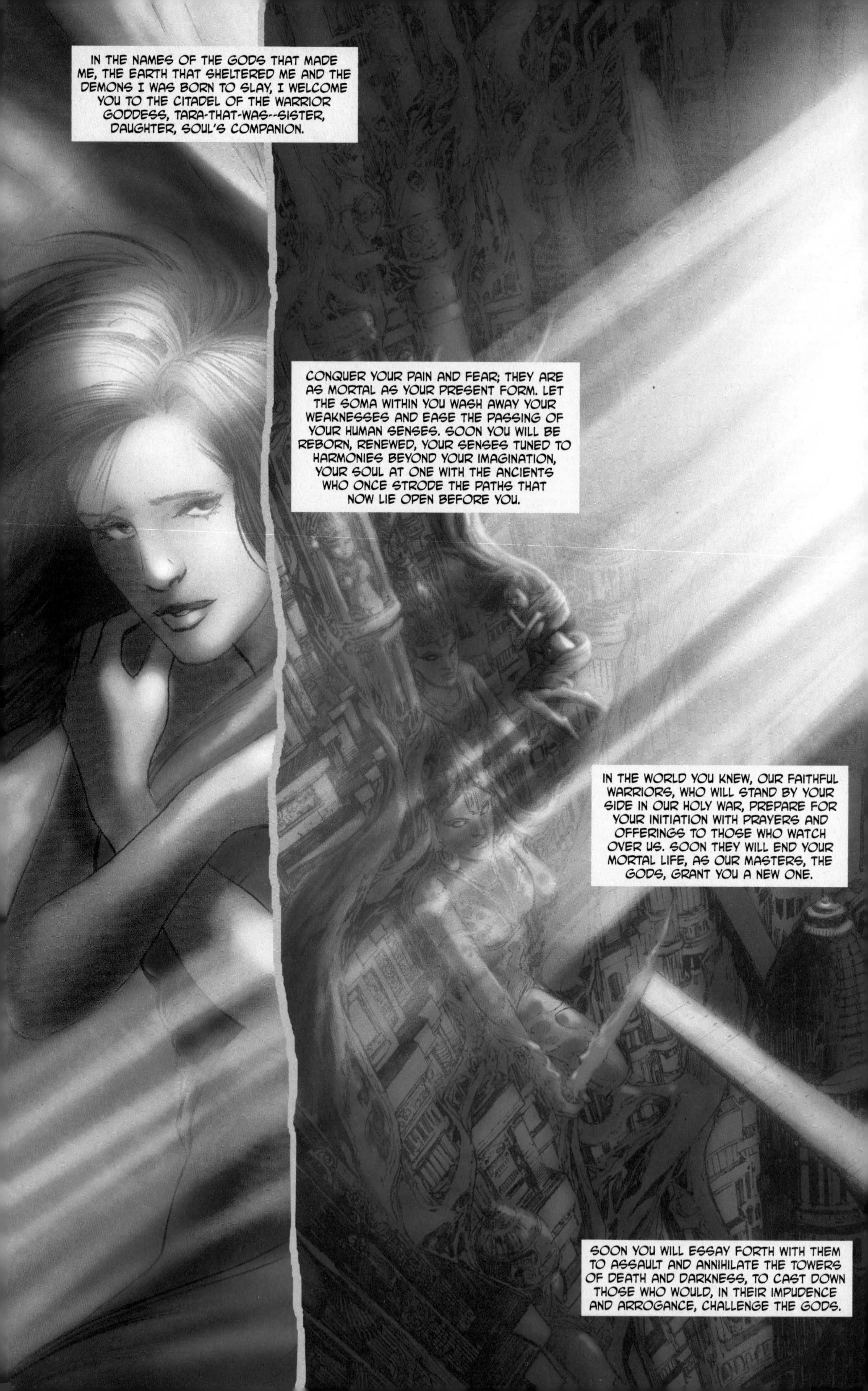
IN THE NAMES OF THE GODS THAT MADE ME, THE EARTH THAT SHELTERED ME AND THE DEMONS I WAS BORN TO SLAY, I WELCOME YOU TO THE CITADEL OF THE WARRIOR GODDESS, TARA-THAT-WAS--SISTER, DAUGHTER, SOUL'S COMPANION.
CONQUER YOUR PAIN AND FEAR; THEY ARE AS MORTAL AS YOUR PRESENT FORM. LET THE SOMA WITHIN YOU WASH AWAY YOUR WEAKNESSES AND EASE THE PASSING OF YOUR HUMAN SENSES. SOON YOU WILL BE REBORN, RENEWED, YOUR SENSES TUNED TO HARMONIES BEYOND YOUR IMAGINATION, YOUR SOUL AT ONE WITH THE ANCIENTS WHO ONCE STRODE THE PATHS THAT NOW LIE OPEN BEFORE YOU.
IN THE WORLD YOU KNEW, OUR FAITHFUL WARRIORS, WHO WILL STAND BY YOUR SIDE IN OUR HOLY WAR, PREPARE FOR YOUR INITIATION WITH PRAYERS AND OFFERINGS TO THOSE WHO WATCH OVER US. SOON THEY WILL END YOUR MORTAL LIFE, AS OUR MASTERS, THE GODS, GRANT YOU A NEW ONE.
SOON YOU WILL ESSAY FORTH WITH THEM TO ASSAULT AND ANNIHILATE THE TOWERS OF DEATH AND DARKNESS, TO CAST DOWN THOSE WHO WOULD, IN THEIR IMPUDENCE AND ARROGANCE, CHALLENGE THE GODS.

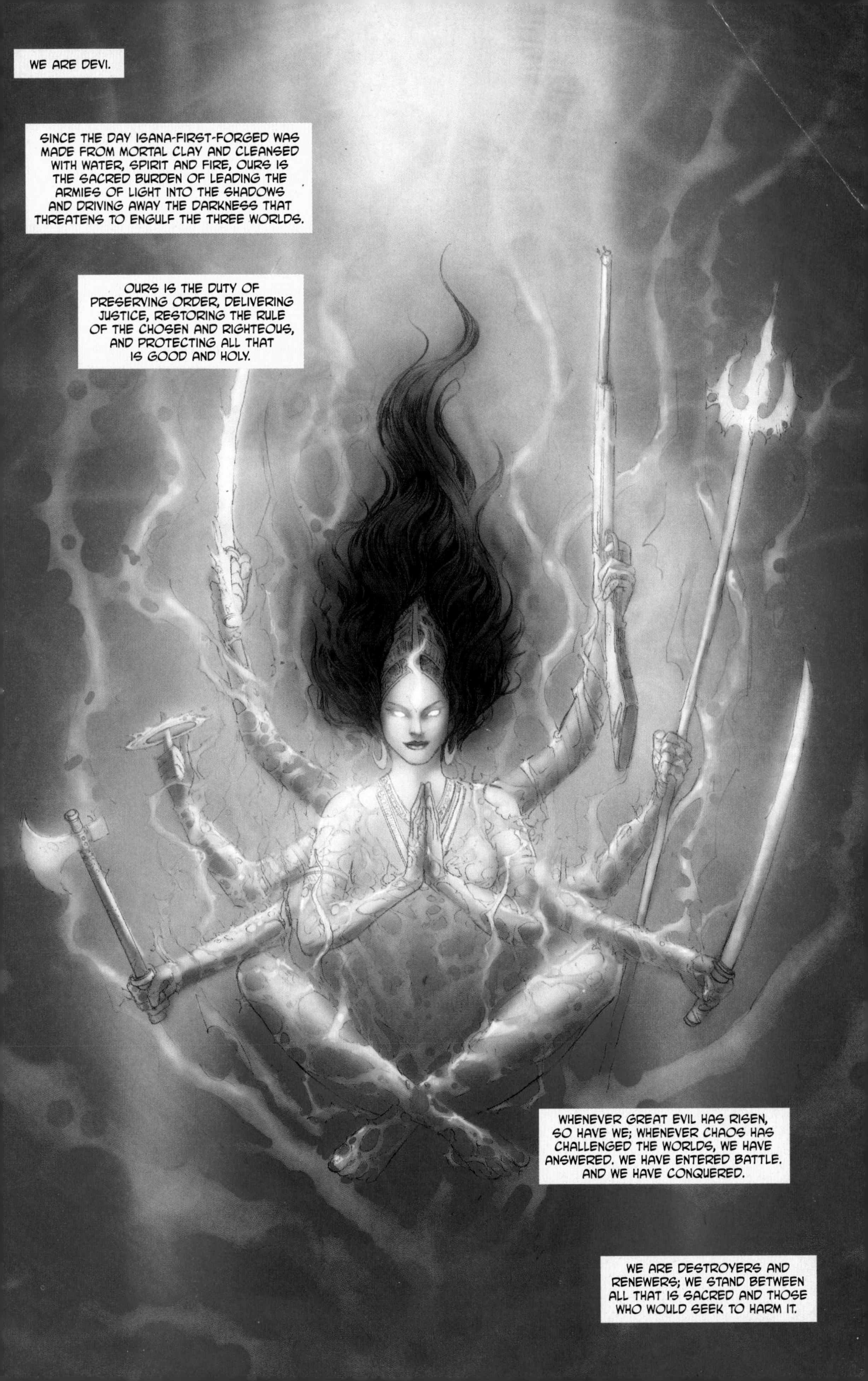
WE ARE DEVI.
SINCE THE DAY ISANA-FIRST-FORGED WAS MADE FROM MORTAL CLAY AND CLEANSED WITH WATER, SPIRIT AND FIRE, OURS IS THE SACRED BURDEN OF LEADING THE ARMIES OF LIGHT INTO THE SHADOWS AND DRIVING AWAY THE DARKNESS THAT THREATENS TO ENGULF THE THREE WORLDS.
OURS IS THE DUTY OF PRESERVING ORDER, DELIVERING JUSTICE, RESTORING THE RULE OF THE CHOSEN AND RIGHTEOUS, AND PROTECTING ALL THAT IS GOOD AND HOLY.
WHENEVER GREAT EVIL HAS RISEN, SO HAVE WE; WHENEVER CHAOS HAS CHALLENGED THE WORLDS, WE HAVE ANSWERED. WE HAVE ENTERED BATTLE. AND WE HAVE CONQUERED.
WE ARE DESTROYERS AND RENEWERS; WE STAND BETWEEN ALL THAT IS SACRED AND THOSE WHO WOULD SEEK TO HARM IT.

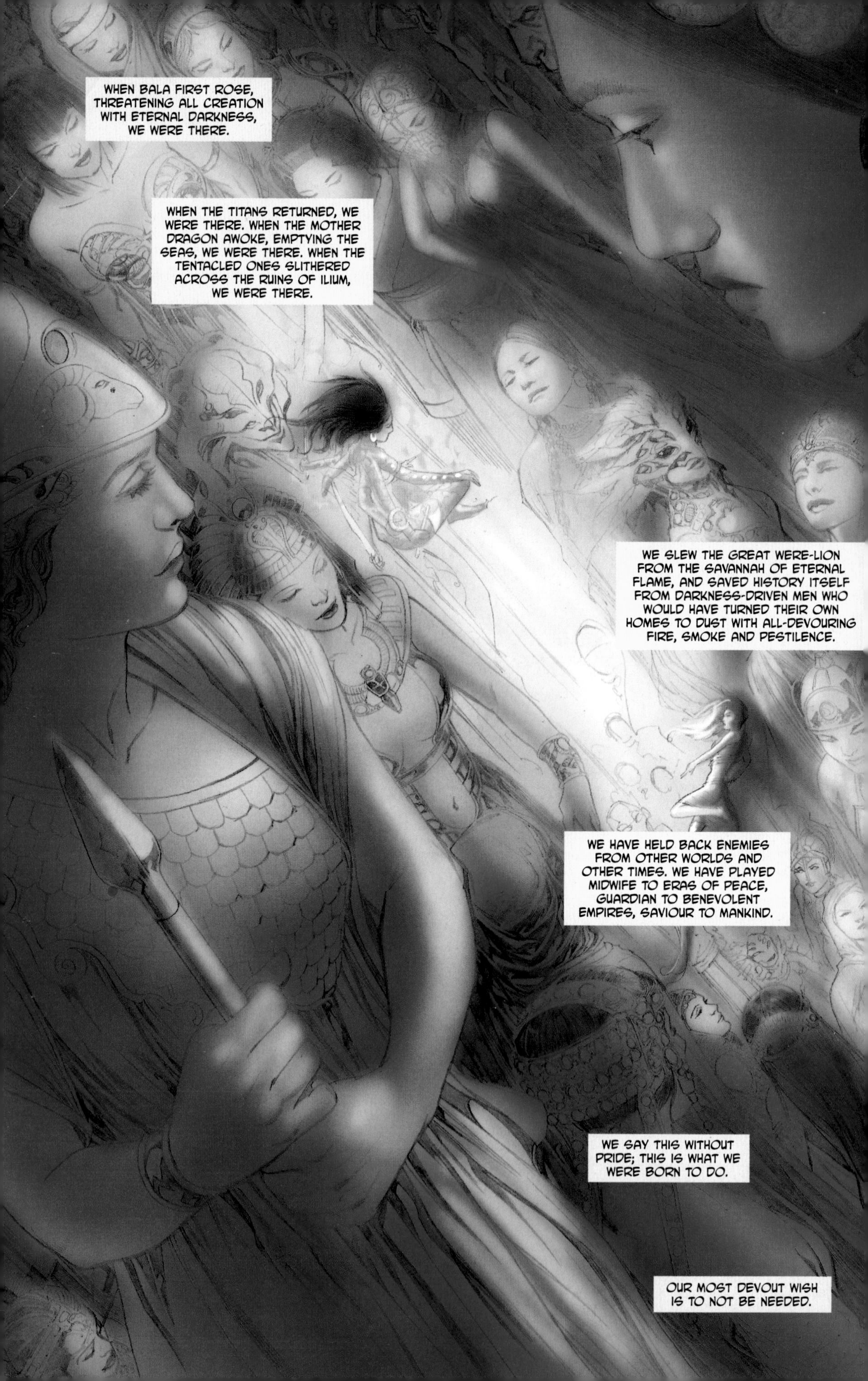
WHEN BALA FIRST ROSE, THREATENING ALL CREATION WITH ETERNAL DARKNESS, WE WERE THERE.
WHEN THE TITANS RETURNED, WE WERE THERE. WHEN THE MOTHER DRAGON AWOKE, EMPTYING THE SEAS, WE WERE THERE. WHEN THE TENTACLED ONES SLITHERED ACROSS THE RUINS OF ILIUM, WE WERE THERE.
WE SLEW THE GREAT WERE-LION FROM THE SAVANNAH OF ETERNAL FLAME, AND SAVED HISTORY ITSELF FROM DARKNESS-DRIVEN MEN WHO WOULD HAVE TURNED THEIR OWN HOMES TO DUST WITH ALL-DEVOURING FIRE, SMOKE AND PESTILENCE.
WE HAVE HELD BACK ENEMIES FROM OTHER WORLDS AND OTHER TIMES. WE HAVE PLAYED MIDWIFE TO ERAS OF PEACE, GUARDIAN TO BENEVOLENT EMPIRES, SAVIOUR TO MANKIND.
WE SAY THIS WITHOUT PRIDE; THIS IS WHAT WE WERE BORN TO DO.
OUR MOST DEVOUT WISH IS TO NOT BE NEEDED.

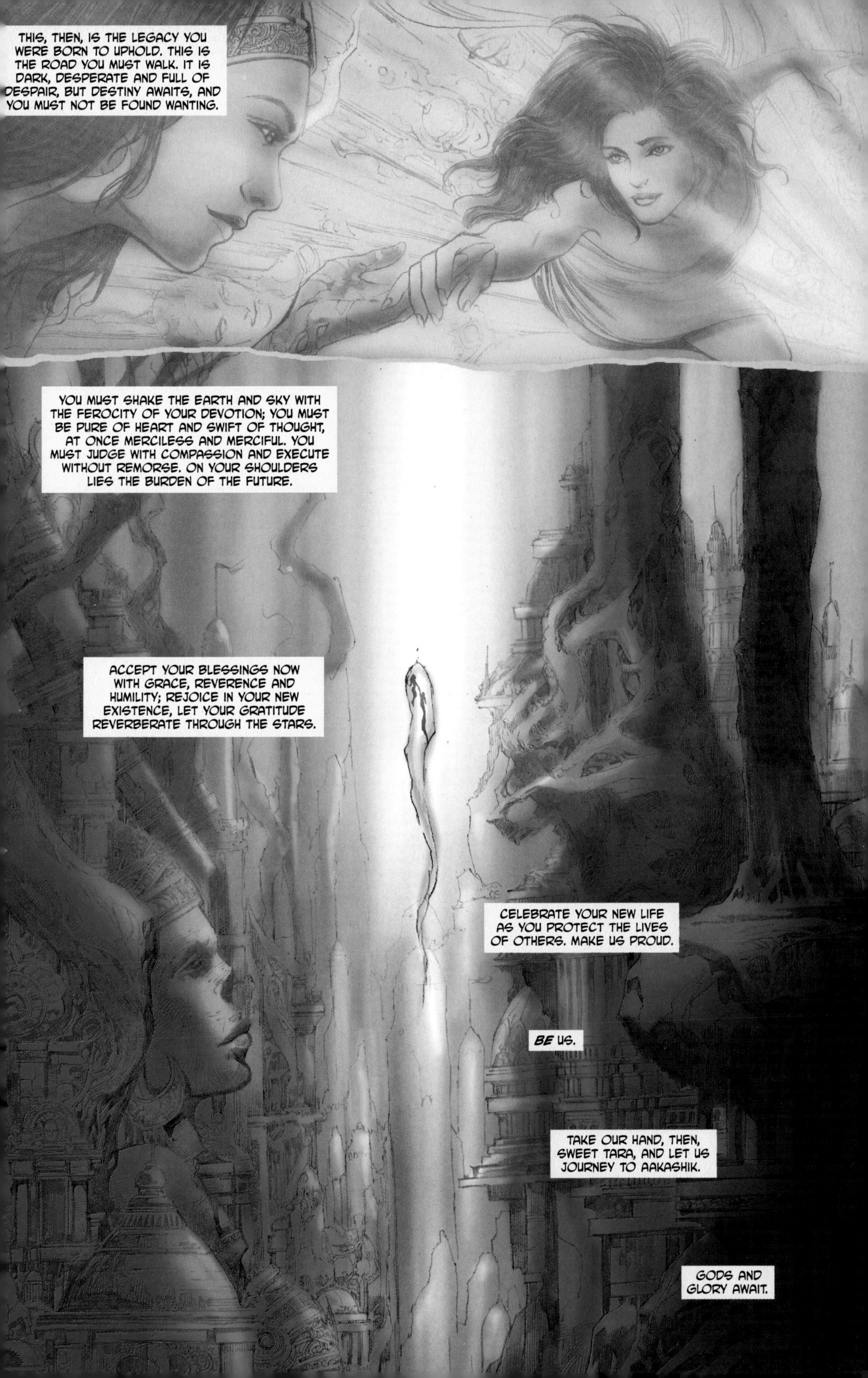
THIS, THEN, IS THE LEGACY YOU WERE BORN TO UPHOLD. THIS IS THE ROAD YOU MUST WALK. IT IS DARK, DESPERATE AND FULL OF DESPAIR, BUT DESTINY AWAITS, AND YOU MUST NOT BE FOUND WANTING.
YOU MUST SHAKE THE EARTH AND SKY WITH THE FEROCITY OF YOUR DEVOTION; YOU MUST BE PURE OF HEART AND SWIFT OF THOUGHT, AT ONCE MERCILESS AND MERCIFUL. YOU MUST JUDGE WITH COMPASSION AND EXECUTE WITHOUT REMORSE. ON YOUR SHOULDERS LIES THE BURDEN OF THE FUTURE.
ACCEPT YOUR BLESSINGS NOW WITH GRACE, REVERENCE AND HUMILITY; REJOICE IN YOUR NEW EXISTENCE, LET YOUR GRATITUDE REVERBERATE THROUGH THE STARS.
CELEBRATE YOUR NEW LIFE AS YOU PROTECT THE LIVES OF OTHERS. MAKE US PROUD.
BE US.
TAKE OUR HAND, THEN, SWEET TARA, AND LET US JOURNEY TO AAKASHIK.
GODS AND GLORY AWAIT.

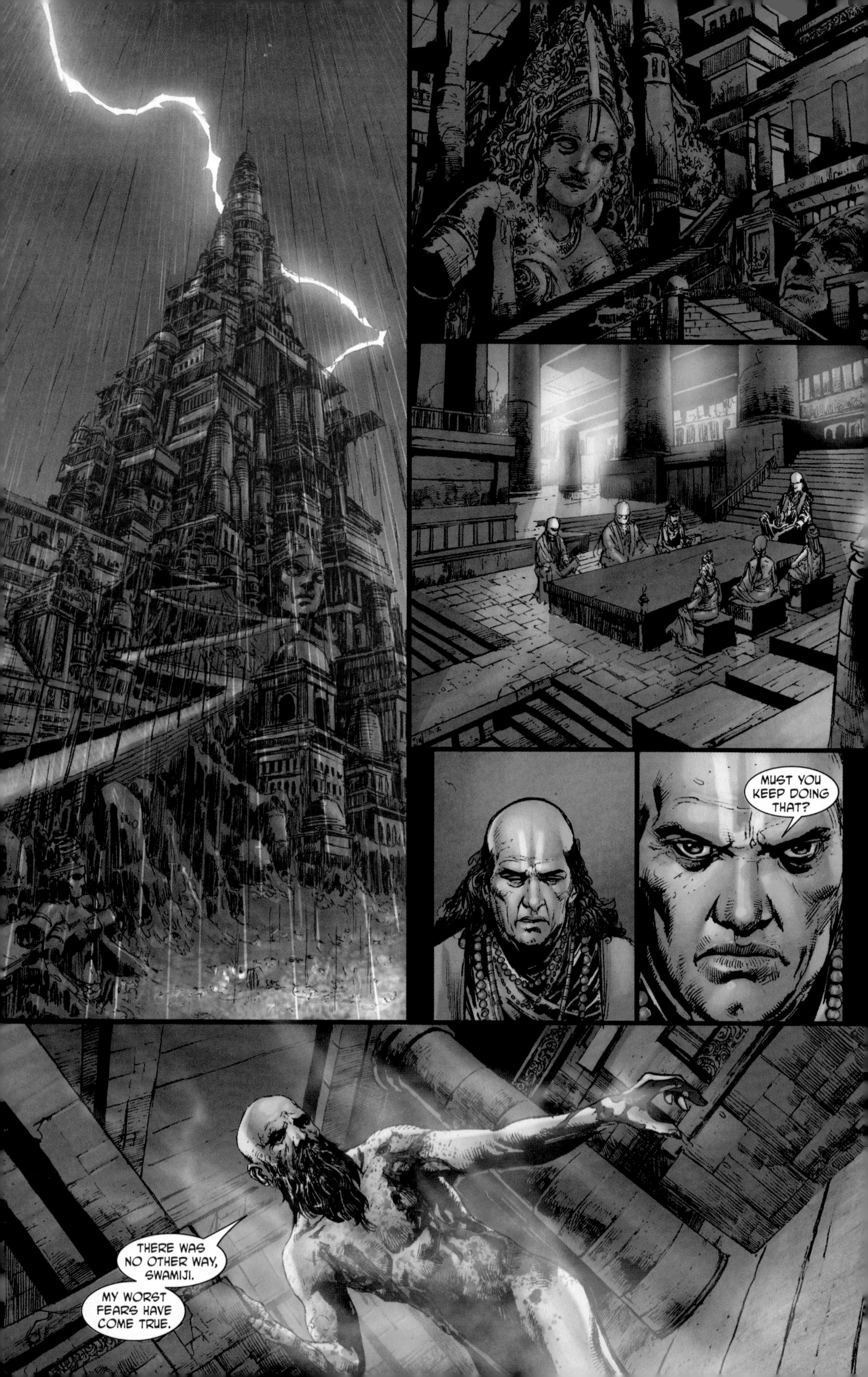
MUST YOU KEEP DOING THAT?
THERE WAS NO OTHER WAY, SWAMIJI.
MY WORST FEARS HAVE COME TRUE.

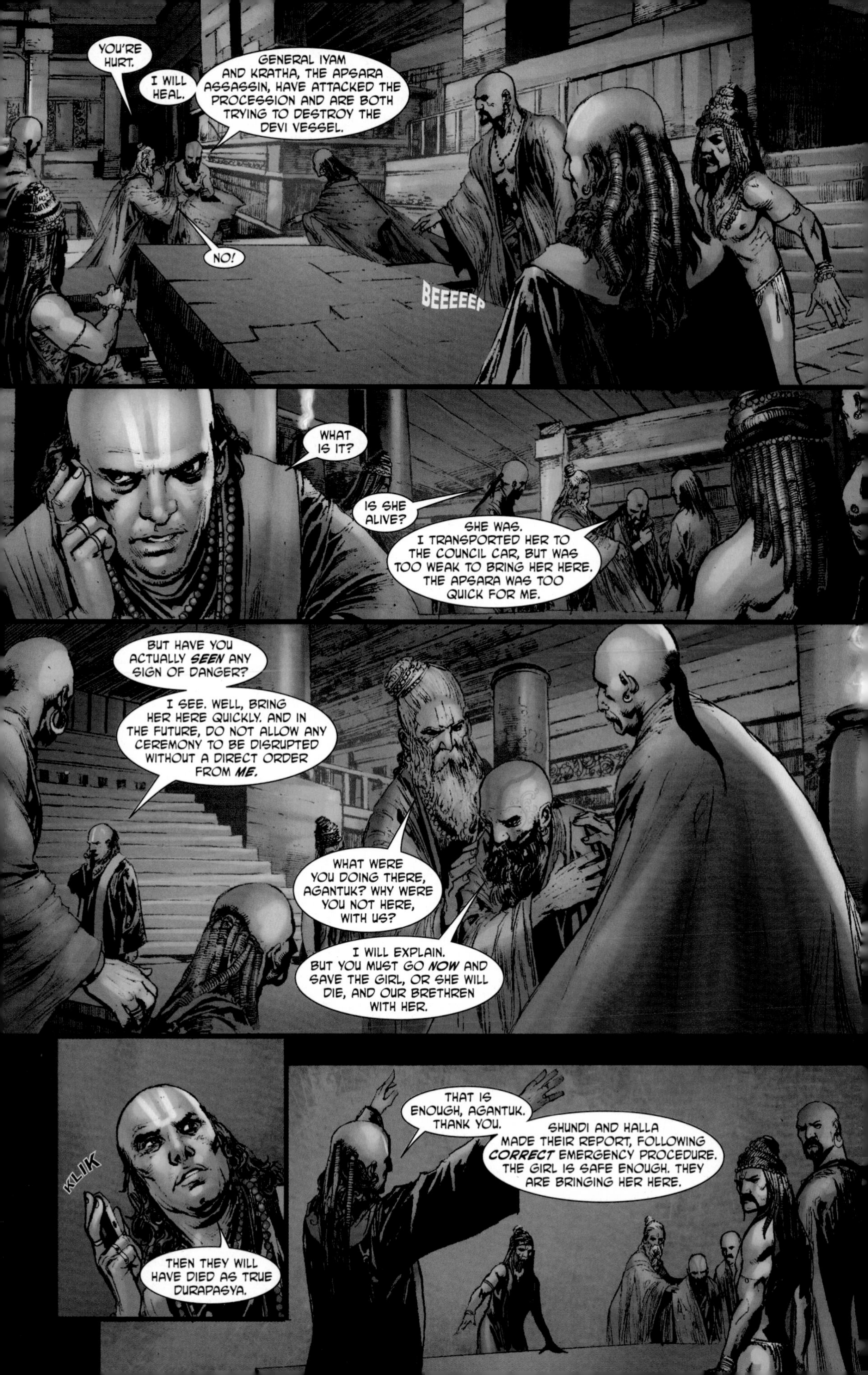
YOU'RE HURT.
I WILL HEAL.
GENERAL IYAM AND KRATHA, THE APSARA ASSASSIN, HAVE ATTACKED THE PROCESSION AND ARE BOTH TRYING TO DESTROY THE DEVI VESSEL.
NO!
BEEEEEP
WHAT IS IT?
IS SHE ALIVE?
SHE WAS. I TRANSPORTED HER TO THE COUNCIL CAR, BUT WAS TOO WEAK TO BRING HER HERE. THE APSARA WAS TOO QUICK FOR ME.
BUT HAVE YOU ACTUALLY *SEEN* ANY SIGN OF DANGER?
I SEE. WELL, BRING HER HERE QUICKLY. AND IN THE FUTURE, DO NOT ALLOW ANY CEREMONY TO BE DISRUPTED WITHOUT A DIRECT ORDER FROM ***ME.***
WHAT WERE YOU DOING THERE, AGANTUK? WHY WERE YOU NOT HERE, WITH US?
I WILL EXPLAIN. BUT YOU MUST GO *NOW* AND SAVE THE GIRL, OR SHE WILL DIE, AND OUR BRETHREN WITH HER.
KLIK
THEN THEY WILL HAVE DIED AS TRUE DURAPASYA.
THAT IS ENOUGH, AGANTUK. THANK YOU.
SHUNDI AND HALLA MADE THEIR REPORT, FOLLOWING *CORRECT* EMERGENCY PROCEDURE. THE GIRL IS SAFE ENOUGH. THEY ARE BRINGING HER HERE.

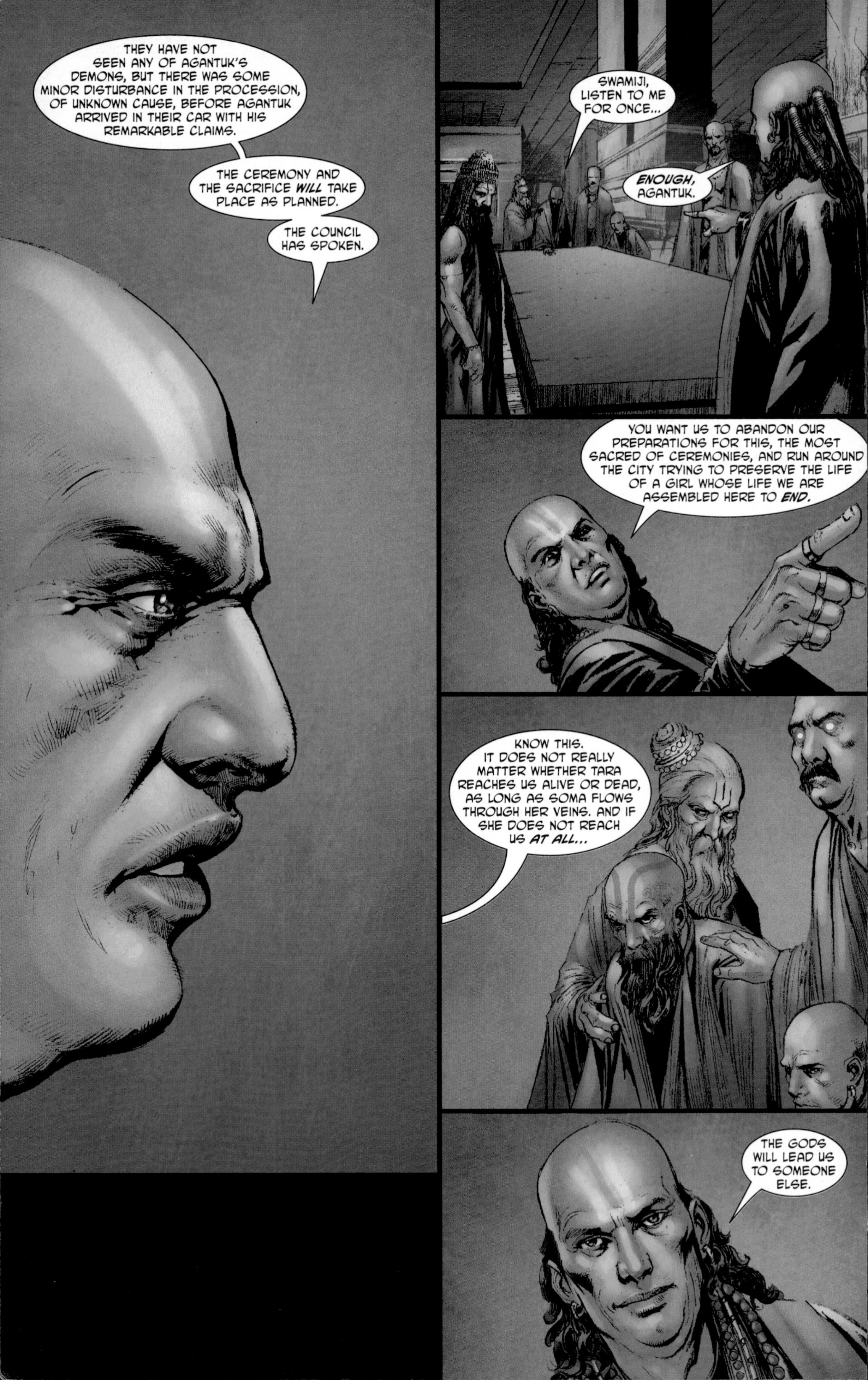
THEY HAVE NOT SEEN ANY OF AGANTUK'S DEMONS, BUT THERE WAS SOME MINOR DISTURBANCE IN THE PROCESSION, OF UNKNOWN CAUSE, BEFORE AGANTUK ARRIVED IN THEIR CAR WITH HIS REMARKABLE CLAIMS.
THE CEREMONY AND THE SACRIFICE *WILL* TAKE PLACE AS PLANNED.
THE COUNCIL HAS SPOKEN.
SWAMIJI, LISTEN TO ME FOR ONCE...
ENOUGH, AGANTUK.
YOU WANT US TO ABANDON OUR PREPARATIONS FOR THIS, THE MOST SACRED OF CEREMONIES, AND RUN AROUND THE CITY TRYING TO PRESERVE THE LIFE OF A GIRL WHOSE LIFE WE ARE ASSEMBLED HERE TO *END.*
KNOW THIS. IT DOES NOT REALLY MATTER WHETHER TARA REACHES US ALIVE OR DEAD, AS LONG AS SOMA FLOWS THROUGH HER VEINS. AND IF SHE DOES NOT REACH US *AT ALL*...
THE GODS WILL LEAD US TO SOMEONE ELSE.

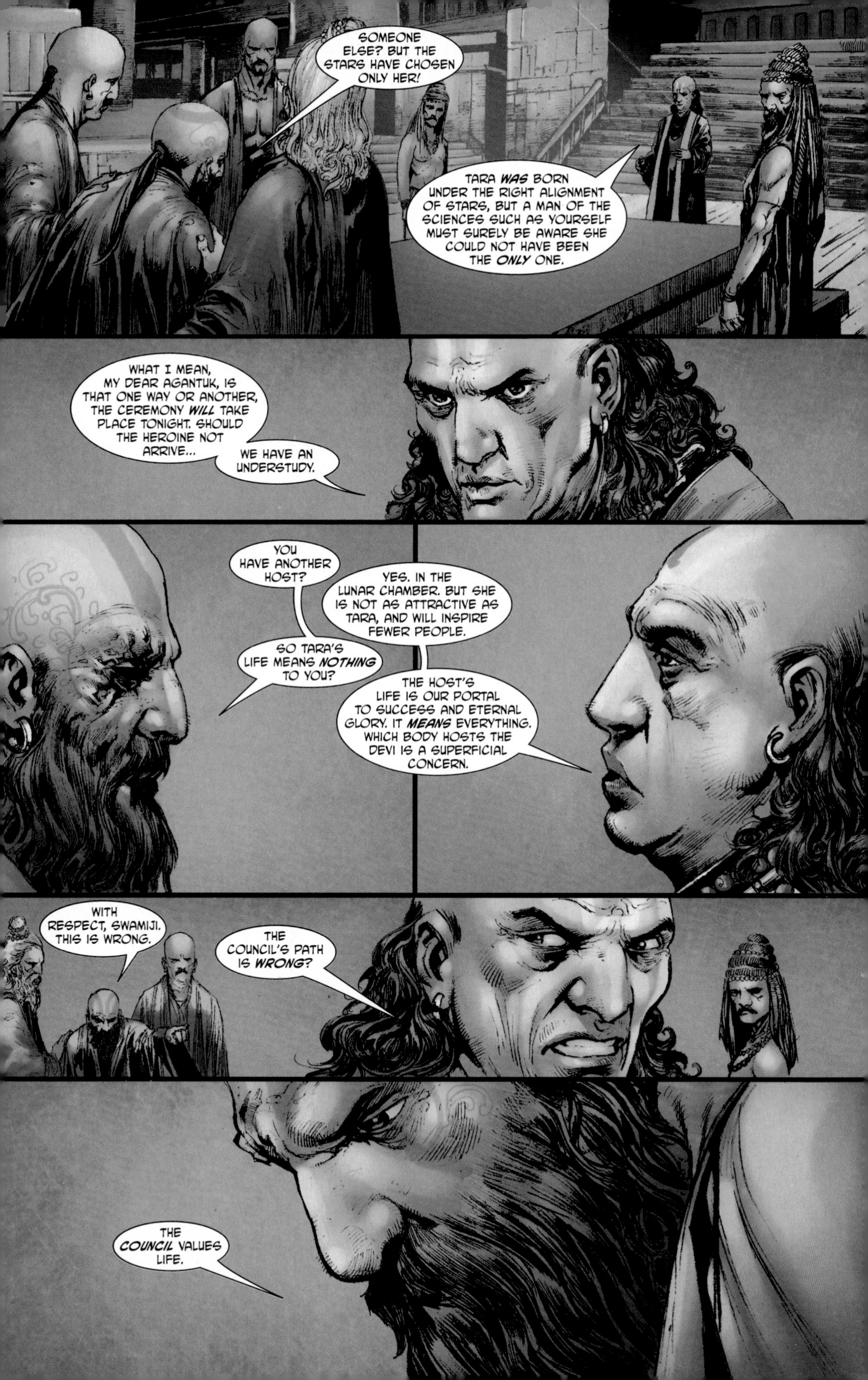
SOMEONE ELSE? BUT THE STARS HAVE CHOSEN ONLY HER!
TARA *WAS* BORN UNDER THE RIGHT ALIGNMENT OF STARS, BUT A MAN OF THE SCIENCES SUCH AS YOURSELF MUST SURELY BE AWARE SHE COULD NOT HAVE BEEN THE *ONLY* ONE.
WHAT I MEAN, MY DEAR AGANTUK, IS THAT ONE WAY OR ANOTHER, THE CEREMONY *WILL* TAKE PLACE TONIGHT. SHOULD THE HEROINE NOT ARRIVE...
WE HAVE AN UNDERSTUDY.
YOU HAVE ANOTHER HOST?
YES. IN THE LUNAR CHAMBER. BUT SHE IS NOT AS ATTRACTIVE AS TARA, AND WILL INSPIRE FEWER PEOPLE.
SO TARA'S LIFE MEANS *NOTHING* TO YOU?
THE HOST'S LIFE IS OUR PORTAL TO SUCCESS AND ETERNAL GLORY. IT *MEANS* EVERYTHING. WHICH BODY HOSTS THE DEVI IS A SUPERFICIAL CONCERN.
WITH RESPECT, SWAMIJI. THIS IS WRONG.
THE COUNCIL'S PATH IS *WRONG*?
THE *COUNCIL* VALUES LIFE.

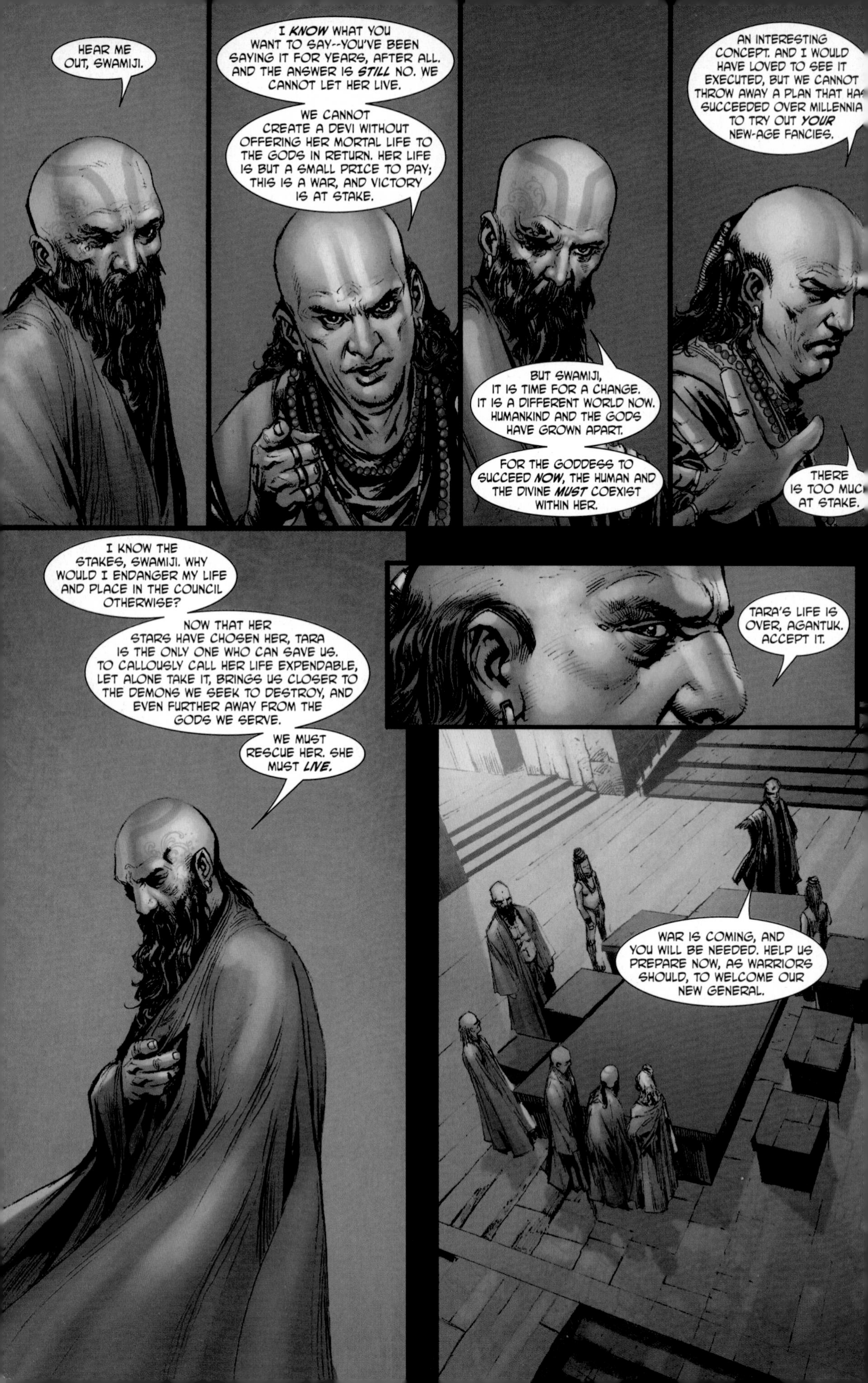
HEAR ME OUT, SWAMIJI.
I KNOW WHAT YOU WANT TO SAY--YOU'VE BEEN SAYING IT FOR YEARS, AFTER ALL. AND THE ANSWER IS STILL NO. WE CANNOT LET HER LIVE.
WE CANNOT CREATE A DEVI WITHOUT OFFERING HER MORTAL LIFE TO THE GODS IN RETURN. HER LIFE IS BUT A SMALL PRICE TO PAY; THIS IS A WAR, AND VICTORY IS AT STAKE.
BUT SWAMIJI, IT IS TIME FOR A CHANGE. IT IS A DIFFERENT WORLD NOW. HUMANKIND AND THE GODS HAVE GROWN APART.
FOR THE GODDESS TO SUCCEED NOW, THE HUMAN AND THE DIVINE MUST COEXIST WITHIN HER.
AN INTERESTING CONCEPT. AND I WOULD HAVE LOVED TO SEE IT EXECUTED, BUT WE CANNOT THROW AWAY A PLAN THAT HA SUCCEEDED OVER MILLENNIA TO TRY OUT YOUR NEW-AGE FANCIES.
THERE IS TOO MUC AT STAKE.
I KNOW THE STAKES, SWAMIJI. WHY WOULD I ENDANGER MY LIFE AND PLACE IN THE COUNCIL OTHERWISE?
NOW THAT HER STARS HAVE CHOSEN HER, TARA IS THE ONLY ONE WHO CAN SAVE US. TO CALLOUSLY CALL HER LIFE EXPENDABLE, LET ALONE TAKE IT, BRINGS US CLOSER TO THE DEMONS WE SEEK TO DESTROY, AND EVEN FURTHER AWAY FROM THE GODS WE SERVE.
WE MUST RESCUE HER. SHE MUST LIVE.
TARA'S LIFE IS OVER, AGANTUK. ACCEPT IT.
WAR IS COMING, AND YOU WILL BE NEEDED. HELP US PREPARE NOW, AS WARRIORS SHOULD, TO WELCOME OUR NEW GENERAL.

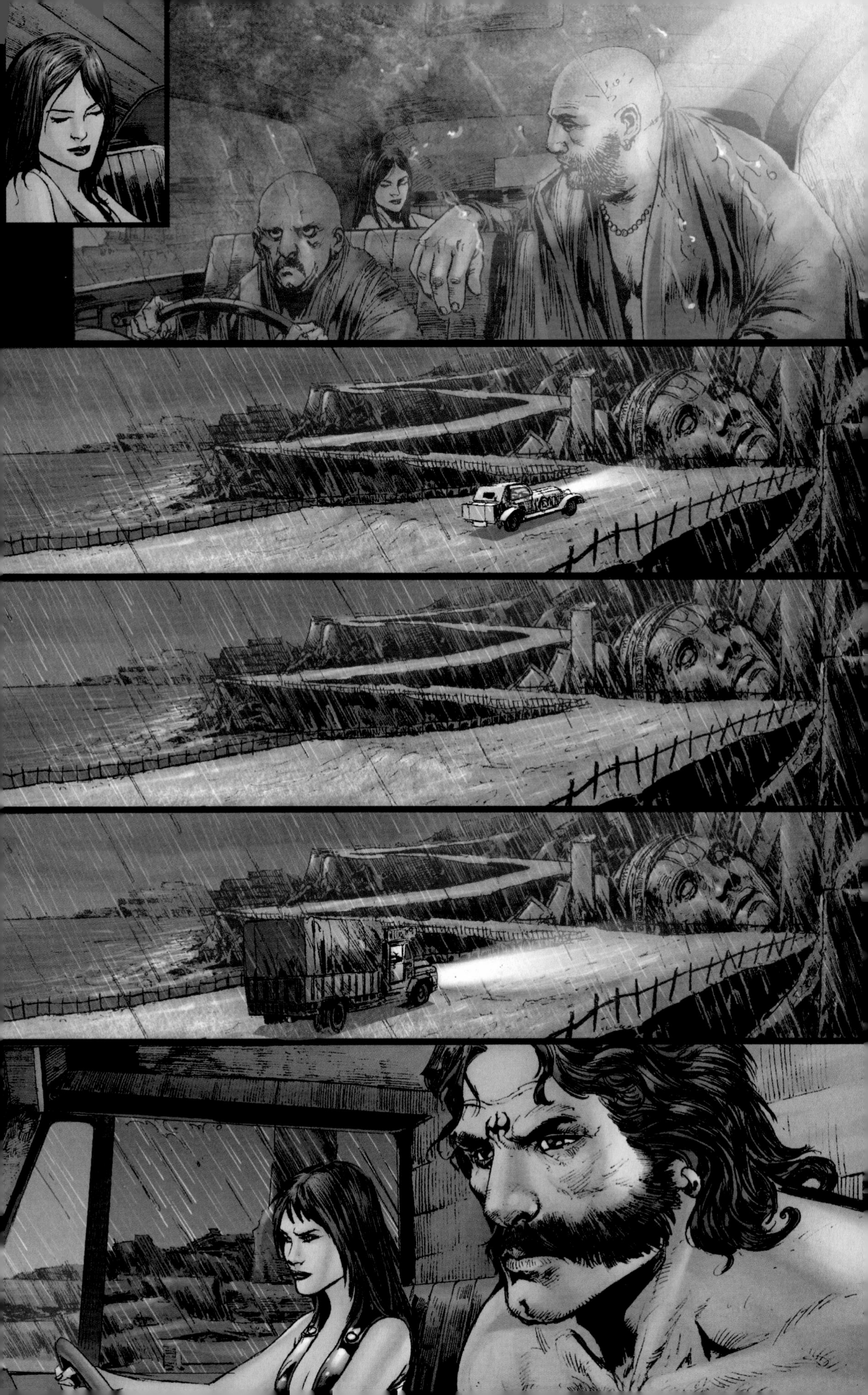

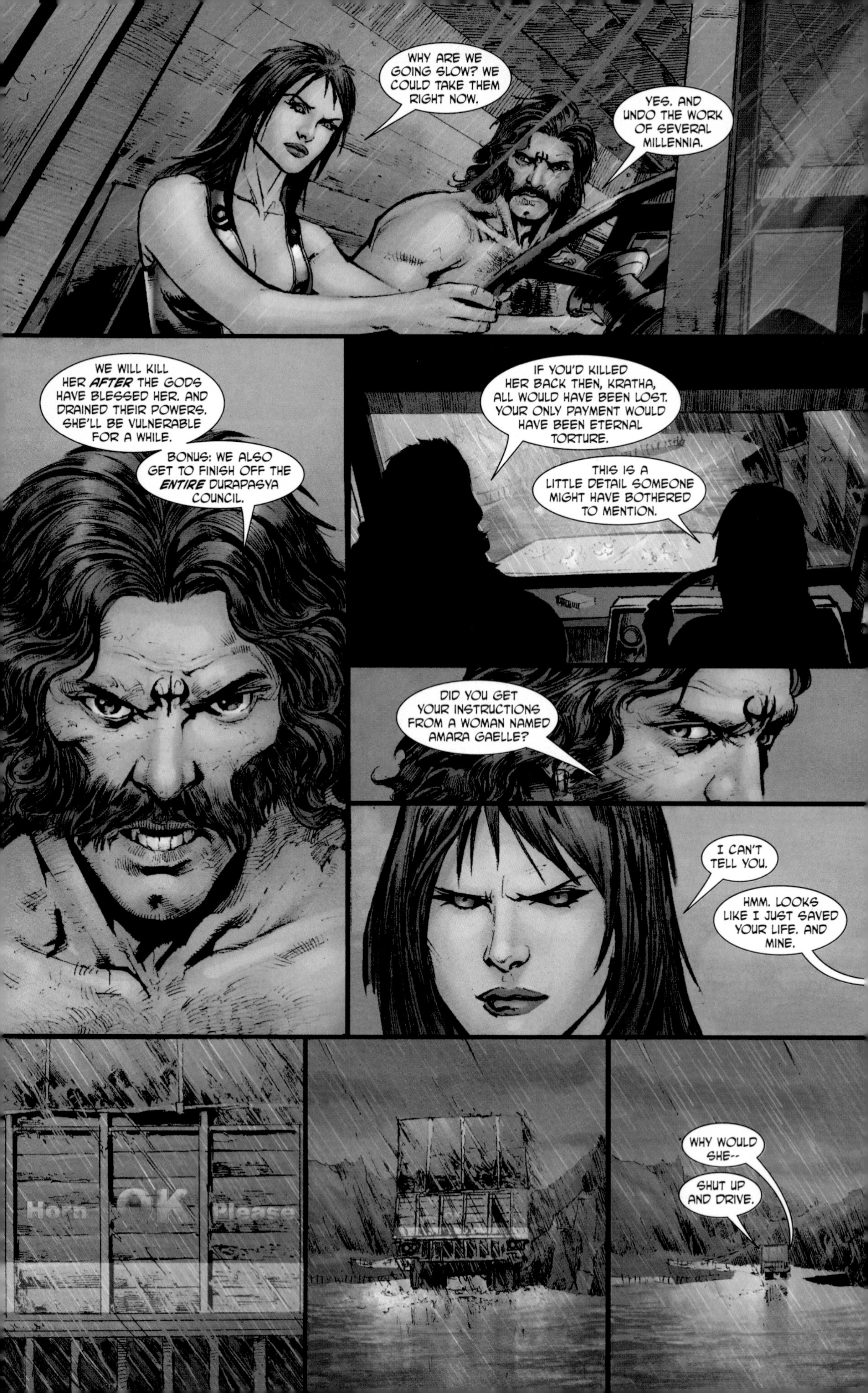
WHY ARE WE GOING SLOW? WE COULD TAKE THEM RIGHT NOW.
YES. AND UNDO THE WORK OF SEVERAL MILLENNIA.
WE WILL KILL HER *AFTER* THE GODS HAVE BLESSED HER. AND DRAINED THEIR POWERS. SHE'LL BE VULNERABLE FOR A WHILE.
BONUS: WE ALSO GET TO FINISH OFF THE *ENTIRE* DURAPASYA COUNCIL.
IF YOU'D KILLED HER BACK THEN, KRATHA, ALL WOULD HAVE BEEN LOST. YOUR ONLY PAYMENT WOULD HAVE BEEN ETERNAL TORTURE.
THIS IS A LITTLE DETAIL SOMEONE MIGHT HAVE BOTHERED TO MENTION.
DID YOU GET YOUR INSTRUCTIONS FROM A WOMAN NAMED AMARA GAELLE?
I CAN'T TELL YOU.
HMM. LOOKS LIKE I JUST SAVED YOUR LIFE. AND MINE.
Horn OK Please
WHY WOULD SHE--
SHUT UP AND DRIVE.

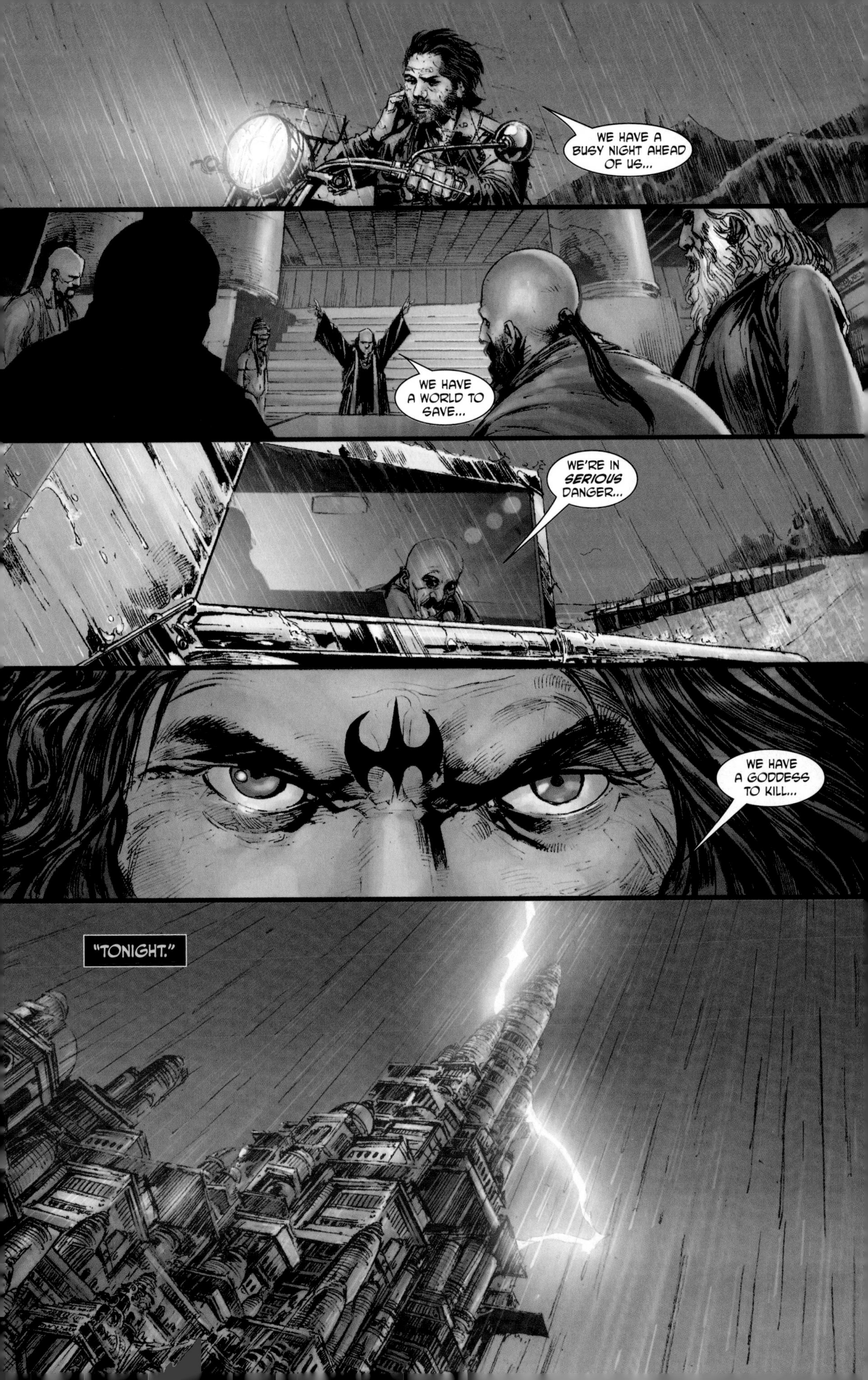
WE HAVE A BUSY NIGHT AHEAD OF US...
WE HAVE A WORLD TO SAVE...
WE'RE IN *SERIOUS* DANGER...
WE HAVE A GODDESS TO KILL...
"TONIGHT."

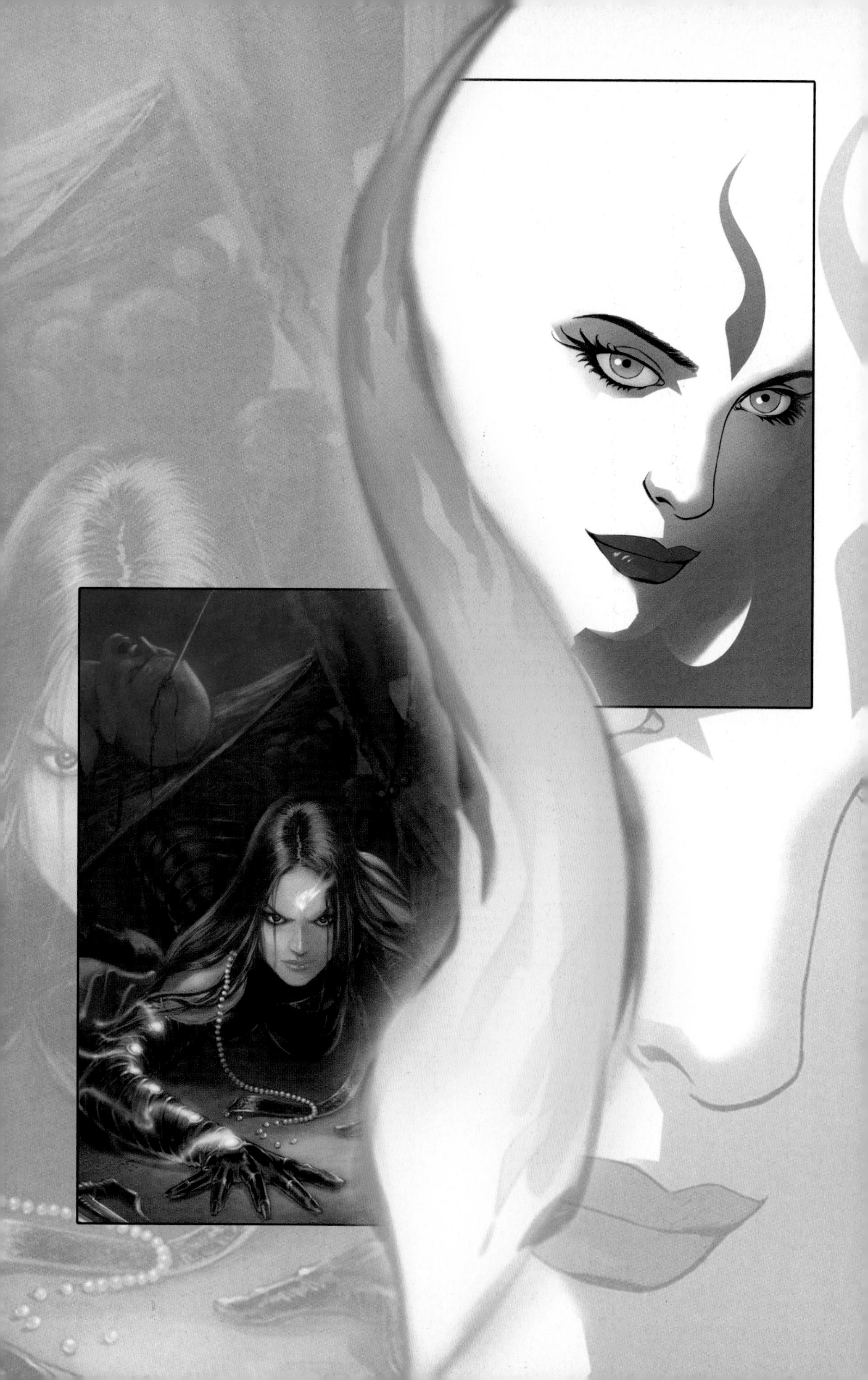

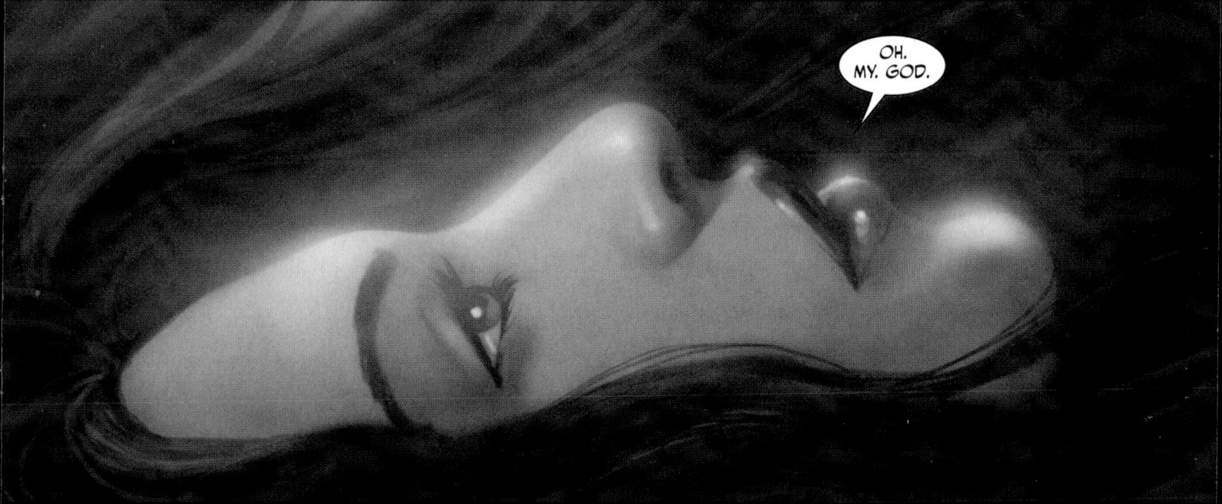
OH. MY. GOD.

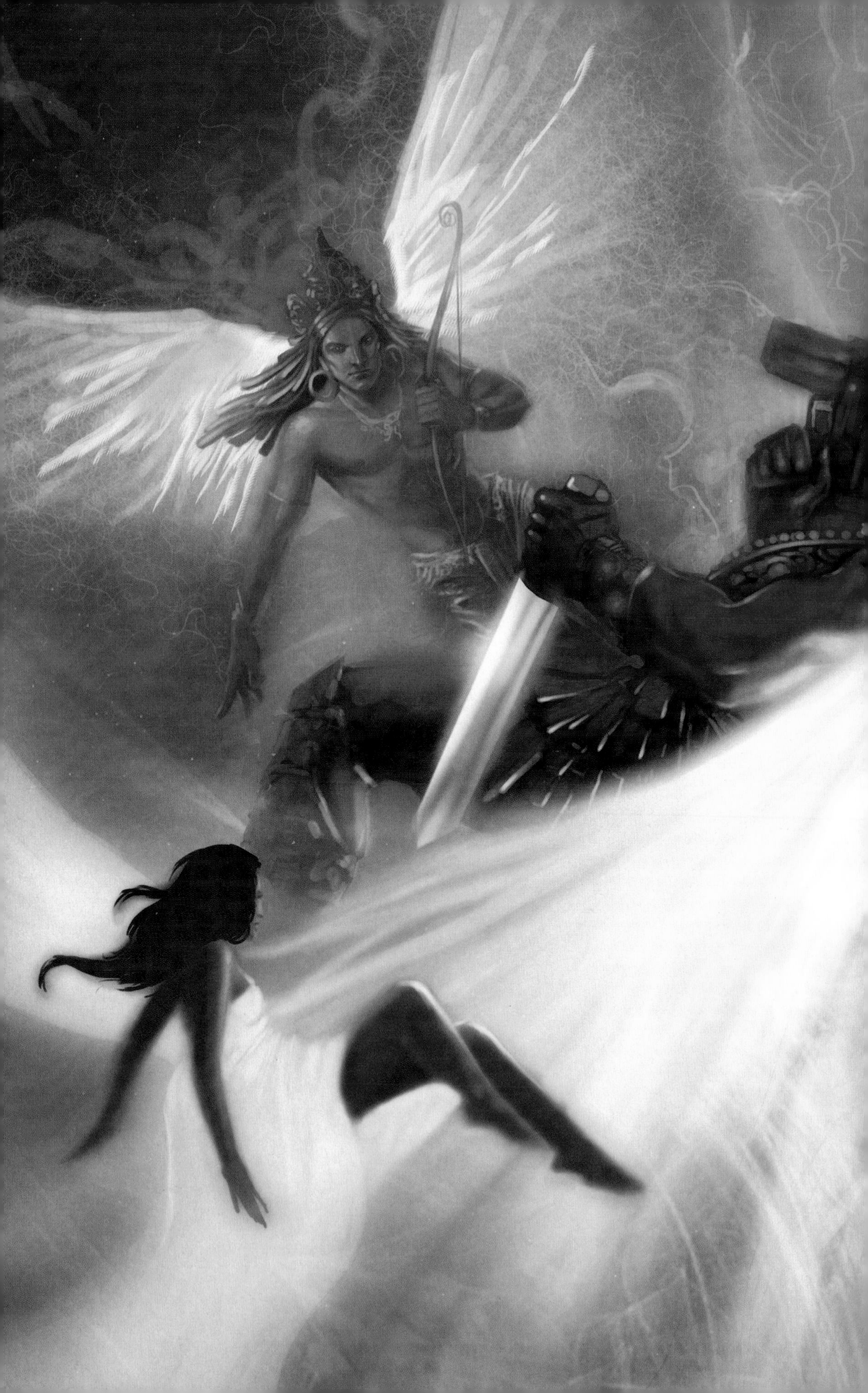

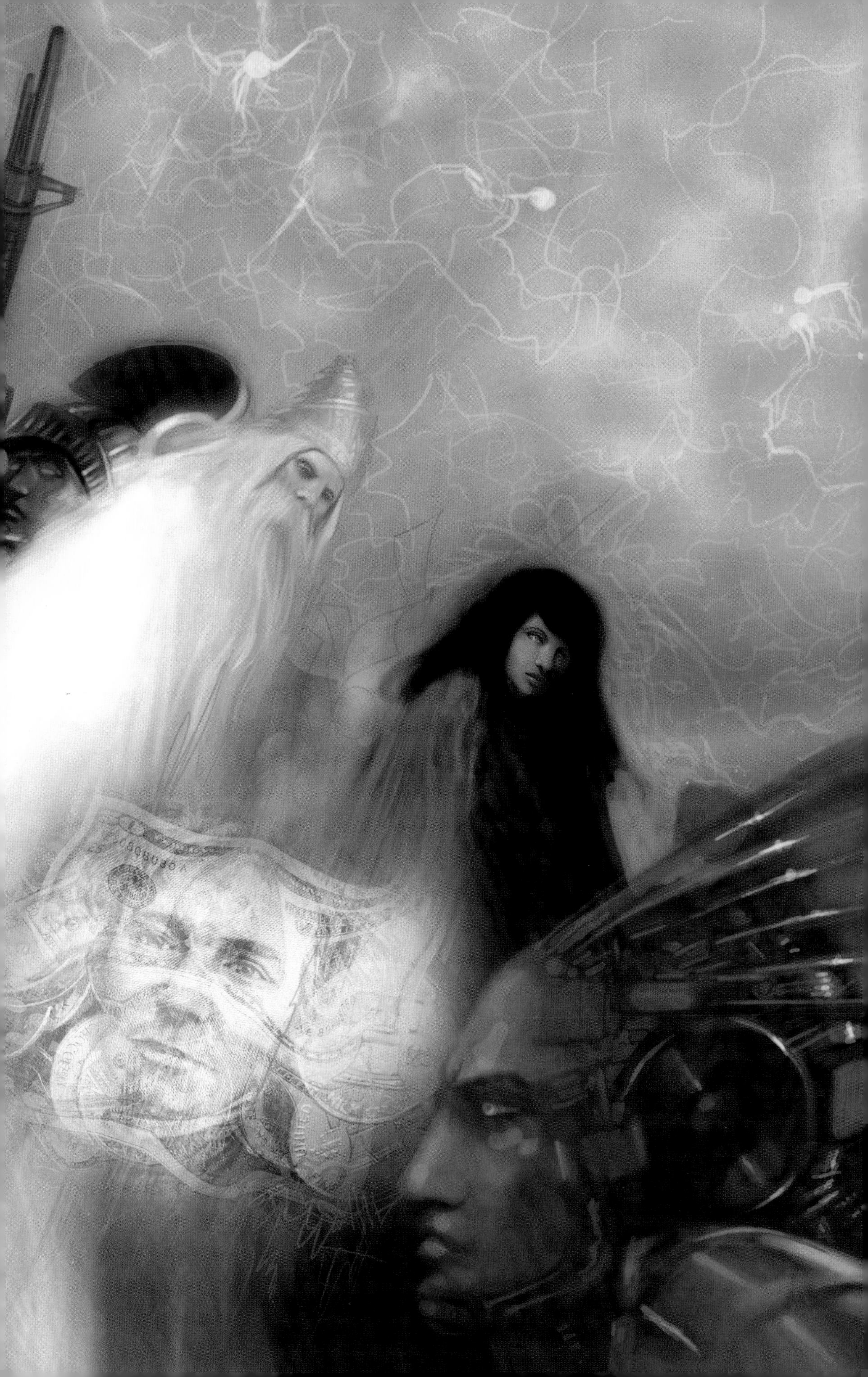

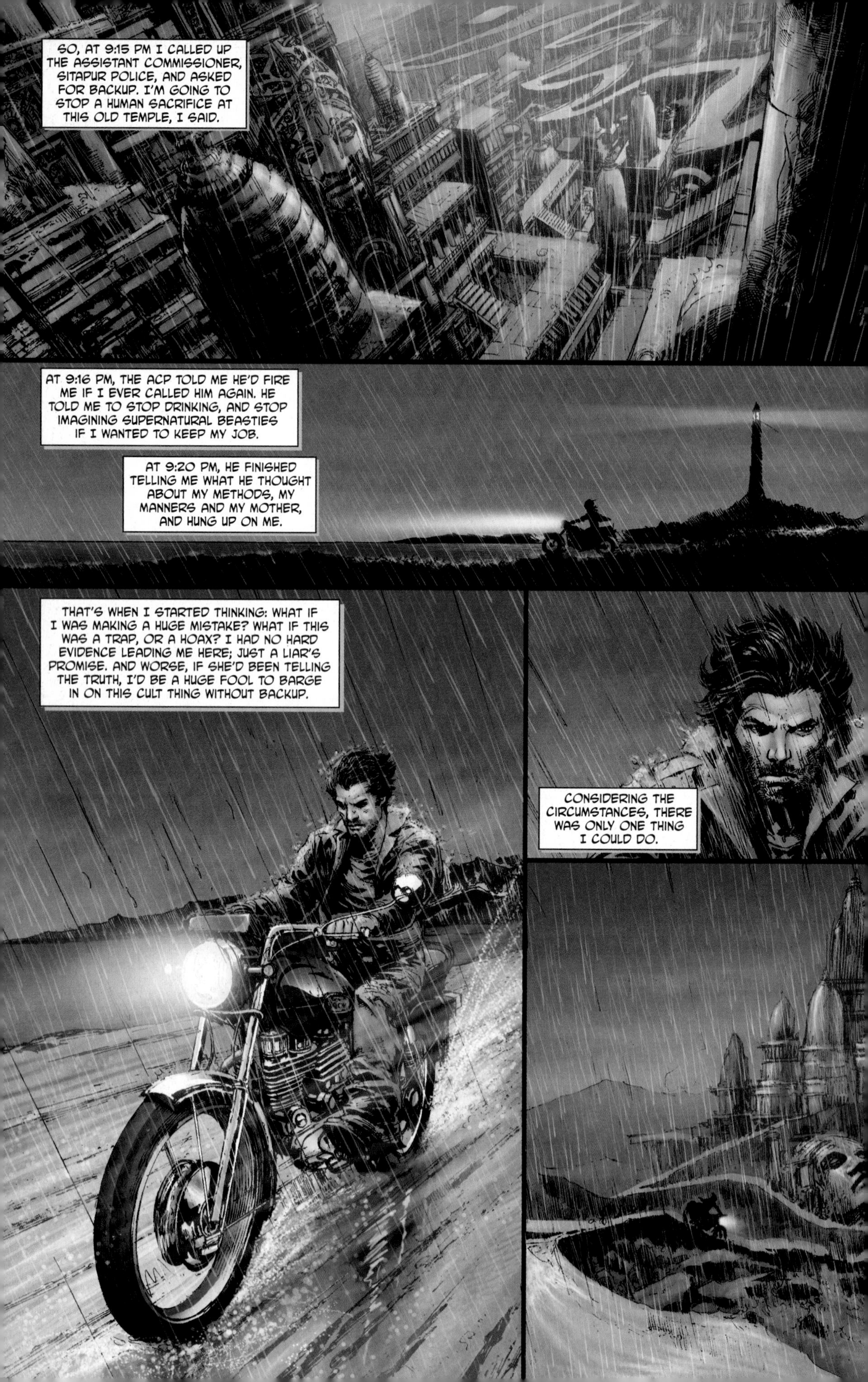
SO, AT 9:15 PM I CALLED UP THE ASSISTANT COMMISSIONER, SITAPUR POLICE, AND ASKED FOR BACKUP. I'M GOING TO STOP A HUMAN SACRIFICE AT THIS OLD TEMPLE, I SAID.
AT 9:16 PM, THE ACP TOLD ME HE'D FIRE ME IF I EVER CALLED HIM AGAIN. HE TOLD ME TO STOP DRINKING, AND STOP IMAGINING SUPERNATURAL BEASTIES IF I WANTED TO KEEP MY JOB.
AT 9:20 PM, HE FINISHED TELLING ME WHAT HE THOUGHT ABOUT MY METHODS, MY MANNERS AND MY MOTHER, AND HUNG UP ON ME.
THAT'S WHEN I STARTED THINKING: WHAT IF I WAS MAKING A HUGE MISTAKE? WHAT IF THIS WAS A TRAP, OR A HOAX? I HAD NO HARD EVIDENCE LEADING ME HERE; JUST A LIAR'S PROMISE. AND WORSE, IF SHE'D BEEN TELLING THE TRUTH, I'D BE A HUGE FOOL TO BARGE IN ON THIS CULT THING WITHOUT BACKUP.
CONSIDERING THE CIRCUMSTANCES, THERE WAS ONLY ONE THING I COULD DO.

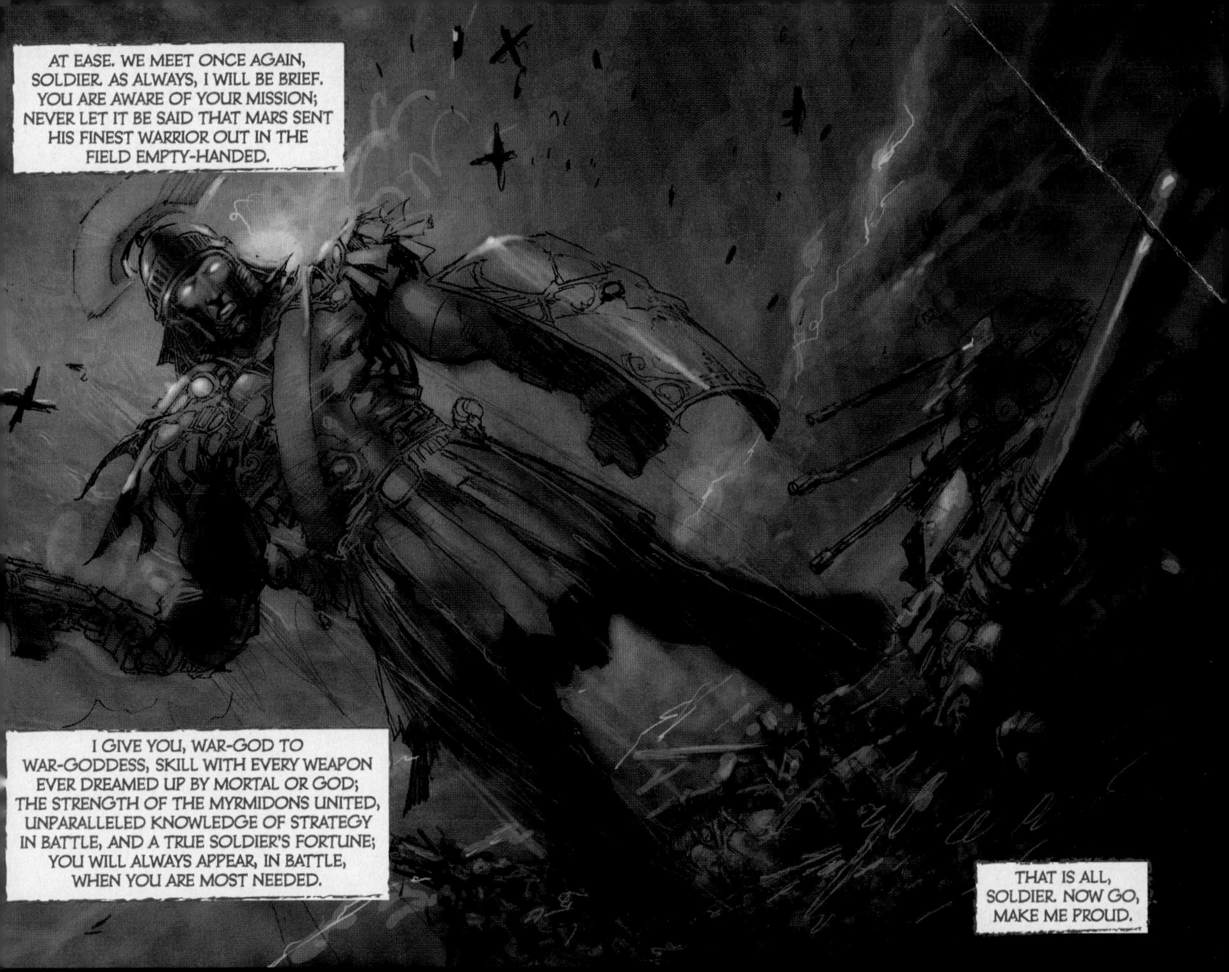
AT EASE. WE MEET ONCE AGAIN, SOLDIER. AS ALWAYS, I WILL BE BRIEF. YOU ARE AWARE OF YOUR MISSION; NEVER LET IT BE SAID THAT MARS SENT HIS FINEST WARRIOR OUT IN THE FIELD EMPTY-HANDED.
I GIVE YOU, WAR-GOD TO WAR-GODDESS, SKILL WITH EVERY WEAPON EVER DREAMED UP BY MORTAL OR GOD; THE STRENGTH OF THE MYRMIDONS UNITED, UNPARALLELED KNOWLEDGE OF STRATEGY IN BATTLE, AND A TRUE SOLDIER'S FORTUNE; YOU WILL ALWAYS APPEAR, IN BATTLE, WHEN YOU ARE MOST NEEDED.
THAT IS ALL, SOLDIER. NOW GO, MAKE ME PROUD.

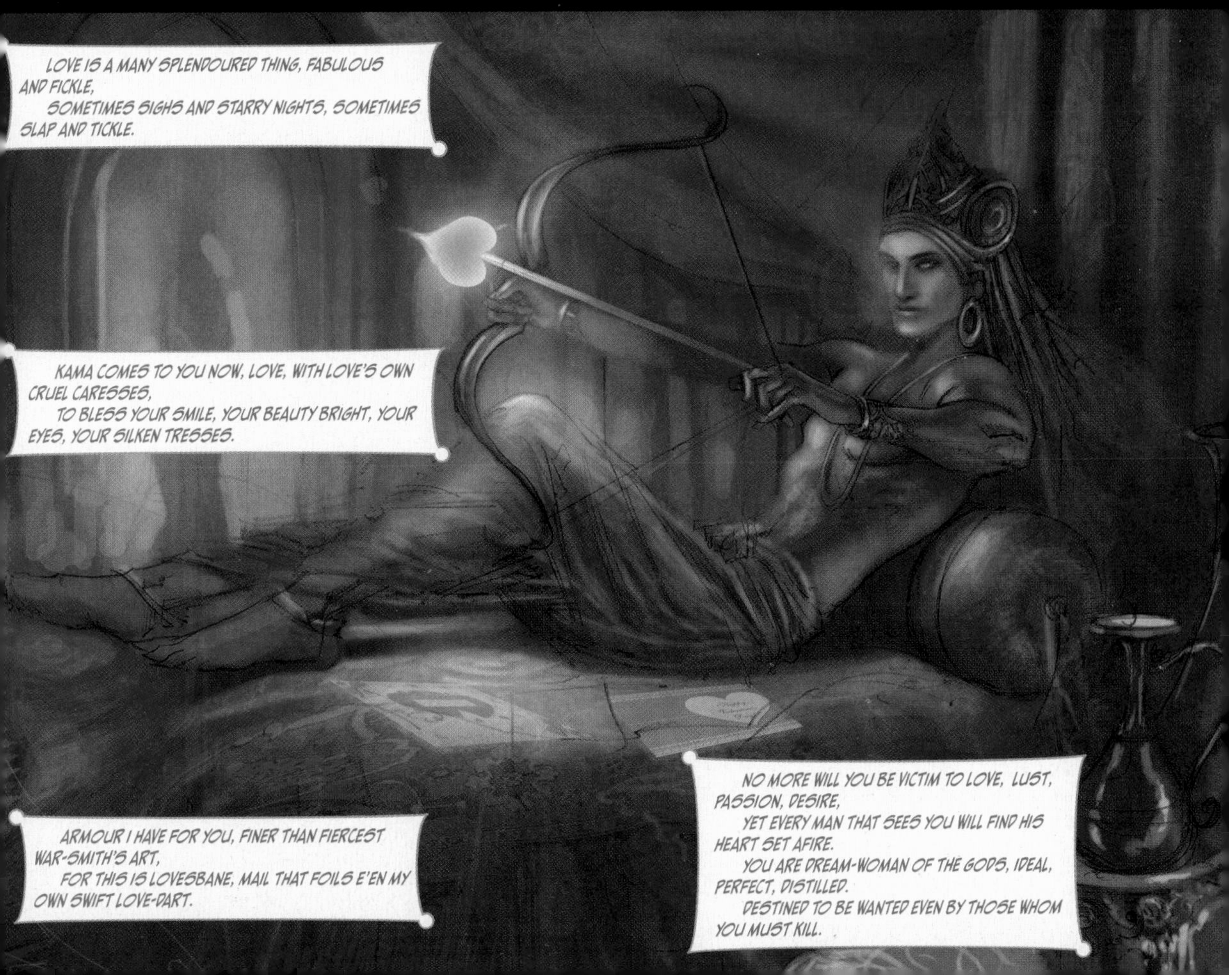
LOVE IS A MANY SPLENDOURED THING, FABULOUS AND FICKLE, SOMETIMES SIGHS AND STARRY NIGHTS, SOMETIMES SLAP AND TICKLE.
KAMA COMES TO YOU NOW, LOVE, WITH LOVE'S OWN CRUEL CARESSES, TO BLESS YOUR SMILE, YOUR BEAUTY BRIGHT, YOUR EYES, YOUR SILKEN TRESSES.
ARMOUR I HAVE FOR YOU, FINER THAN FIERCEST WAR-SMITH'S ART, FOR THIS IS LOVESBANE, MAIL THAT FOILS E'EN MY OWN SWIFT LOVE-DART.
NO MORE WILL YOU BE VICTIM TO LOVE, LUST, PASSION, DESIRE, YET EVERY MAN THAT SEES YOU WILL FIND HIS HEART SET AFIRE. YOU ARE DREAM-WOMAN OF THE GODS, IDEAL, PERFECT, DISTILLED. DESTINED TO BE WANTED EVEN BY THOSE WHOM YOU MUST KILL.

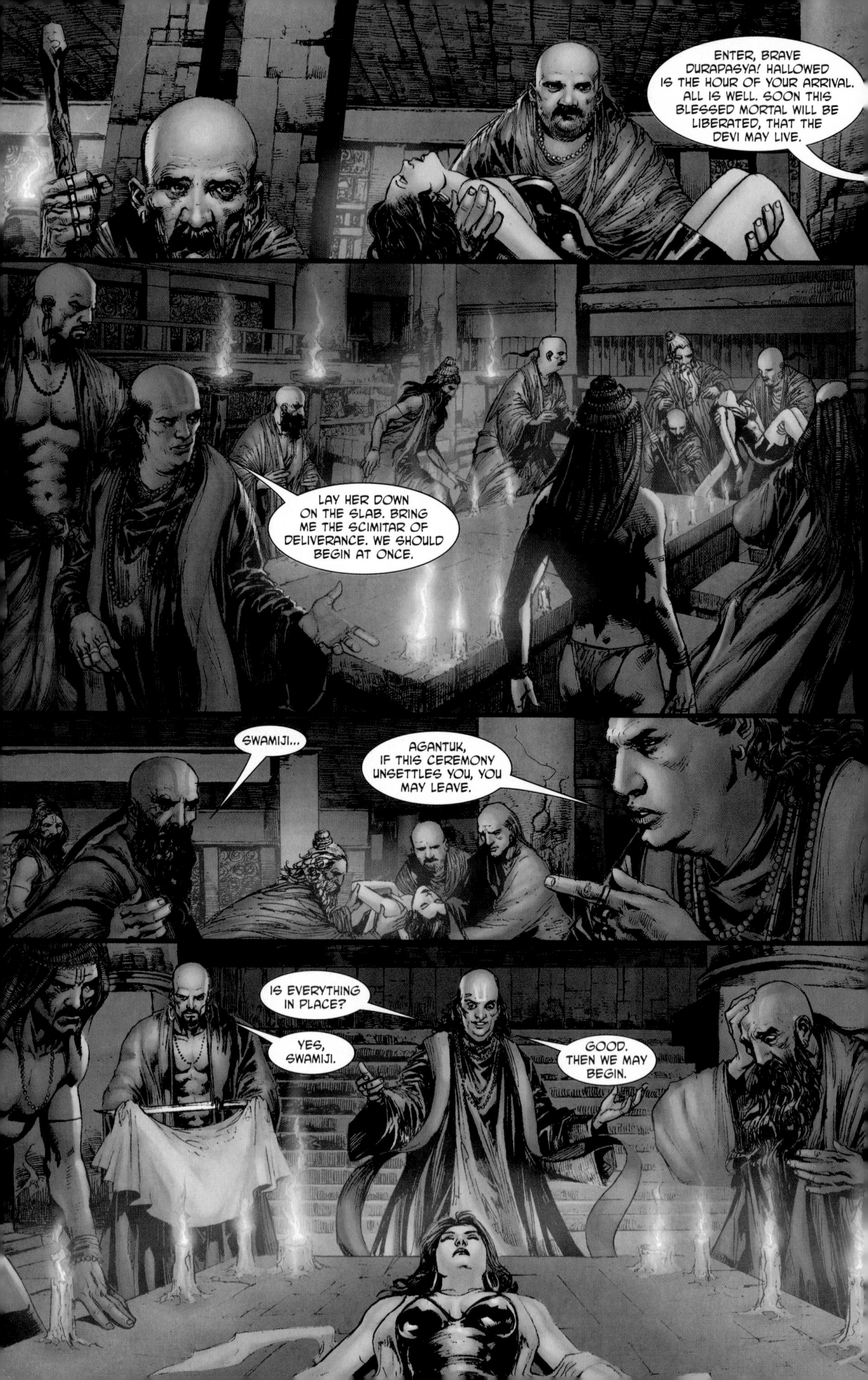
ENTER, BRAVE DURAPASYA! HALLOWED IS THE HOUR OF YOUR ARRIVAL. ALL IS WELL. SOON THIS BLESSED MORTAL WILL BE LIBERATED, THAT THE DEVI MAY LIVE.
LAY HER DOWN ON THE SLAB. BRING ME THE SCIMITAR OF DELIVERANCE. WE SHOULD BEGIN AT ONCE.
SWAMIJI...
AGANTUK, IF THIS CEREMONY UNSETTLES YOU, YOU MAY LEAVE.
IS EVERYTHING IN PLACE?
YES, SWAMIJI.
GOOD. THEN WE MAY BEGIN.

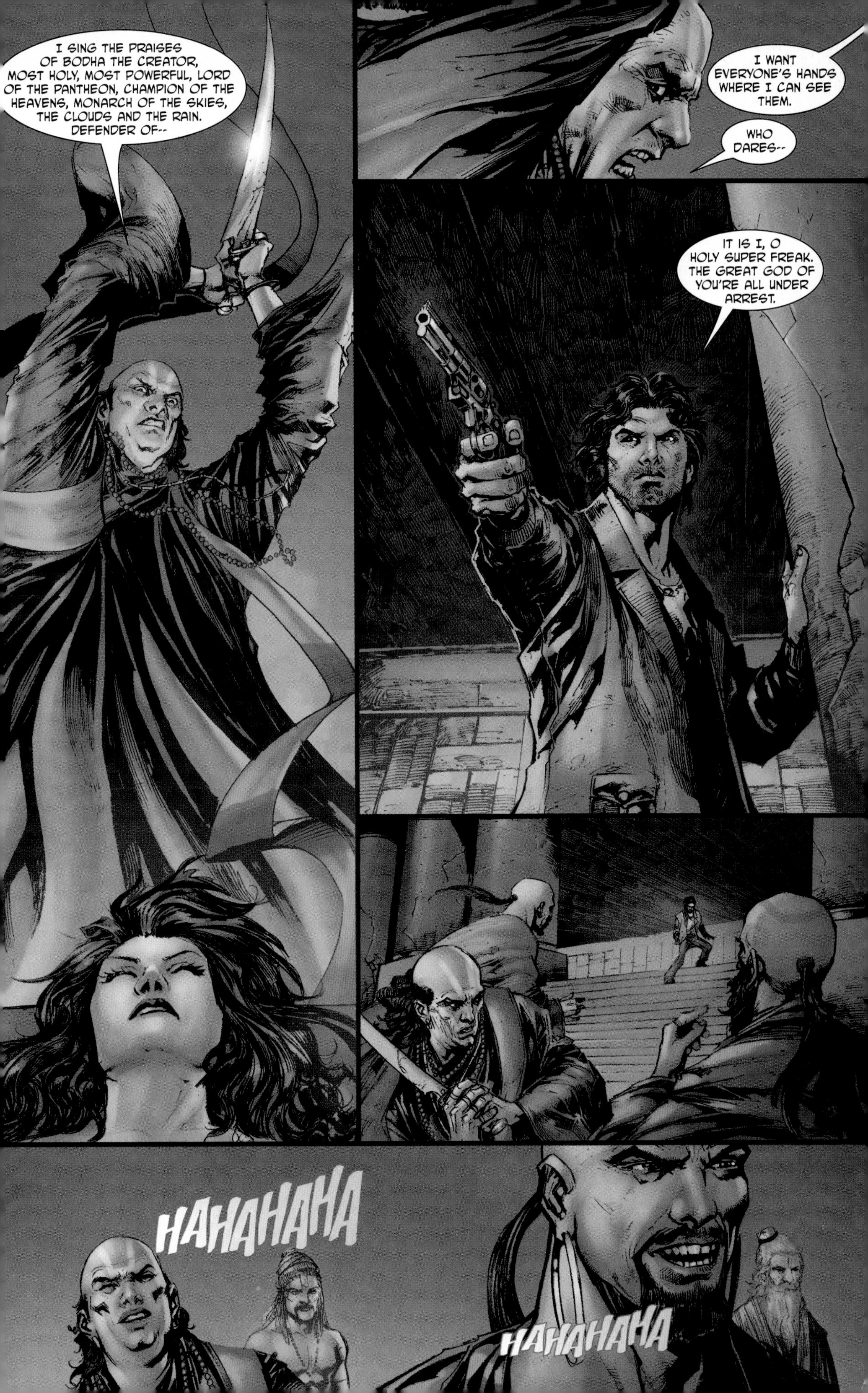
I SING THE PRAISES OF BODHA THE CREATOR, MOST HOLY, MOST POWERFUL, LORD OF THE PANTHEON, CHAMPION OF THE HEAVENS, MONARCH OF THE SKIES, THE CLOUDS AND THE RAIN. DEFENDER OF--
I WANT EVERYONE'S HANDS WHERE I CAN SEE THEM.
WHO DARES--
IT IS I, O HOLY SUPER FREAK. THE GREAT GOD OF YOU'RE ALL UNDER ARREST.
HAHAHAHA
HAHAHAHA

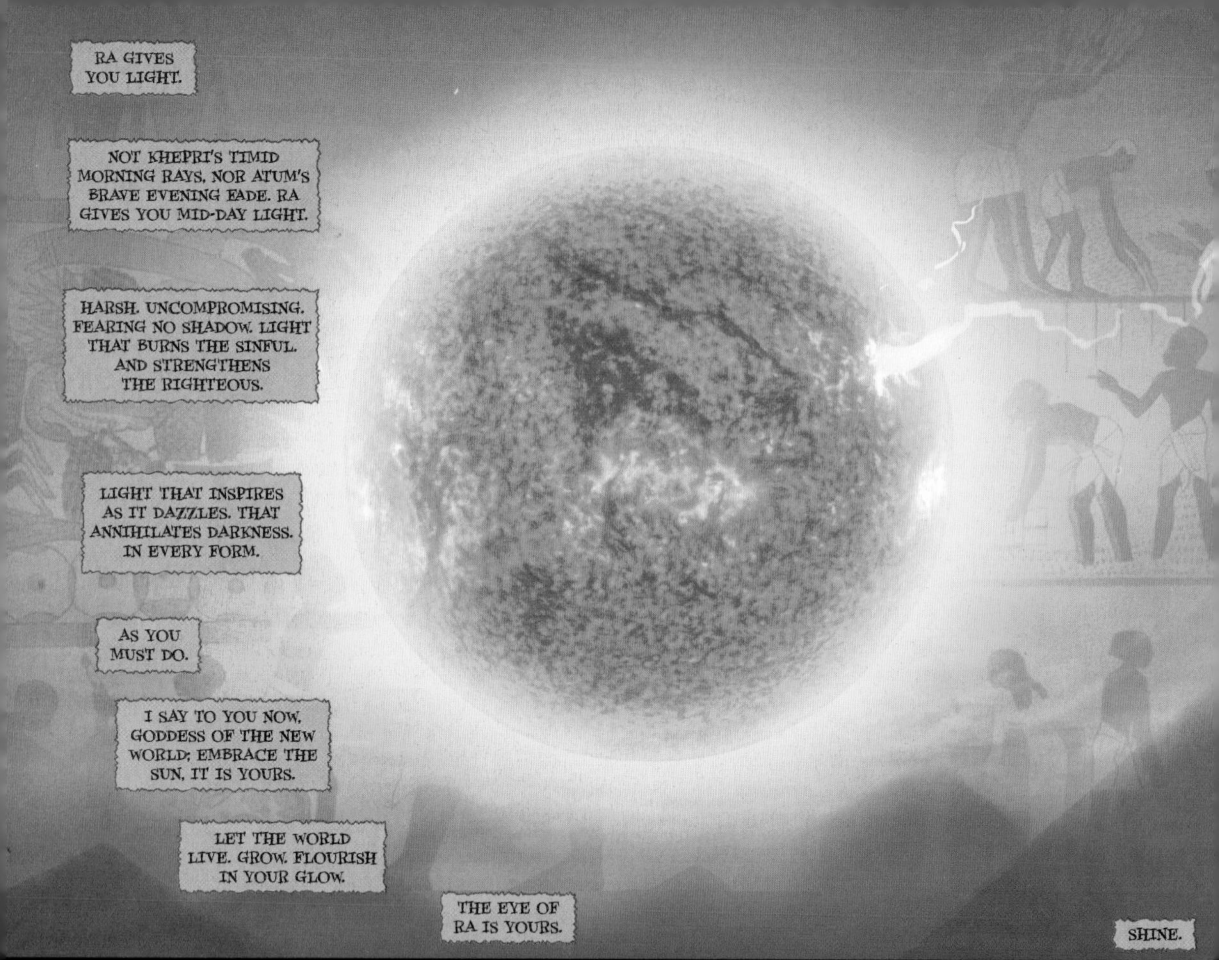

RA GIVES YOU LIGHT.
NOT KHEPRI'S TIMID MORNING RAYS, NOR ATUM'S BRAVE EVENING FADE. RA GIVES YOU MID-DAY LIGHT.
HARSH. UNCOMPROMISING. FEARING NO SHADOW. LIGHT THAT BURNS THE SINFUL. AND STRENGTHENS THE RIGHTEOUS.
LIGHT THAT INSPIRES AS IT DAZZLES. THAT ANNIHILATES DARKNESS. IN EVERY FORM.
AS YOU MUST DO.
I SAY TO YOU NOW, GODDESS OF THE NEW WORLD; EMBRACE THE SUN. IT IS YOURS.
LET THE WORLD LIVE. GROW. FLOURISH IN YOUR GLOW.
THE EYE OF RA IS YOURS.
SHINE.

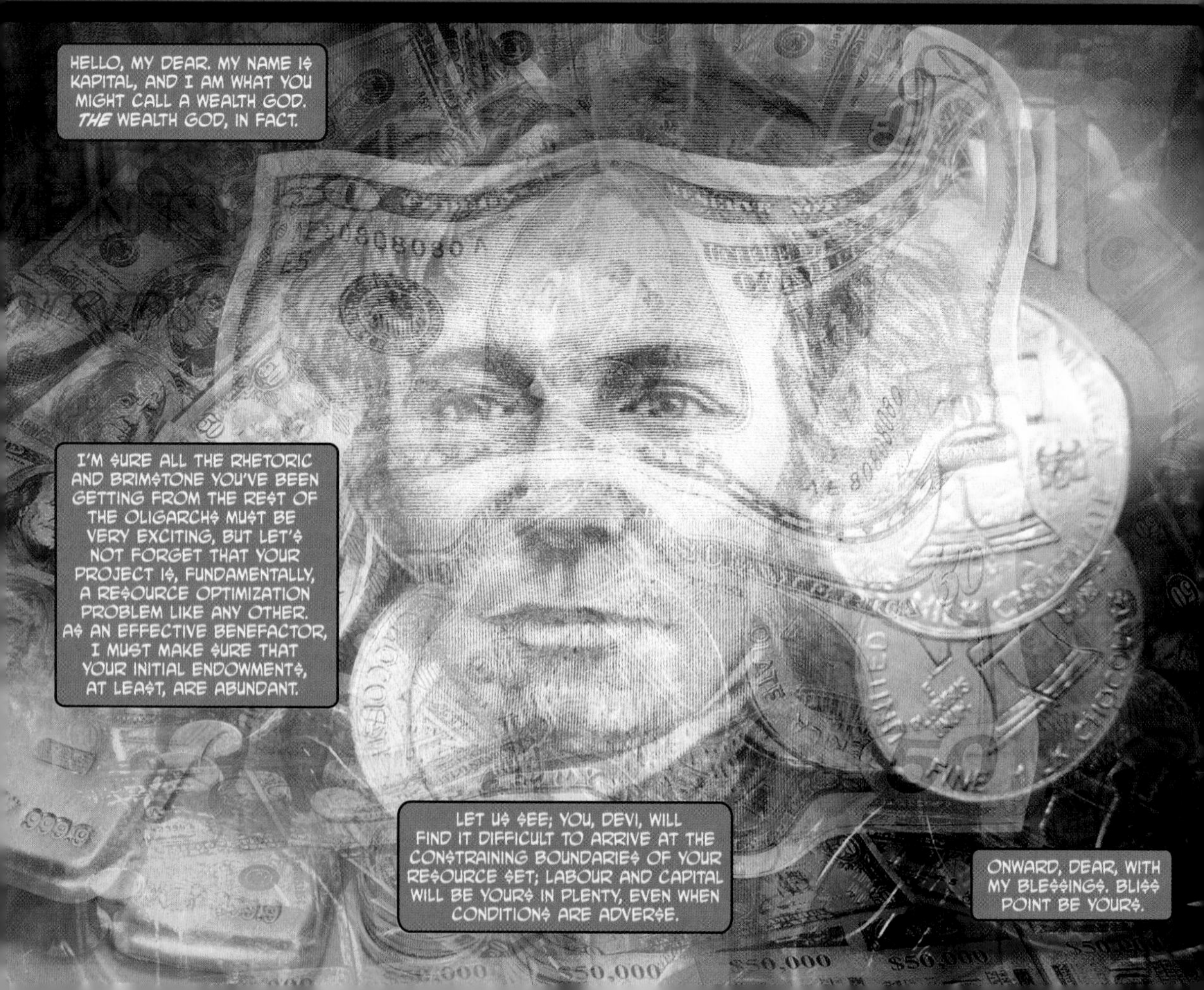

HELLO, MY DEAR. MY NAME I$ KAPITAL, AND I AM WHAT YOU MIGHT CALL A WEALTH GOD. *THE* WEALTH GOD, IN FACT.
I'M $URE ALL THE RHETORIC AND BRIM$TONE YOU'VE BEEN GETTING FROM THE RE$T OF THE OLIGARCH$ MU$T BE VERY EXCITING, BUT LET'$ NOT FORGET THAT YOUR PROJECT I$, FUNDAMENTALLY, A RE$OURCE OPTIMIZATION PROBLEM LIKE ANY OTHER. A$ AN EFFECTIVE BENEFACTOR, I MUST MAKE $URE THAT YOUR INITIAL ENDOWMENT$, AT LEA$T, ARE ABUNDANT.
LET U$ $EE; YOU, DEVI, WILL FIND IT DIFFICULT TO ARRIVE AT THE CON$TRAINING BOUNDARIE$ OF YOUR RE$OURCE $ET; LABOUR AND CAPITAL WILL BE YOUR$ IN PLENTY, EVEN WHEN CONDITION$ ARE ADVER$E.
ONWARD, DEAR, WITH MY BLE$$ING$. BLI$$ POINT BE YOUR$.

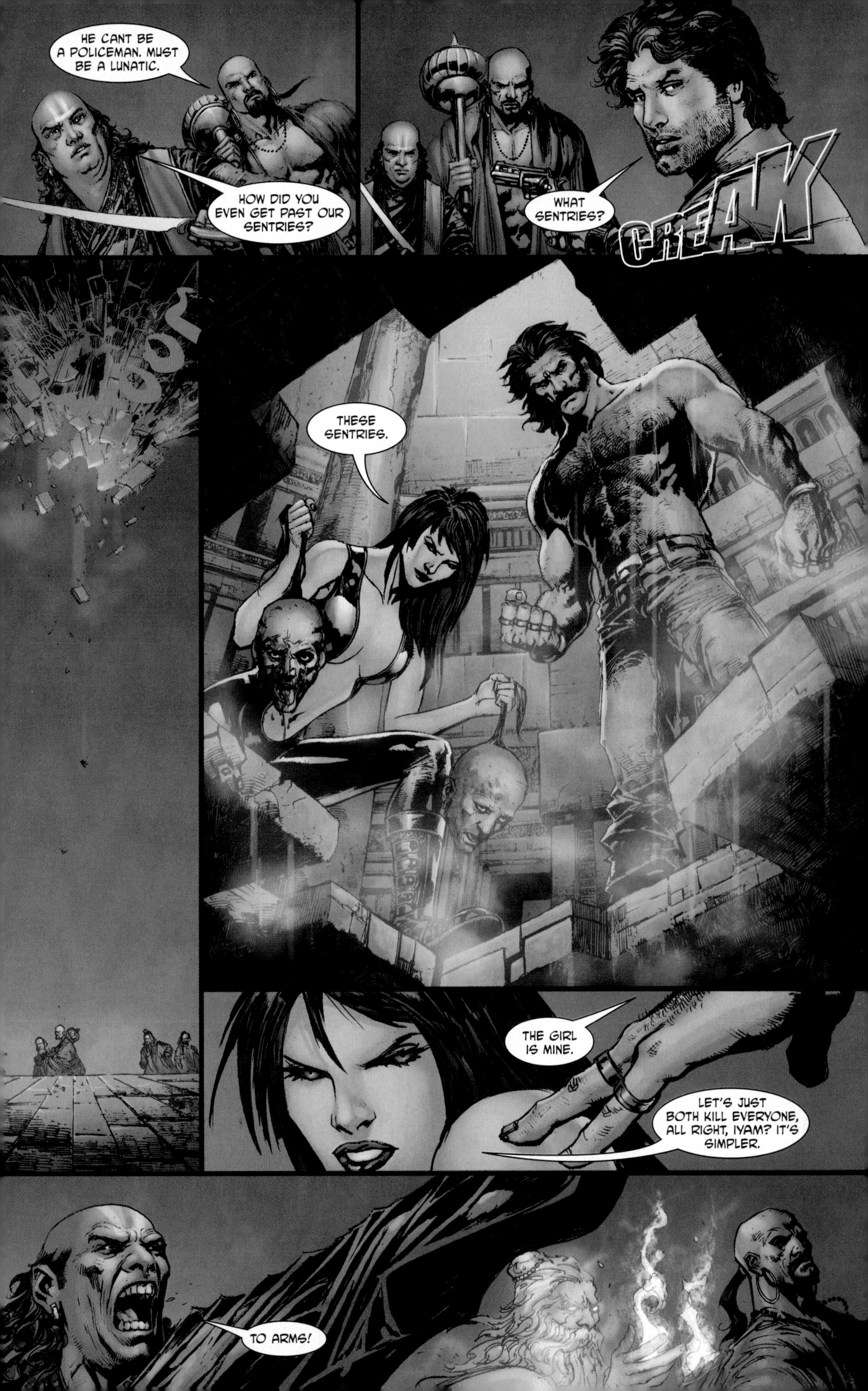
HE CANT BE A POLICEMAN. MUST BE A LUNATIC.
HOW DID YOU EVEN GET PAST OUR SENTRIES?
WHAT SENTRIES?
CREAK
THESE SENTRIES.
THE GIRL IS MINE.
LET'S JUST BOTH KILL EVERYONE, ALL RIGHT, IYAM? IT'S SIMPLER.
TO ARMS!

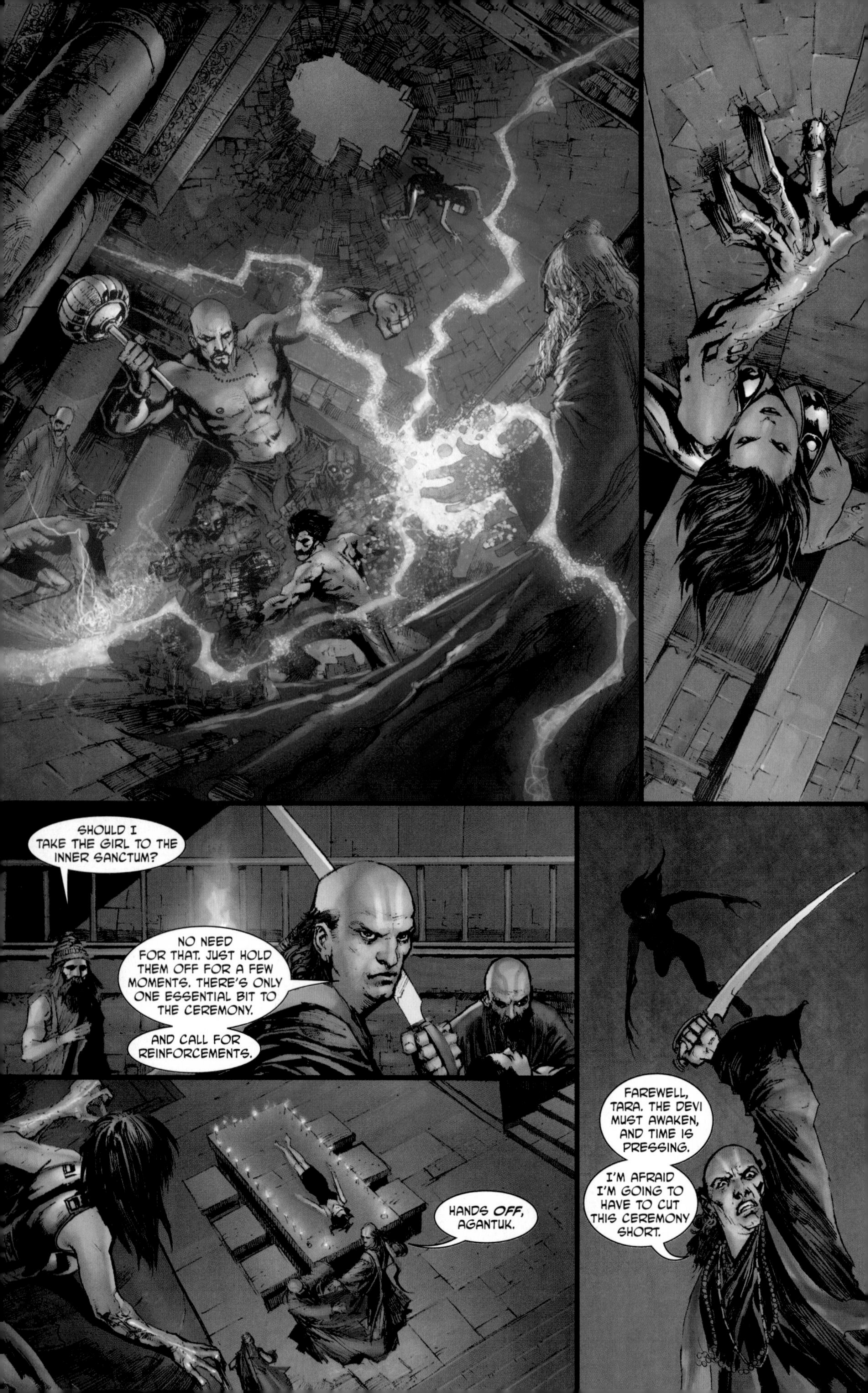
SHOULD I TAKE THE GIRL TO THE INNER SANCTUM?
NO NEED FOR THAT. JUST HOLD THEM OFF FOR A FEW MOMENTS. THERE'S ONLY ONE ESSENTIAL BIT TO THE CEREMONY.
AND CALL FOR REINFORCEMENTS.
HANDS *OFF*, AGANTUK.
FAREWELL, TARA. THE DEVI MUST AWAKEN, AND TIME IS PRESSING.
I'M AFRAID I'M GOING TO HAVE TO CUT THIS CEREMONY SHORT.

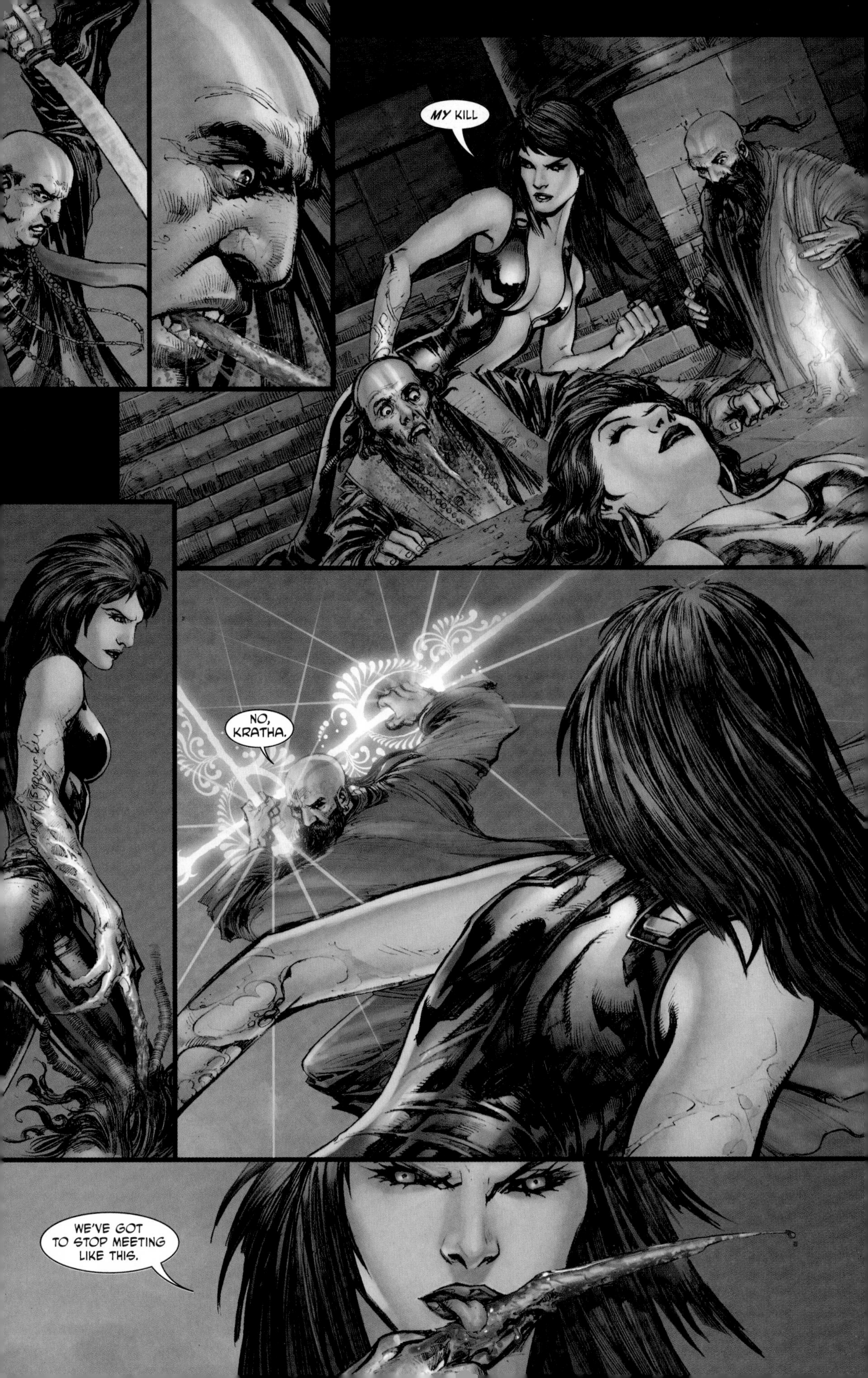
MY KILL
NO, KRATHA.
WE'VE GOT TO STOP MEETING LIKE THIS.

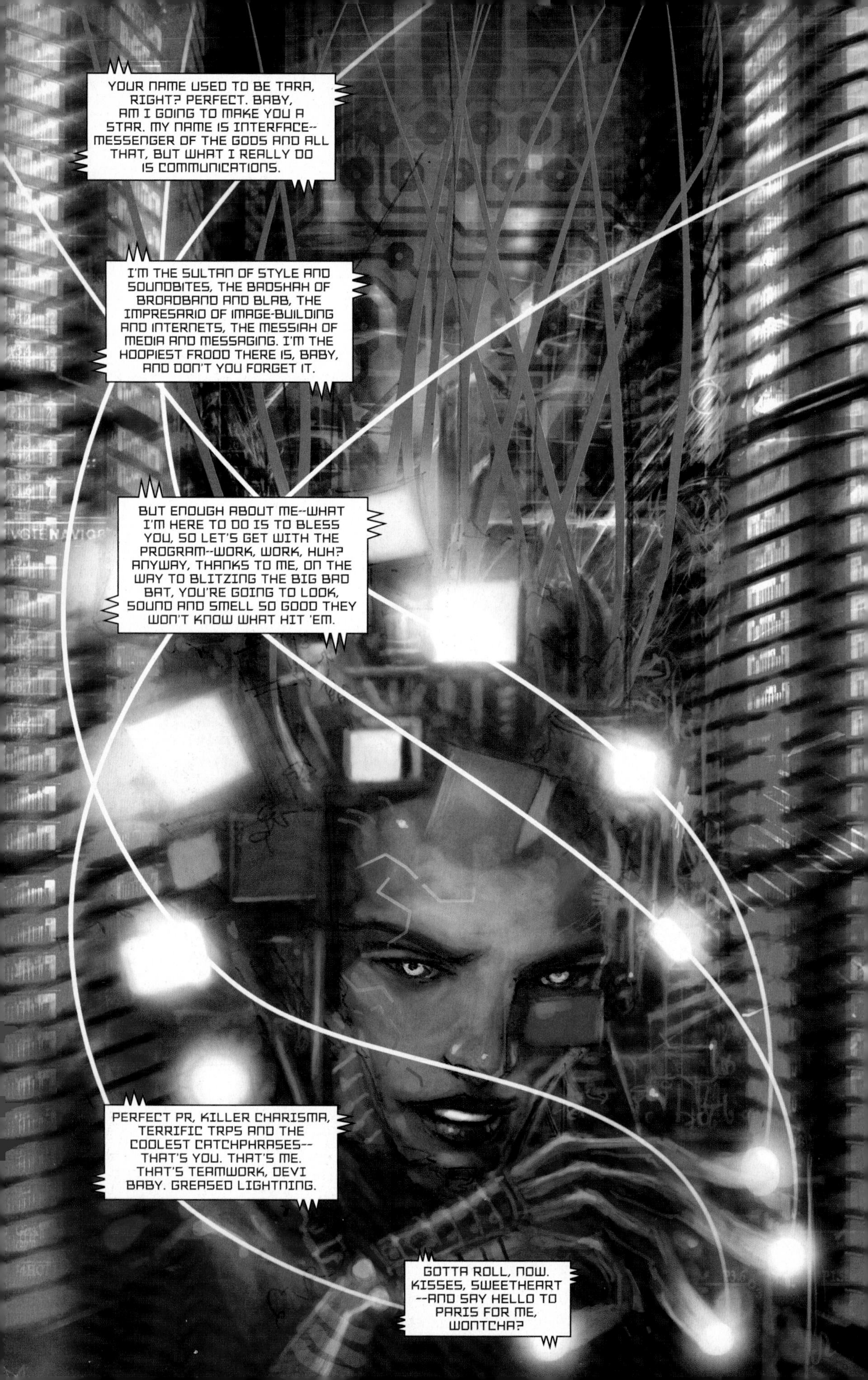
YOUR NAME USED TO BE TARA, RIGHT? PERFECT. BABY, AM I GOING TO MAKE YOU A STAR. MY NAME IS INTERFACE--MESSENGER OF THE GODS AND ALL THAT, BUT WHAT I REALLY DO IS COMMUNICATIONS.
I'M THE SULTAN OF STYLE AND SOUNDBITES, THE BADSHAH OF BROADBAND AND BLAB, THE IMPRESARIO OF IMAGE-BUILDING AND INTERNETS, THE MESSIAH OF MEDIA AND MESSAGING. I'M THE HOOPIEST FROOD THERE IS, BABY, AND DON'T YOU FORGET IT.
BUT ENOUGH ABOUT ME--WHAT I'M HERE TO DO IS TO BLESS YOU, SO LET'S GET WITH THE PROGRAM--WORK, WORK, HUH? ANYWAY, THANKS TO ME, ON THE WAY TO BLITZING THE BIG BAD BAT, YOU'RE GOING TO LOOK, SOUND AND SMELL SO GOOD THEY WON'T KNOW WHAT HIT 'EM.
PERFECT PR, KILLER CHARISMA, TERRIFIC TRPS AND THE COOLEST CATCHPHRASES--THAT'S YOU. THAT'S ME. THAT'S TEAMWORK, DEVI BABY. GREASED LIGHTNING.
GOTTA ROLL, NOW. KISSES, SWEETHEART --AND SAY HELLO TO PARIS FOR ME, WONTCHA?

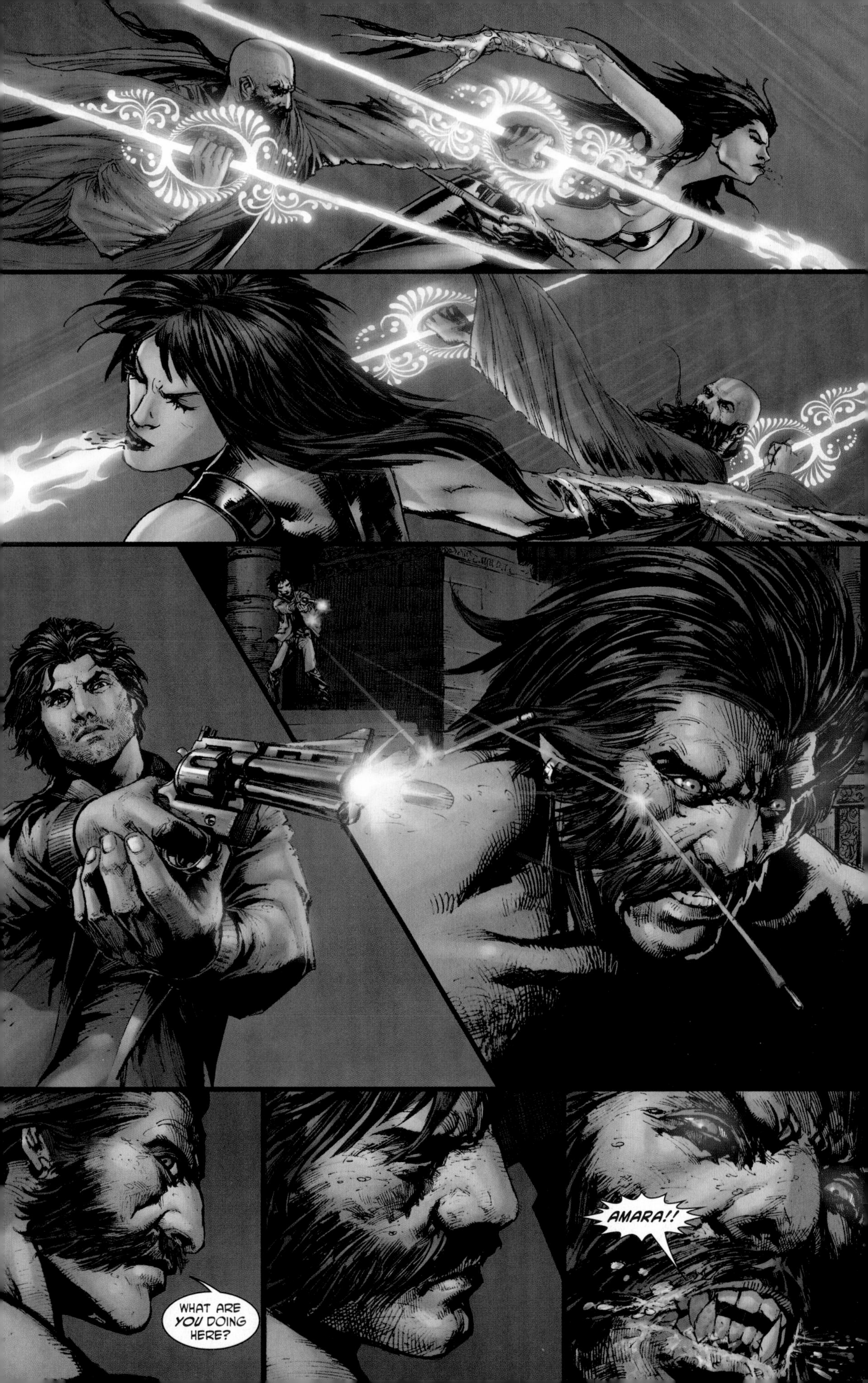
WHAT ARE YOU DOING HERE?
AMARA!!

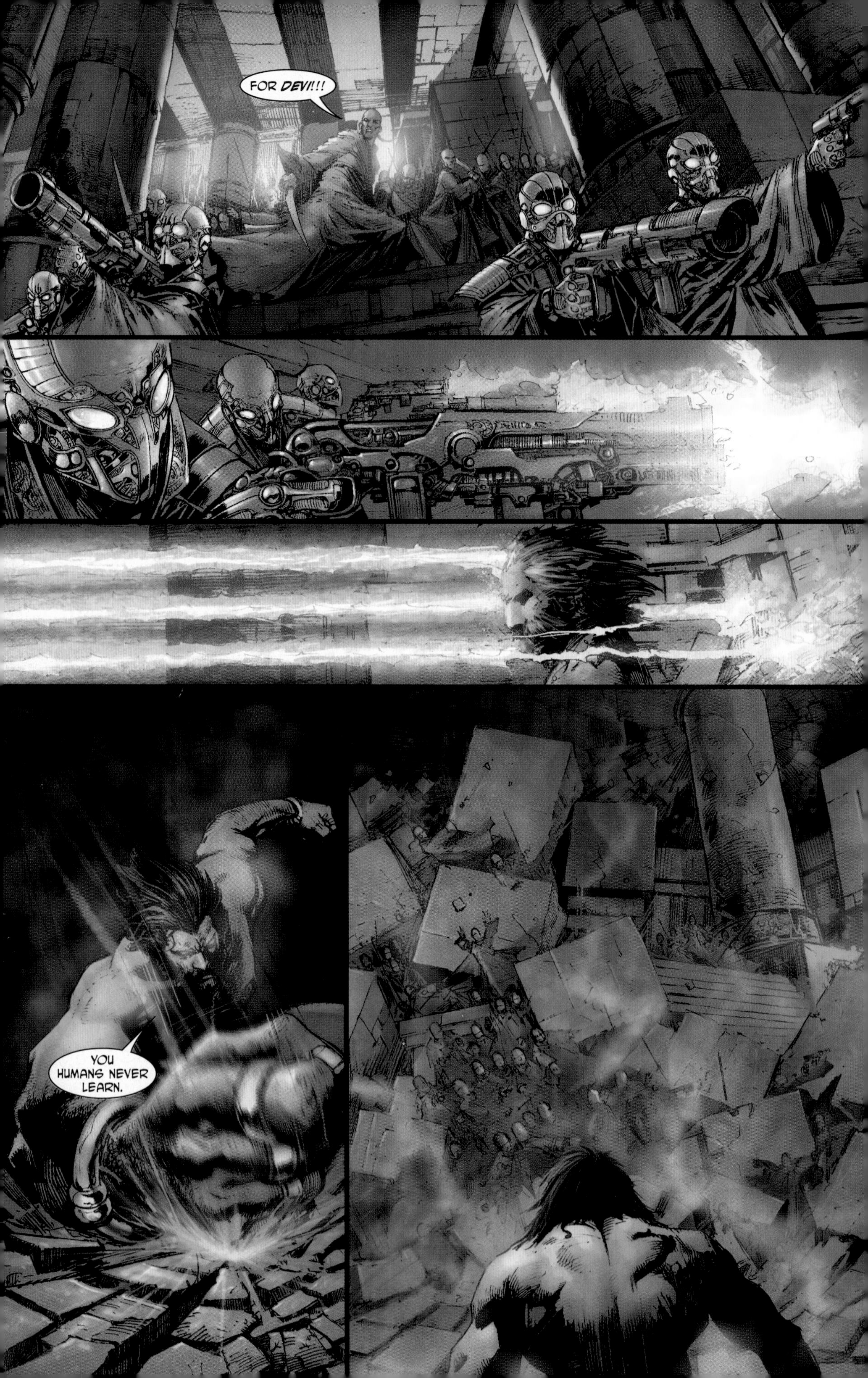
FOR DEVI!!!
YOU HUMANS NEVER LEARN.

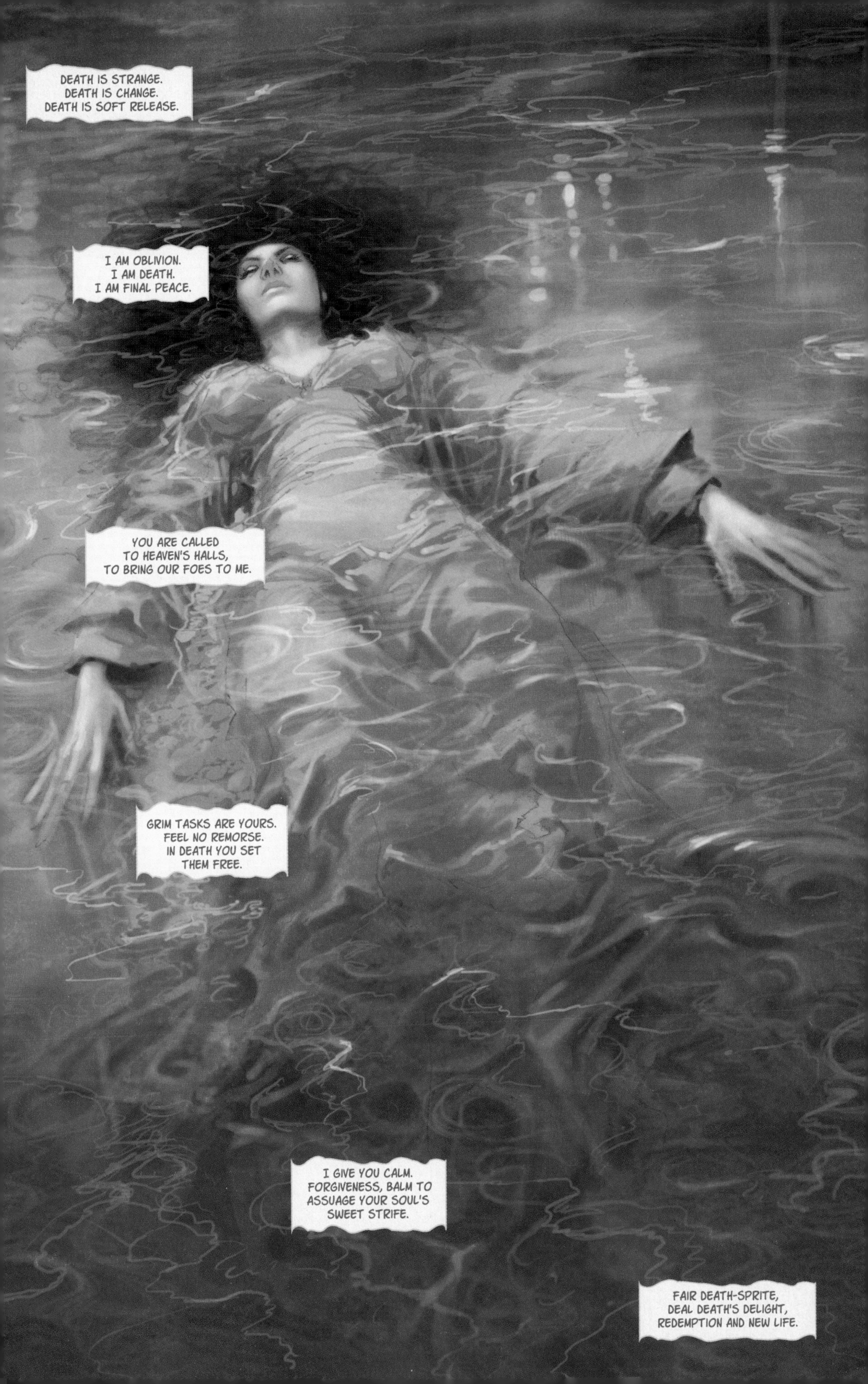
DEATH IS STRANGE. DEATH IS CHANGE. DEATH IS SOFT RELEASE.
I AM OBLIVION. I AM DEATH. I AM FINAL PEACE.
YOU ARE CALLED TO HEAVEN'S HALLS, TO BRING OUR FOES TO ME.
GRIM TASKS ARE YOURS. FEEL NO REMORSE. IN DEATH YOU SET THEM FREE.
I GIVE YOU CALM. FORGIVENESS, BALM TO ASSUAGE YOUR SOUL'S SWEET STRIFE.
FAIR DEATH-SPRITE, DEAL DEATH'S DELIGHT, REDEMPTION AND NEW LIFE.

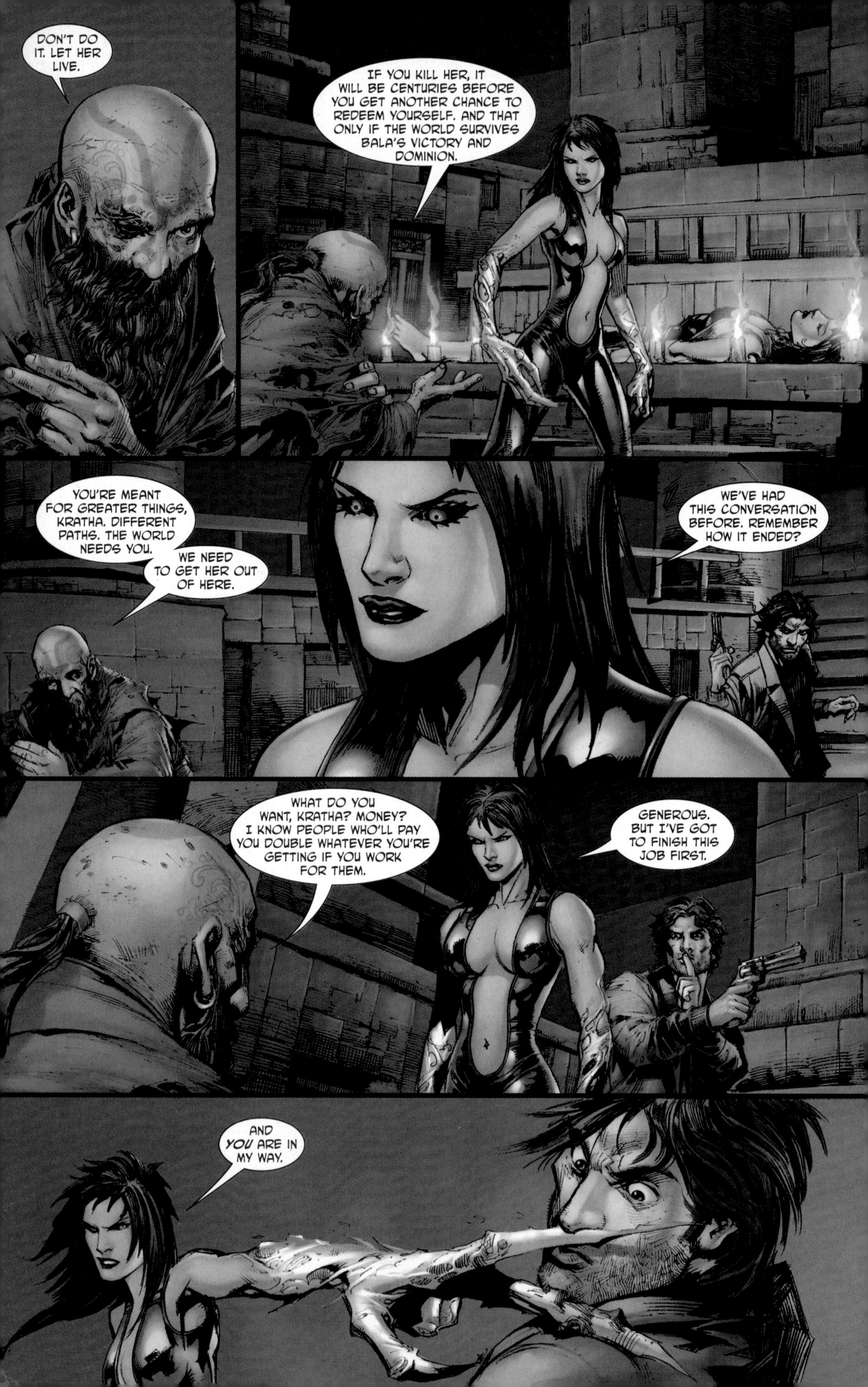
DON'T DO IT. LET HER LIVE.
IF YOU KILL HER, IT WILL BE CENTURIES BEFORE YOU GET ANOTHER CHANCE TO REDEEM YOURSELF. AND THAT ONLY IF THE WORLD SURVIVES BALA'S VICTORY AND DOMINION.
YOU'RE MEANT FOR GREATER THINGS, KRATHA. DIFFERENT PATHS. THE WORLD NEEDS YOU.
WE NEED TO GET HER OUT OF HERE.
WE'VE HAD THIS CONVERSATION BEFORE. REMEMBER HOW IT ENDED?
WHAT DO YOU WANT, KRATHA? MONEY? I KNOW PEOPLE WHO'LL PAY YOU DOUBLE WHATEVER YOU'RE GETTING IF YOU WORK FOR THEM.
GENEROUS. BUT I'VE GOT TO FINISH THIS JOB FIRST.
AND *YOU* ARE IN MY WAY.

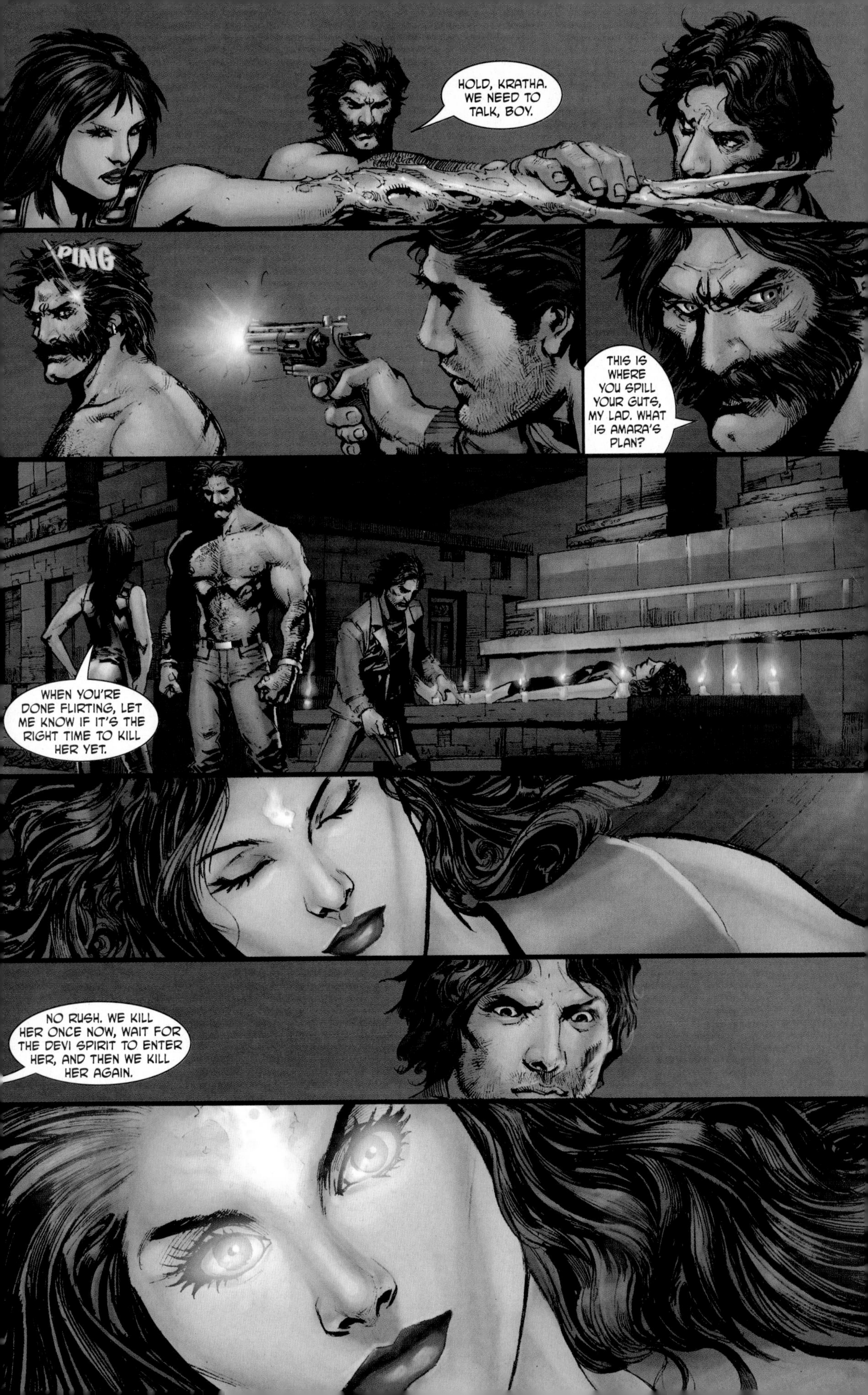
HOLD, KRATHA. WE NEED TO TALK, BOY.
PING
THIS IS WHERE YOU SPILL YOUR GUTS, MY LAD. WHAT IS AMARA'S PLAN?
WHEN YOU'RE DONE FLIRTING, LET ME KNOW IF IT'S THE RIGHT TIME TO KILL HER YET.
NO RUSH. WE KILL HER ONCE NOW, WAIT FOR THE DEVI SPIRIT TO ENTER HER, AND THEN WE KILL HER AGAIN.

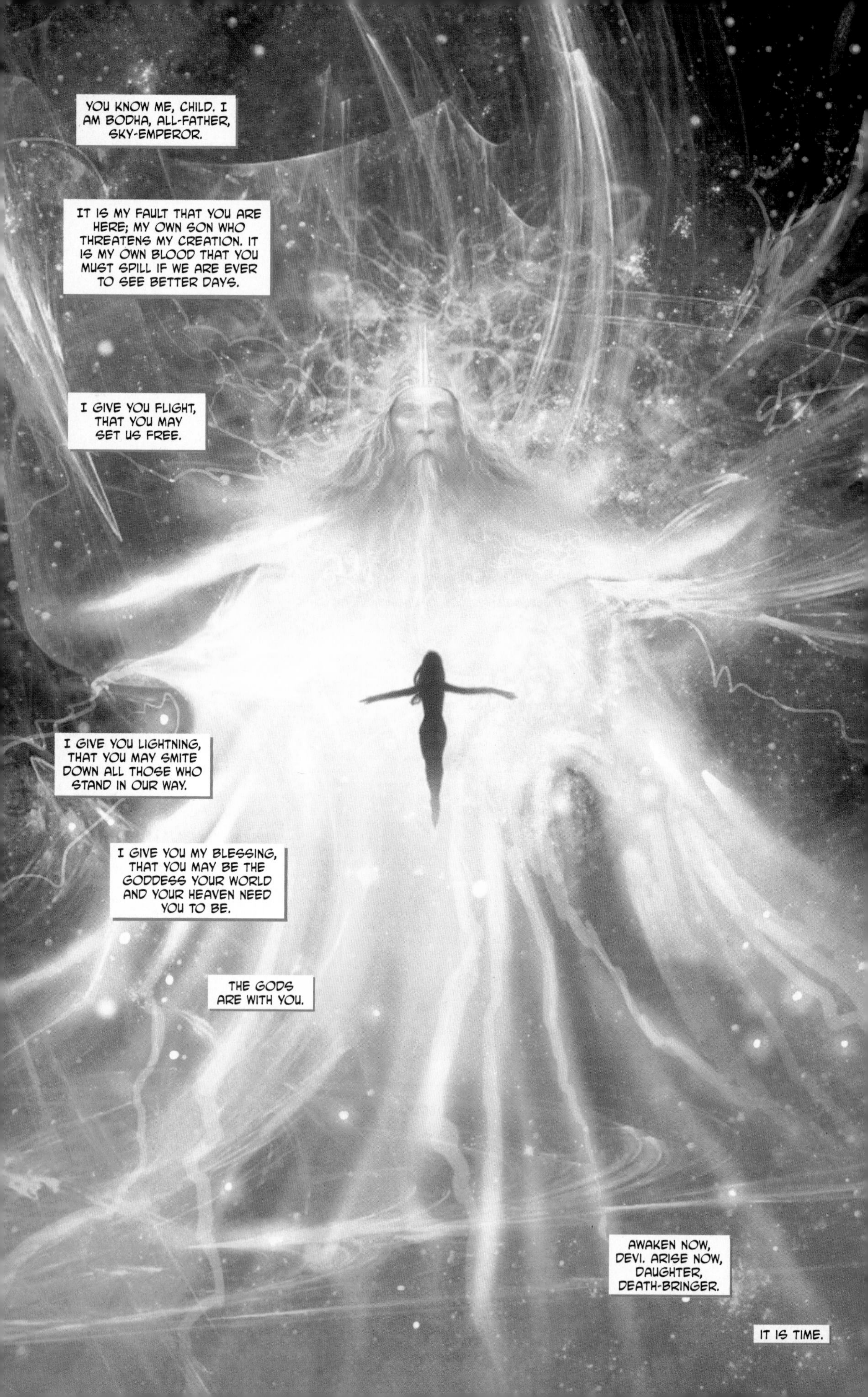
YOU KNOW ME, CHILD. I AM BODHA, ALL-FATHER, SKY-EMPEROR.
IT IS MY FAULT THAT YOU ARE HERE; MY OWN SON WHO THREATENS MY CREATION. IT IS MY OWN BLOOD THAT YOU MUST SPILL IF WE ARE EVER TO SEE BETTER DAYS.
I GIVE YOU FLIGHT, THAT YOU MAY SET US FREE.
I GIVE YOU LIGHTNING, THAT YOU MAY SMITE DOWN ALL THOSE WHO STAND IN OUR WAY.
I GIVE YOU MY BLESSING, THAT YOU MAY BE THE GODDESS YOUR WORLD AND YOUR HEAVEN NEED YOU TO BE.
THE GODS ARE WITH YOU.
AWAKEN NOW, DEVI. ARISE NOW, DAUGHTER, DEATH-BRINGER.
IT IS TIME.

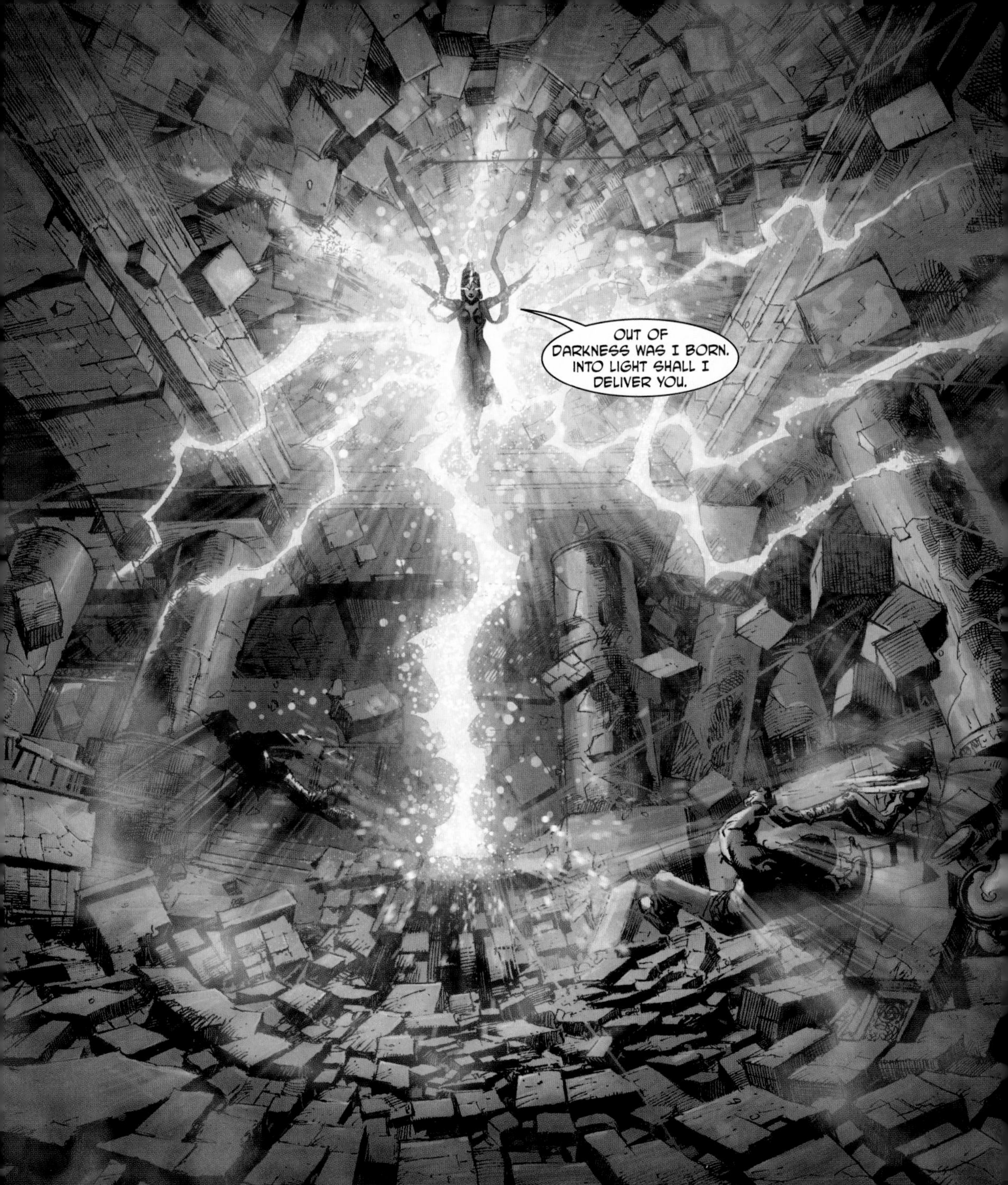
OUT OF DARKNESS WAS I BORN. INTO LIGHT SHALL I DELIVER YOU.

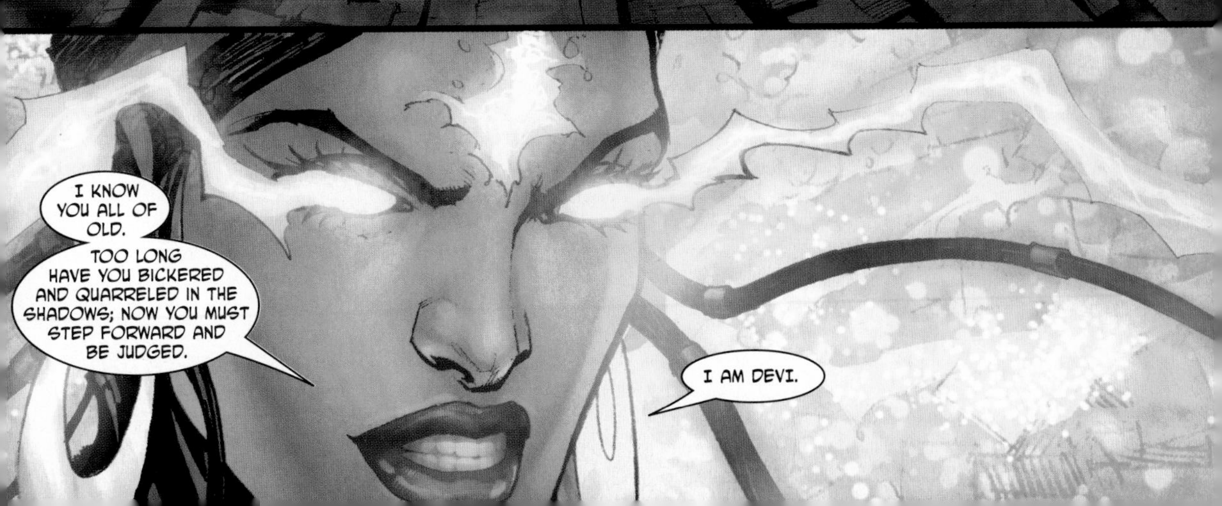
I KNOW YOU ALL OF OLD.
TOO LONG HAVE YOU BICKERED AND QUARRELED IN THE SHADOWS; NOW YOU MUST STEP FORWARD AND BE JUDGED.
I AM DEVI.

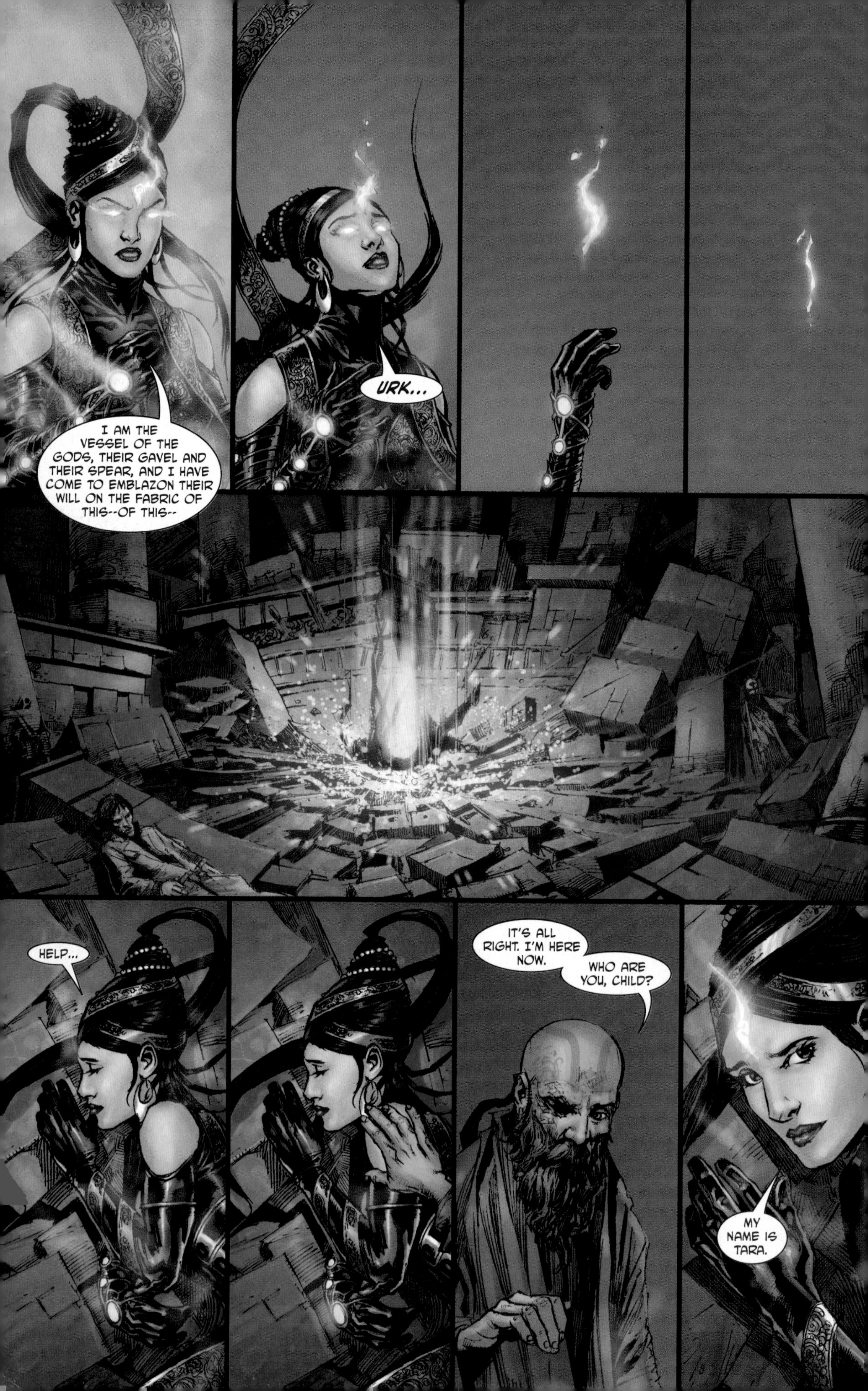
I AM THE VESSEL OF THE GODS, THEIR GAVEL AND THEIR SPEAR, AND I HAVE COME TO EMBLAZON THEIR WILL ON THE FABRIC OF THIS--OF THIS--
URK...
HELP...
IT'S ALL RIGHT. I'M HERE NOW.
WHO ARE YOU, CHILD?
MY NAME IS TARA.

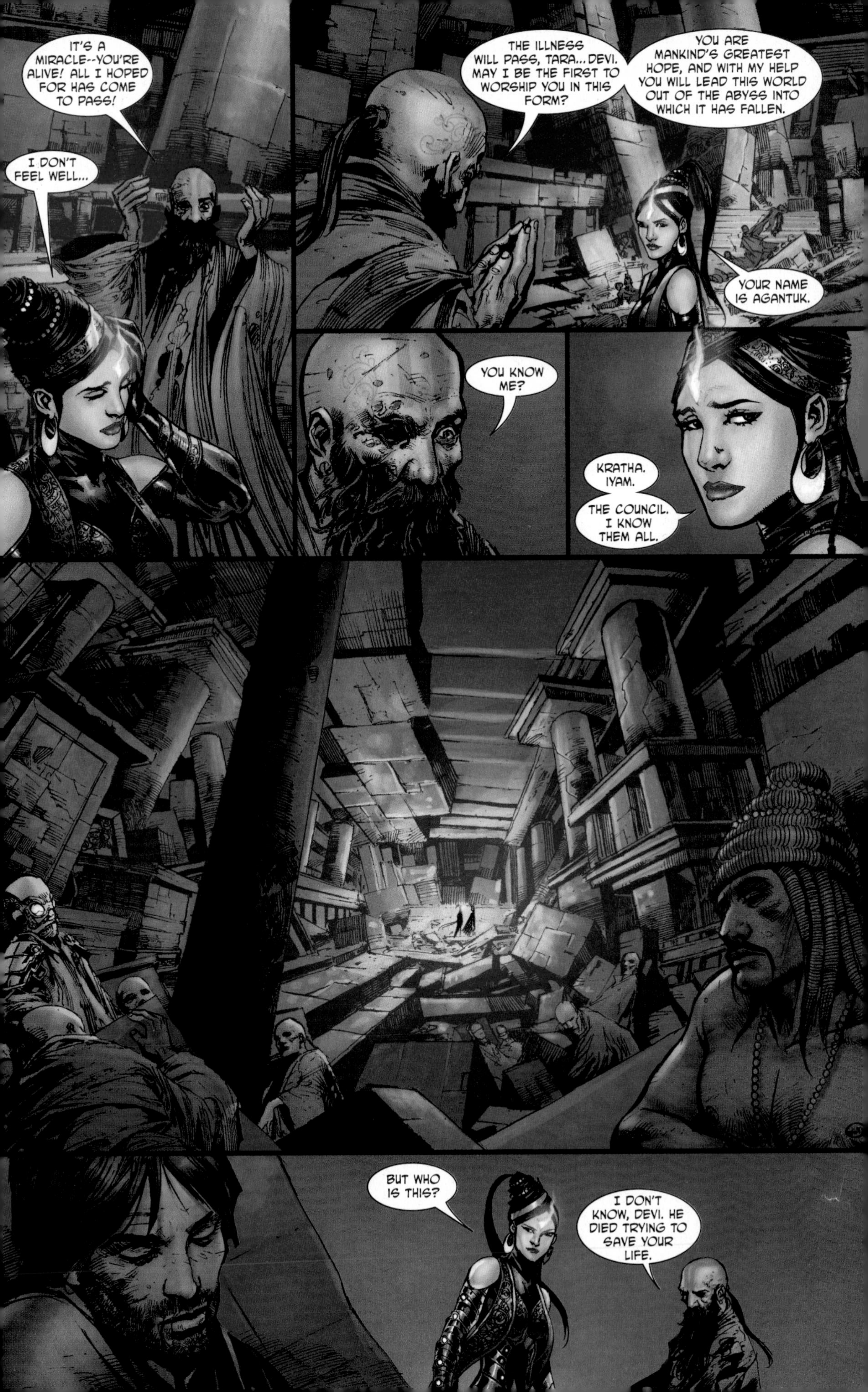
IT'S A MIRACLE--YOU'RE ALIVE! ALL I HOPED FOR HAS COME TO PASS!
I DON'T FEEL WELL...
THE ILLNESS WILL PASS, TARA...DEVI. MAY I BE THE FIRST TO WORSHIP YOU IN THIS FORM?
YOU ARE MANKIND'S GREATEST HOPE, AND WITH MY HELP YOU WILL LEAD THIS WORLD OUT OF THE ABYSS INTO WHICH IT HAS FALLEN.
YOUR NAME IS AGANTUK.
YOU KNOW ME?
KRATHA. IYAM.
THE COUNCIL. I KNOW THEM ALL.
BUT WHO IS THIS?
I DON'T KNOW, DEVI. HE DIED TRYING TO SAVE YOUR LIFE.

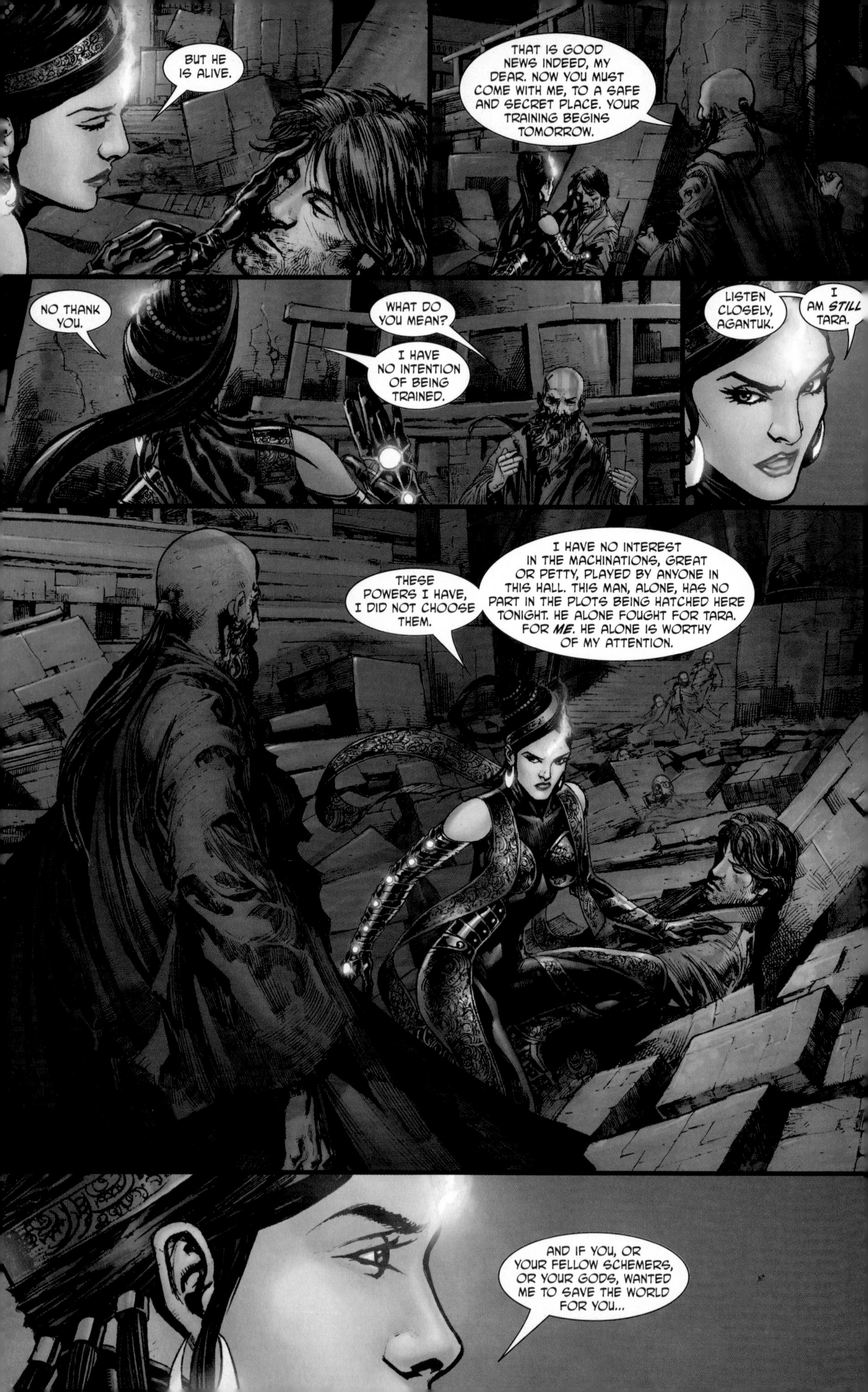
BUT HE IS ALIVE.
THAT IS GOOD NEWS INDEED, MY DEAR. NOW YOU MUST COME WITH ME, TO A SAFE AND SECRET PLACE. YOUR TRAINING BEGINS TOMORROW.
NO THANK YOU.
WHAT DO YOU MEAN?
I HAVE NO INTENTION OF BEING TRAINED.
LISTEN CLOSELY, AGANTUK.
I AM *STILL* TARA.
THESE POWERS I HAVE, I DID NOT CHOOSE THEM.
I HAVE NO INTEREST IN THE MACHINATIONS, GREAT OR PETTY, PLAYED BY ANYONE IN THIS HALL. THIS MAN, ALONE, HAS NO PART IN THE PLOTS BEING HATCHED HERE TONIGHT. HE ALONE FOUGHT FOR TARA. FOR ***ME***. HE ALONE IS WORTHY OF MY ATTENTION.
AND IF YOU, OR YOUR FELLOW SCHEMERS, OR YOUR GODS, WANTED ME TO SAVE THE WORLD FOR YOU...

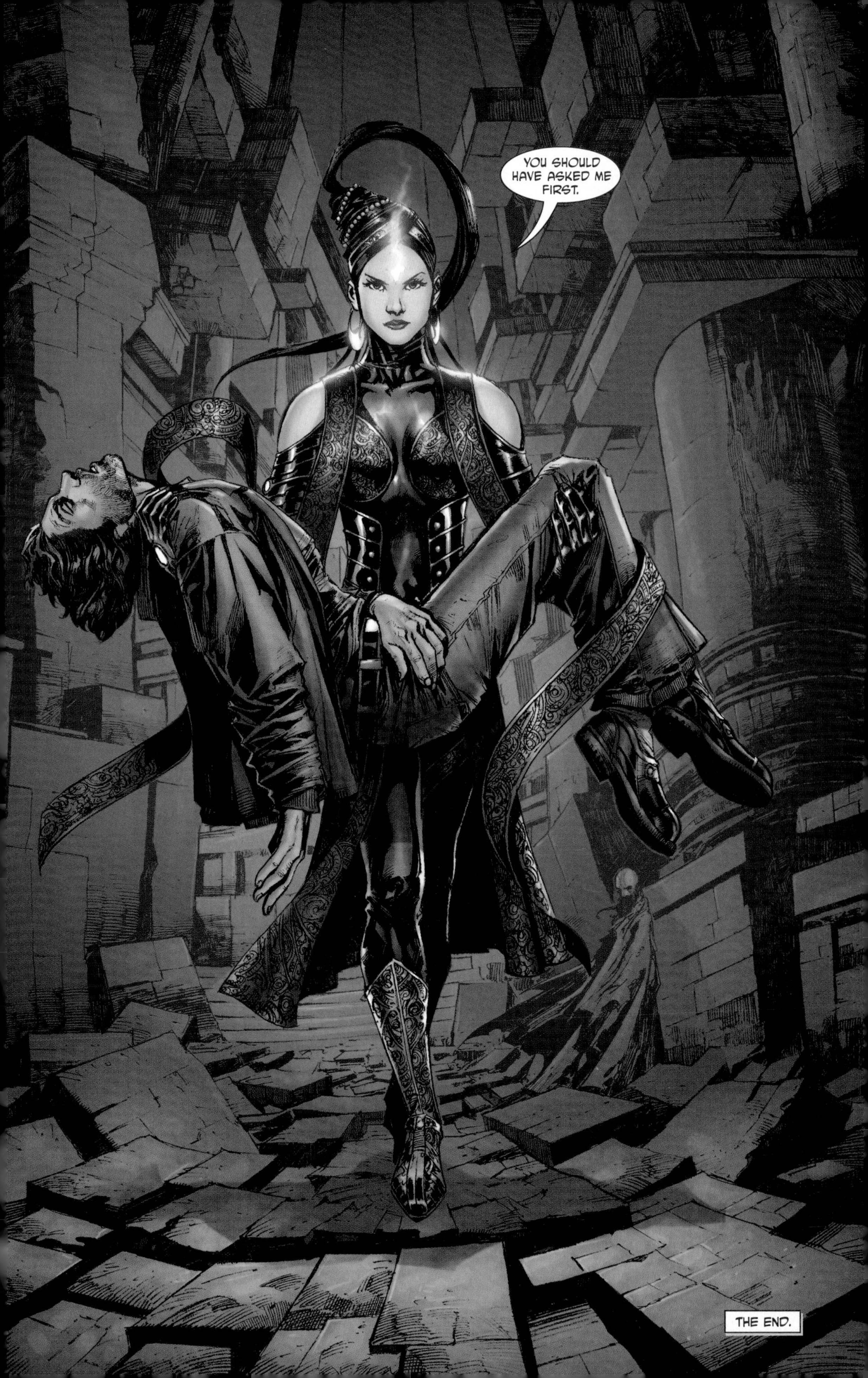
YOU SHOULD HAVE ASKED ME FIRST.
THE END.

DEVI-MYTH, LEGEND, OR LEATHER-CLAD SUPERBABE?

Who is the *Devi?* No, we don't mean just our own half-woman half-goddess leather clad superheroine from the streets of Sitapur, but the iconic Hindu goddess who inspired the story of Tara Mehta, Shekhar Kapur's *Devi*. In Sanskrit and Hindi, "Devi" literally means "Goddess". The word dates back 3,300 years to when the Vedas—Ancient Hindu scriptures from 1,300 BC—were written. And the stories told in the Vedas form the basis of the Hindu faith, which has close to a billion followers around the world.

They say in these scriptures that upon the Universe's conception, two primordial forces emerged—including within God, itself. Like the female *Yin*, and the masculine *Yang*, that are the cornerstones of Taoist philosophy, the Hindu Supreme Being was given a male aspect *Shiva*, which represents consciousness and perception, and a female aspect, which represents energy or *Shakti*. Without *Shakti*, the male aspect is rendered powerless—impotent. And unlike other supreme Gods, like the Greek *Hera*, or the Egyptian *Isis*, the *Devi* is the direct female manifestation of the Supreme Being. In India, every Goddess in the wide pantheon is derived from her.

Devi's three main avatars are wealth, wisdom and nature, manifested in *Lakshmi, Saraswathi,* and *Durga* respectively. As the All-Mother, she apportions both life and death, joy and pain. She is a Goddess of fertility, rain, health, and nature. And like the Greek Earth-Goddess *Gaia*, she holds the universe in her womb.

In modern India still, hundreds of millions of people worship Devi in all her forms, to seek her blessings and to thank her for her gifts with the firm belief that she will give them strength to overcome obstacles, and bring prosperity to their lots. There are many different celebrations during the year including *Durga Puja*, when clay idols of the Goddess Durga are lovingly adorned and paraded through the city, and *Dasara*, when people worship their work places and tools (some, even their calculators) to grant them prosperity in their businesses. And then there is *Divali*, the festival of lights which takes place in October, where a billion lamps are lit and tremendous fireworks shows are performed, all in an effort once again to draw the attention of Devi and her blessings.

At the core of all these celebrations is an acknowledgement by the people that Devi protects and provides for them, whether she is a super heroine who fights a demon to save a child, or a harbinger of prosperity for all walks of life. Devi is the All-Mother who empowers us with her myriad faces and in a thousand different ways. But talk to the sages of India, and they will whisper a last definitive secret regarding Devi to all those that will listen. Devi is not an idol simply worthy of worship, or a mere colorful icon or statue placed upon a pedestal; just as she was embedded within the Universe during its birth, so too does she exist in the embryo of each one of us. Worship her, nurture her, love her, and she will reveal herself within you to truly be the greatest super hero ever known.

Following is a tale of the Devi and her
human cohort, inspector Rahul Singh, battling
the things that go bump in the night. Though it does
not take place in the same timeline as the previous
story, it offers further evidence that, in our world,
where the divine and diabolical struggle for
supremacy, there is hope in the form of
a young woman and goddess.
She is Devi...

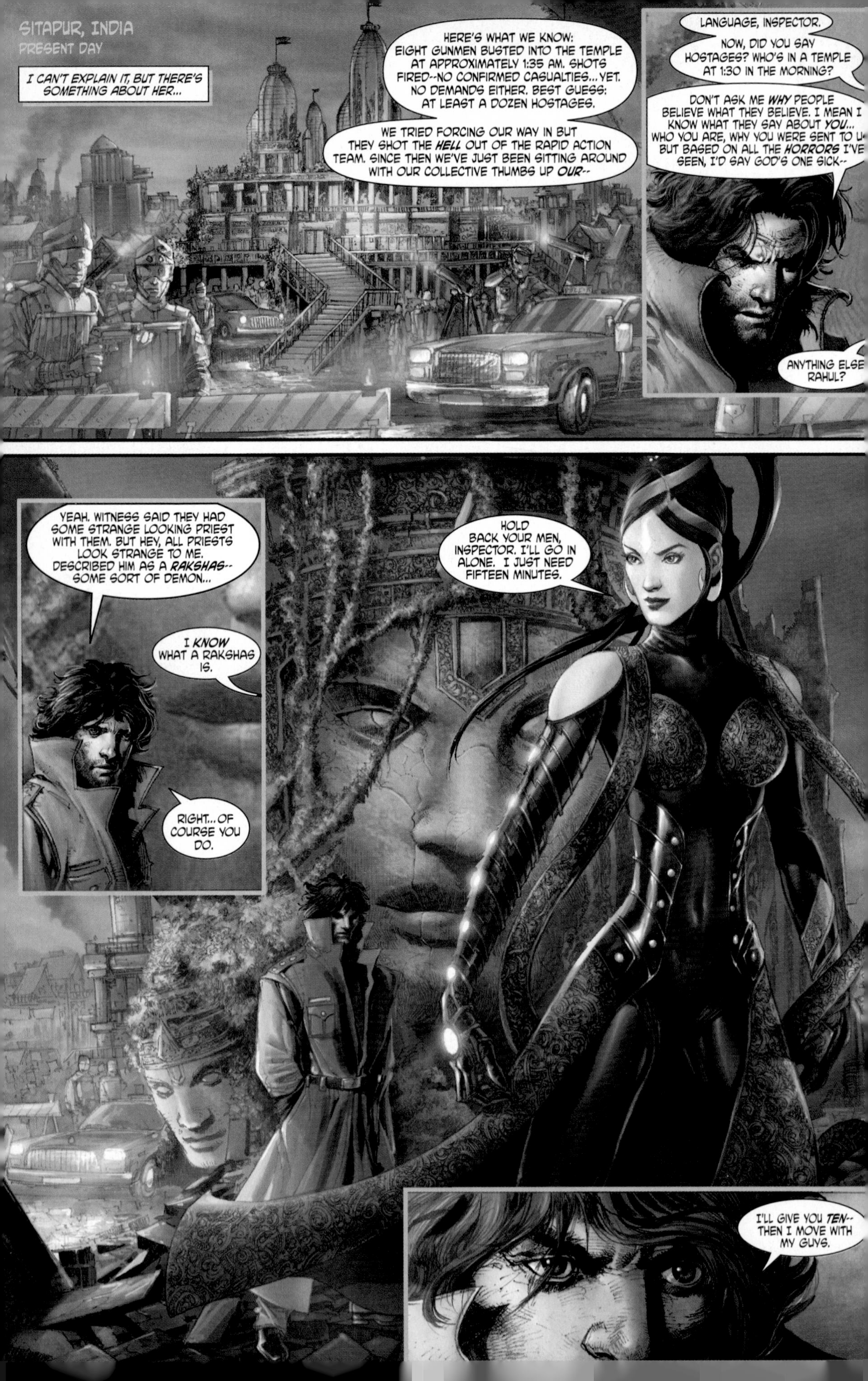
SITAPUR, INDIA
PRESENT DAY
I CAN'T EXPLAIN IT, BUT THERE'S SOMETHING ABOUT HER...
HERE'S WHAT WE KNOW: EIGHT GUNMEN BUSTED INTO THE TEMPLE AT APPROXIMATELY 1:35 AM. SHOTS FIRED--NO CONFIRMED CASUALTIES... YET. NO DEMANDS EITHER. BEST GUESS: AT LEAST A DOZEN HOSTAGES.
WE TRIED FORCING OUR WAY IN BUT THEY SHOT THE HELL OUT OF THE RAPID ACTION TEAM. SINCE THEN WE'VE JUST BEEN SITTING AROUND WITH OUR COLLECTIVE THUMBS UP OUR--
LANGUAGE, INSPECTOR.
NOW, DID YOU SAY HOSTAGES? WHO'S IN A TEMPLE AT 1:30 IN THE MORNING?
DON'T ASK ME WHY PEOPLE BELIEVE WHAT THEY BELIEVE. I MEAN I KNOW WHAT THEY SAY ABOUT YOU... WHO YOU ARE, WHY YOU WERE SENT TO U- BUT BASED ON ALL THE HORRORS I'VE SEEN, I'D SAY GOD'S ONE SICK--
ANYTHING ELSE RAHUL?
YEAH. WITNESS SAID THEY HAD SOME STRANGE LOOKING PRIEST WITH THEM. BUT HEY, ALL PRIESTS LOOK STRANGE TO ME. DESCRIBED HIM AS A RAKSHAS-- SOME SORT OF DEMON...
I KNOW WHAT A RAKSHAS IS.
RIGHT... OF COURSE YOU DO.
HOLD BACK YOUR MEN, INSPECTOR. I'LL GO IN ALONE. I JUST NEED FIFTEEN MINUTES.
I'LL GIVE YOU TEN-- THEN I MOVE WITH MY GUYS.

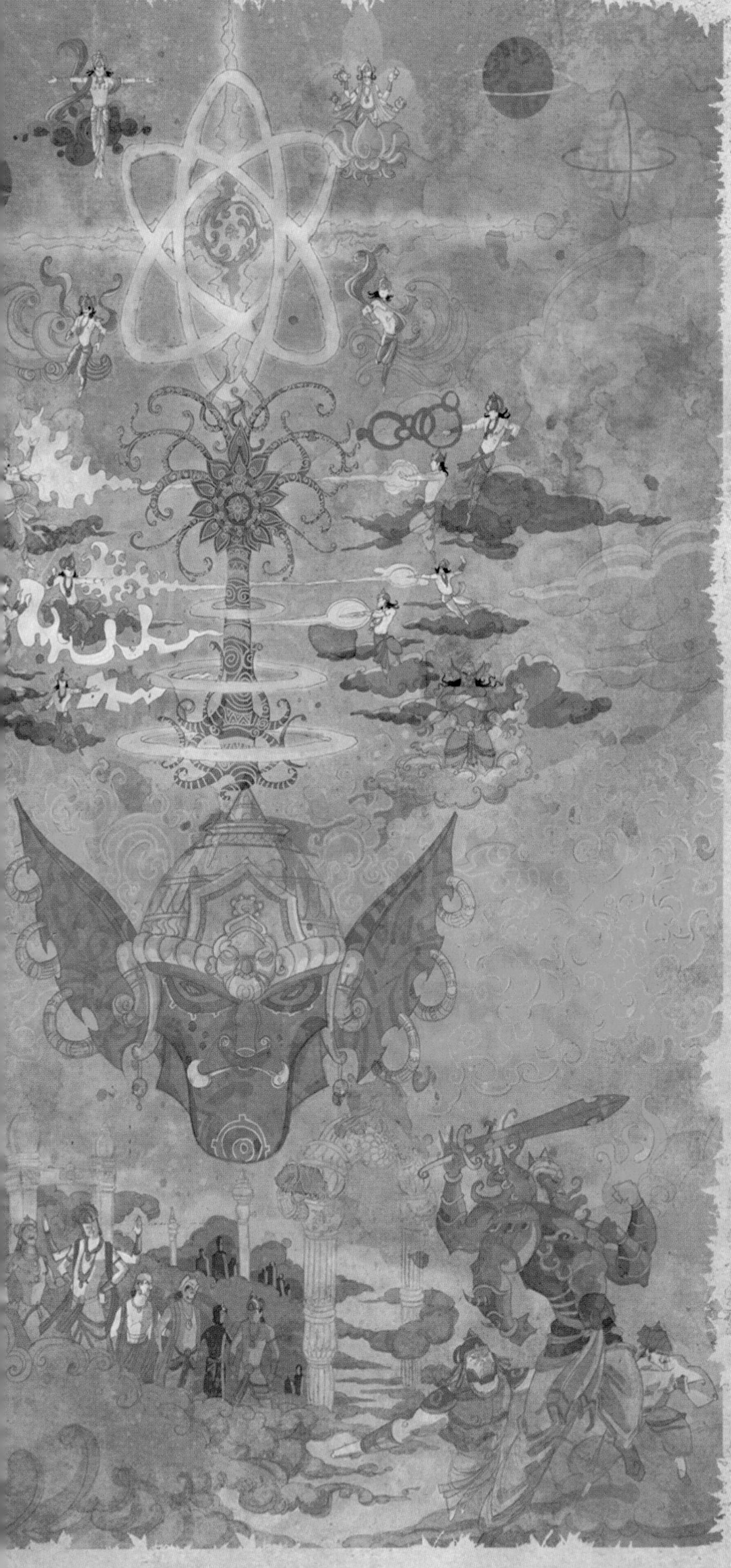

In the beginning there was perfection.

The cosmos danced the celestial ballet accompanied by a chorus of light. Bright, beautiful light. This was the time that was.

This was the age of innocence.

The Gods were born from this light. Like children, their laughter sounded in the song of the spheres.

For a time they played and explored the farthest reaches of space. And when they had learnt all that could be revealed to them, they turned their minds to another goal.

The Gods of Light created Prakriti. They created life!

But they never claimed dominion over creation. When one world was completed the Gods would move to the next, leaving the new life to grow and prosper. It had not occurred to them to claim mastery over any living thing.

For the Gods, the joy of existence lay solely in the art of making. The universe was nearly infinite and there were many creations yet to be undertaken.

But there was one amongst them who was unhappy. There was one who thought his work was most beautiful.

He had something that the other Gods did not possess. He had an ego and that ego demanded that all others should pay him tribute for his craft.

And that all should submit to his will.

The more he was denied his recognition the more discontented he became.

This God was named Bala and his heart had grown dark with jealousy for the work of other Gods.

When it was decided that the Gods would undertake the creation of man, Bala refused to join in unless he was given sole control over the making.

The Gods tried to dissuade him. But Bala's resolve was unmovable.

He stormed out of the Halls of Akashik and was not heard from for a long time.

Where he went or what he did during that **Yagya*** is not known to any.

* *Self-imposed exile.*

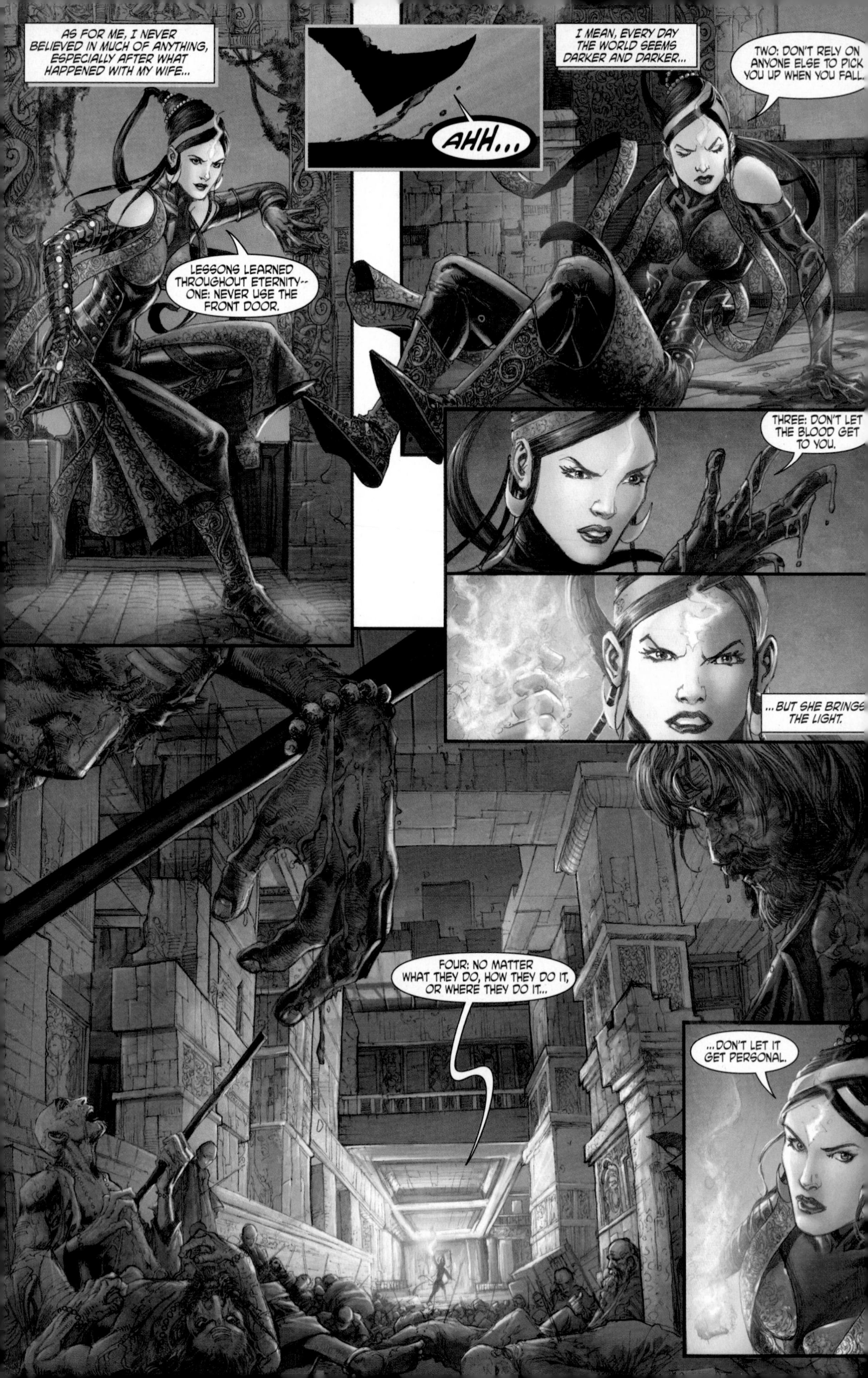
AS FOR ME, I NEVER BELIEVED IN MUCH OF ANYTHING, ESPECIALLY AFTER WHAT HAPPENED WITH MY WIFE...
LESSONS LEARNED THROUGHOUT ETERNITY-- ONE: NEVER USE THE FRONT DOOR.
AHH...
I MEAN, EVERY DAY THE WORLD SEEMS DARKER AND DARKER...
TWO: DON'T RELY ON ANYONE ELSE TO PICK YOU UP WHEN YOU FALL.
THREE: DON'T LET THE BLOOD GET TO YOU.
...BUT SHE BRINGS THE LIGHT.
FOUR: NO MATTER WHAT THEY DO, HOW THEY DO IT, OR WHERE THEY DO IT...
...DON'T LET IT GET PERSONAL.

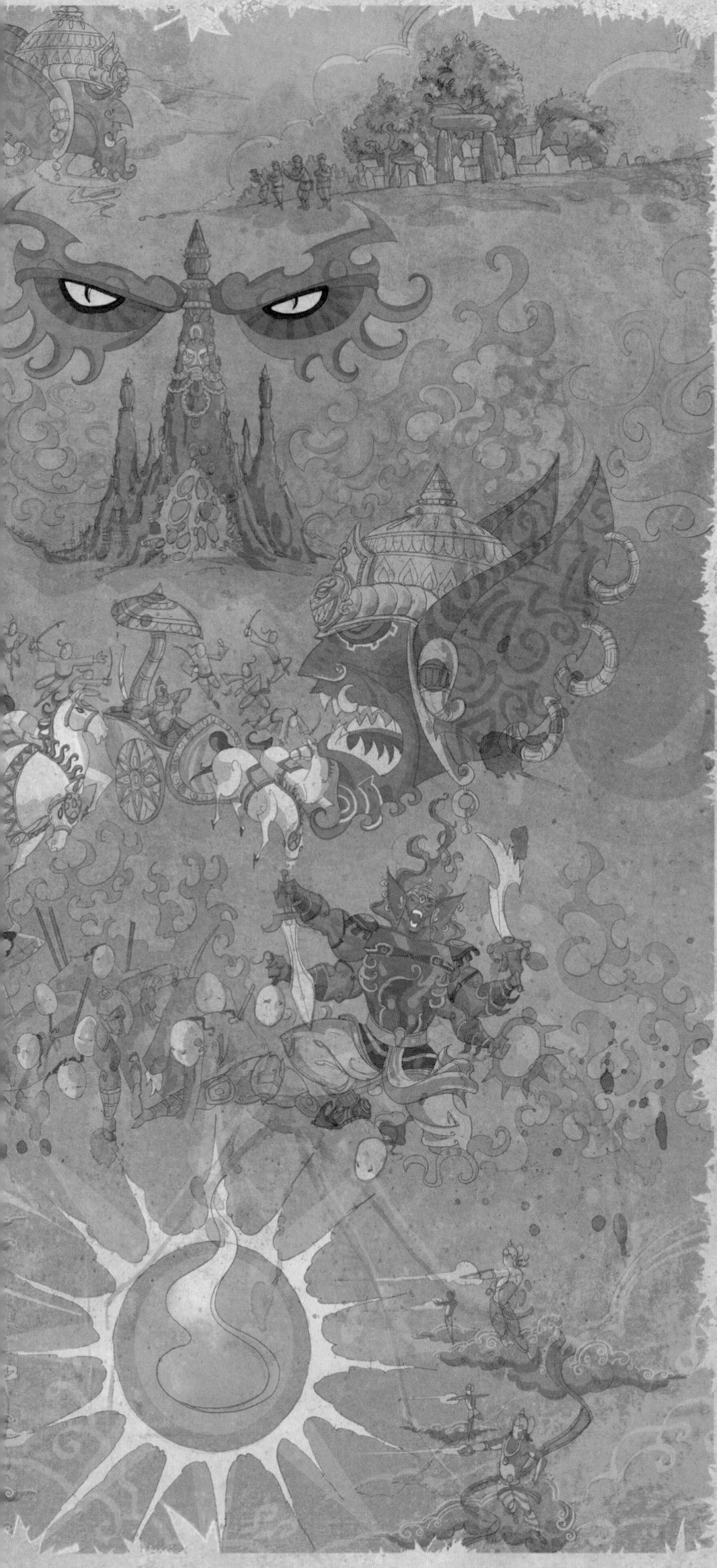

Bala came to earth after the race of men had been created. Not as a God but in human form, for it is said that this is the only way the Gods can walk amongst men.

But his body was deformed into a bat-being! His whole visage a mockery of the creation called man. His voice defiant of the Gods--the brothers on whom he had turned his back.

Using the help of his three generals, Gods who had been seduced by his lies, Bala enslaved the human race and was known as the Dread Lord!

Together, they rained much hardship on the defenseless humans, forcing them to build a dark empire in the center of the world where once stood the World Tree.

The Pure Gods eventually discovered Bala's atrocities. Indeed the Dread Lord did not cloak his actions in secrecy.

When their appeal to Bala to change his ways fell on deaf ears, the Gods attacked the Dread Lord.

But Bala had grown too powerful on the forced worship of men--the Pantheon was no match for him.

Eventually, many of the humans rebelled against Bala and allied themselves with the Gods. They were called the Durapasya, Warriors of the Light.

Despite all their efforts all who went up against Bala himself fell before the might of the Dread Lord.

The pure Gods realized that individually they were no match for Bala. So under the instruction of Bodha, King of the Gods, they sacrificed a part of their divine power to create a single entity.

Bodha blessed this divine being of power and named her **Devi**.

The Gods were so wounded by Bala's betrayal that they did not give this entity an immortal form, for they were afraid of what might come to pass if ever such a great power decided to turn on them.

Instead, they gave the Durapasya the secret rites for infusing the Devi entity into a human host. Thus making her more than human--an avatar of Divine power.

A goddess with a thousand faces.

A Devi!

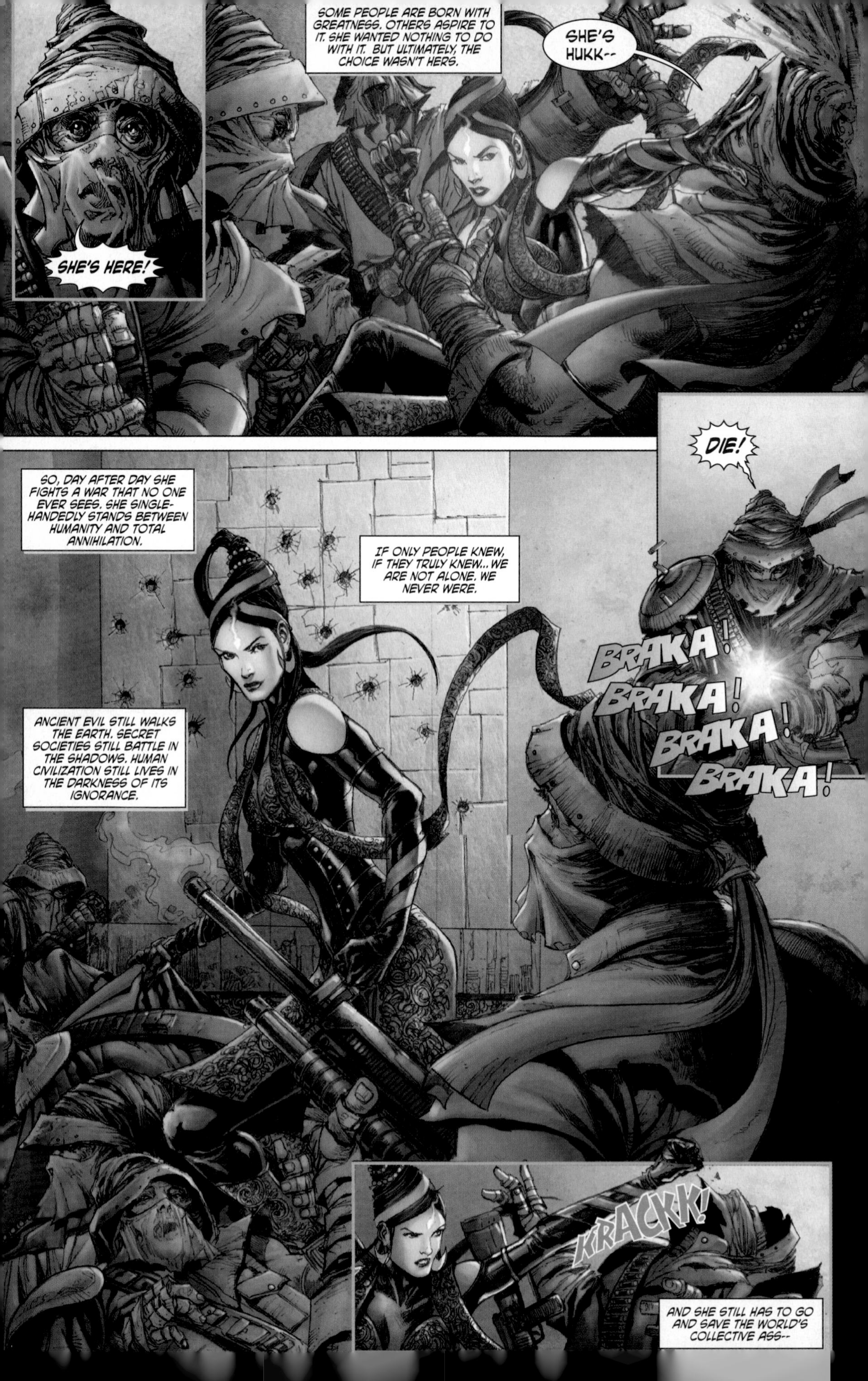
SOME PEOPLE ARE BORN WITH GREATNESS. OTHERS ASPIRE TO IT. SHE WANTED NOTHING TO DO WITH IT. BUT ULTIMATELY, THE CHOICE WASN'T HERS.
SHE'S HERE!
SHE'S HUKK--
SO, DAY AFTER DAY SHE FIGHTS A WAR THAT NO ONE EVER SEES. SHE SINGLE-HANDEDLY STANDS BETWEEN HUMANITY AND TOTAL ANNIHILATION.
IF ONLY PEOPLE KNEW, IF THEY TRULY KNEW... WE ARE NOT ALONE. WE NEVER WERE.
DIE!
BRAKA! BRAKA! BRAKA! BRAKA!
ANCIENT EVIL STILL WALKS THE EARTH. SECRET SOCIETIES STILL BATTLE IN THE SHADOWS. HUMAN CIVILIZATION STILL LIVES IN THE DARKNESS OF ITS IGNORANCE.
KRACKK!
AND SHE STILL HAS TO GO AND SAVE THE WORLD'S COLLECTIVE ASS--

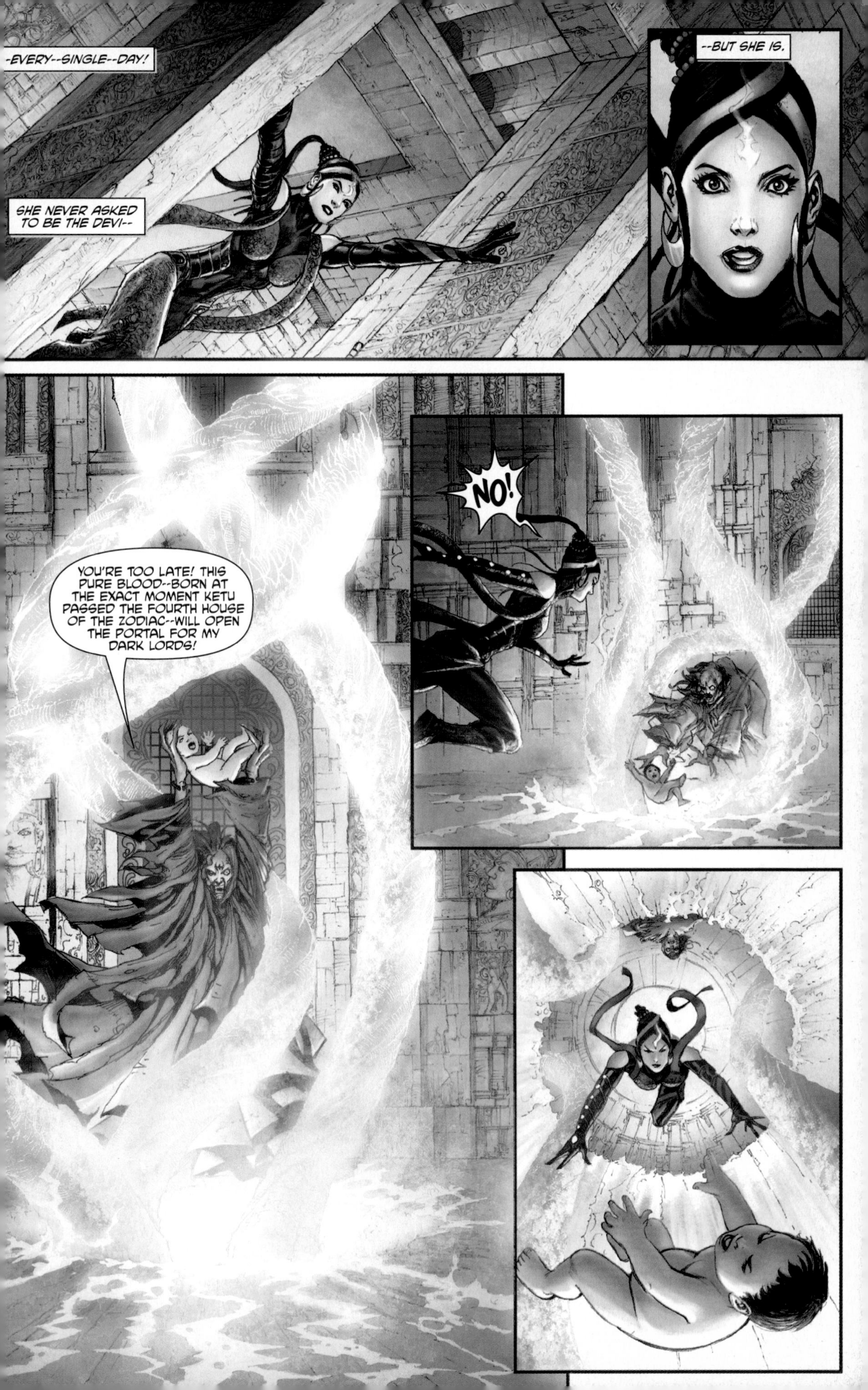
-EVERY--SINGLE--DAY!
SHE NEVER ASKED TO BE THE DEVI--
--BUT SHE IS.
YOU'RE TOO LATE! THIS PURE BLOOD--BORN AT THE EXACT MOMENT KETU PASSED THE FOURTH HOUSE OF THE ZODIAC--WILL OPEN THE PORTAL FOR MY DARK LORDS!
NO!

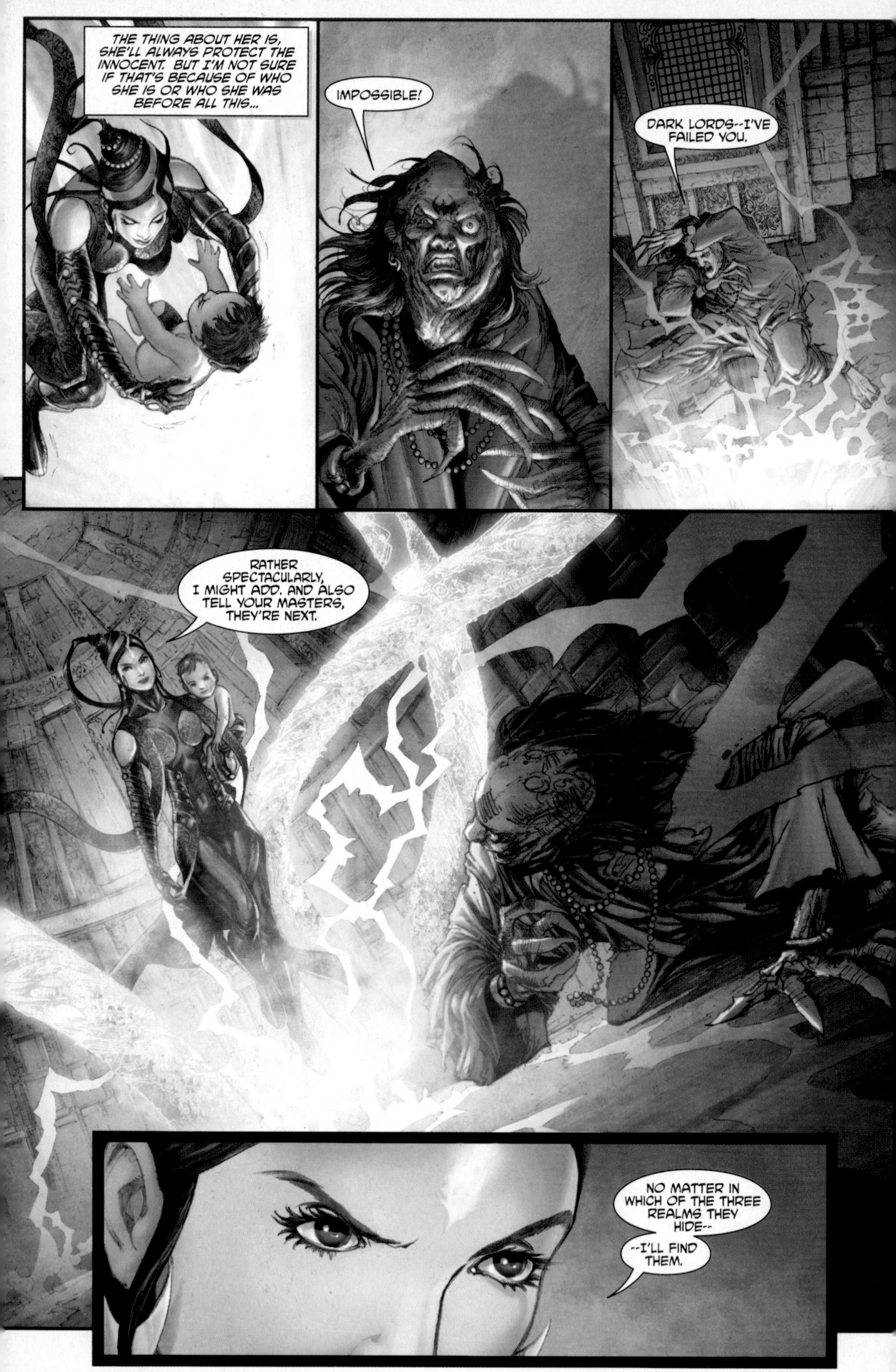
THE THING ABOUT HER IS, SHE'LL ALWAYS PROTECT THE INNOCENT. BUT I'M NOT SURE IF THAT'S BECAUSE OF WHO SHE IS OR WHO SHE WAS BEFORE ALL THIS...
IMPOSSIBLE!
DARK LORDS--I'VE FAILED YOU.
RATHER SPECTACULARLY, I MIGHT ADD. AND ALSO TELL YOUR MASTERS, THEY'RE NEXT.
NO MATTER IN WHICH OF THE THREE REALMS THEY HIDE--
--I'LL FIND THEM.

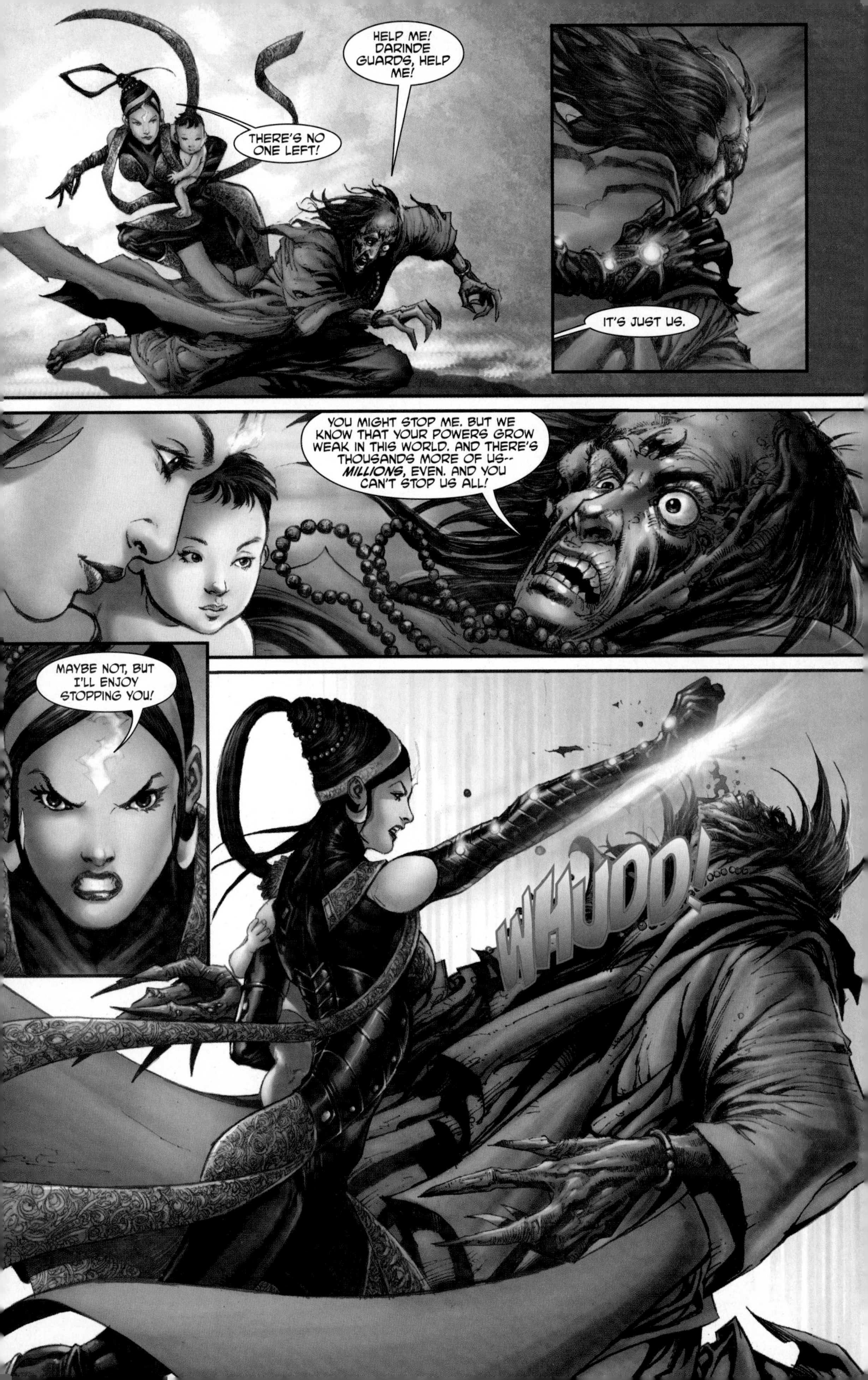

HELP ME! DARINDE GUARDS, HELP ME!
THERE'S NO ONE LEFT!
IT'S JUST US.
YOU MIGHT STOP ME. BUT WE KNOW THAT YOUR POWERS GROW WEAK IN THIS WORLD. AND THERE'S THOUSANDS MORE OF US-- *MILLIONS*, EVEN. AND YOU CAN'T STOP US ALL!
MAYBE NOT, BUT I'LL ENJOY STOPPING YOU!
WHUDD!

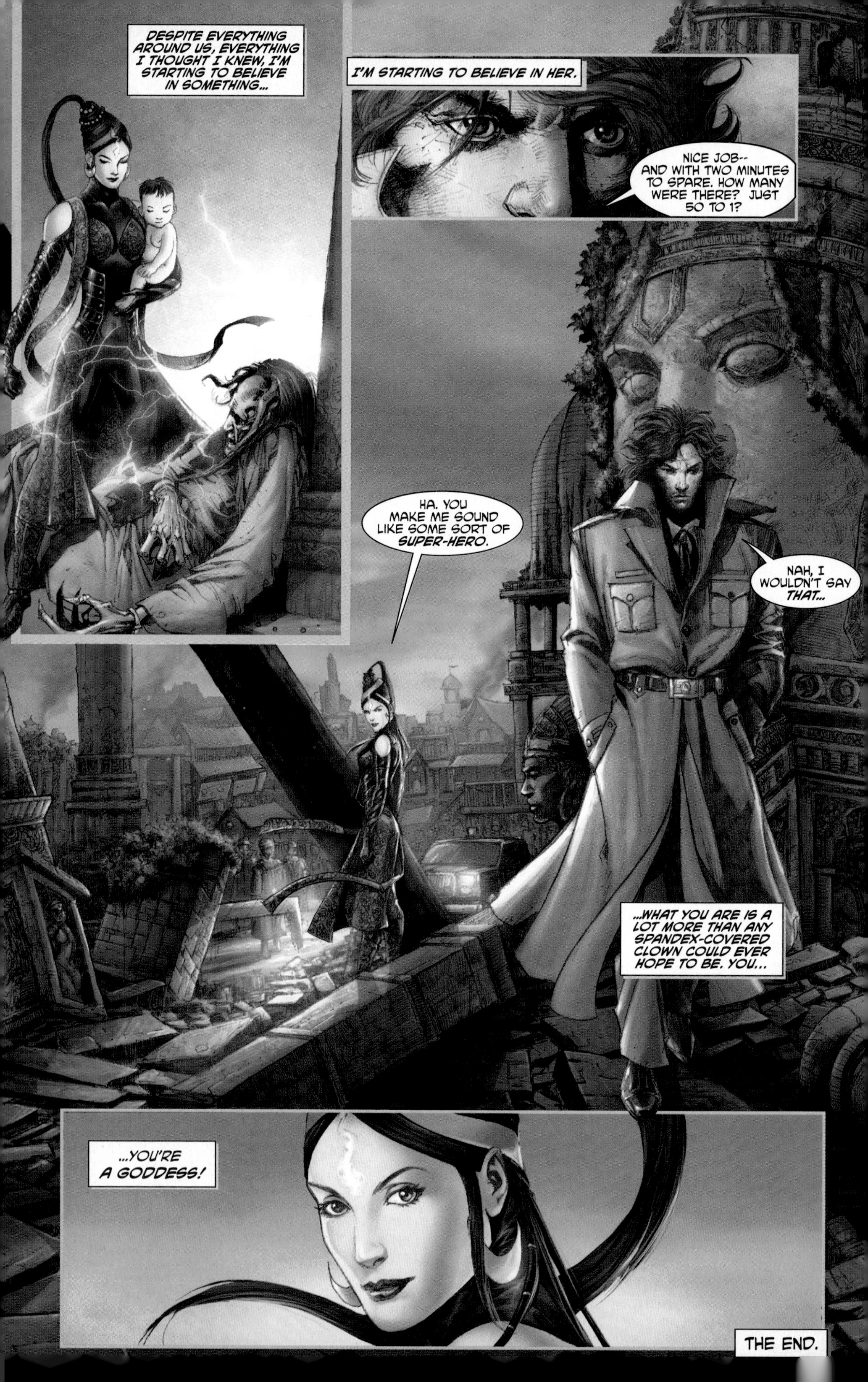
DESPITE EVERYTHING AROUND US, EVERYTHING I THOUGHT I KNEW, I'M STARTING TO BELIEVE IN SOMETHING...
I'M STARTING TO BELIEVE IN HER.
NICE JOB-- AND WITH TWO MINUTES TO SPARE. HOW MANY WERE THERE? JUST 50 TO 1?
HA. YOU MAKE ME SOUND LIKE SOME SORT OF SUPER-HERO.
NAH, I WOULDN'T SAY THAT...
...WHAT YOU ARE IS A LOT MORE THAN ANY SPANDEX-COVERED CLOWN COULD EVER HOPE TO BE. YOU...
...YOU'RE A GODDESS!
THE END.

GET INSIDE WRITER SAMIT BASU'S MIND

One of the first things the creative team behind Devi discussed about this issue was the Dreamstate, the other world where Tara was blessed by the gods and given her powers. I found the idea fascinating as I plotted it; the parallel journeys, ascension on the vast, serene astral plane towards divinity and a higher destiny and descent on the murky, chaotic mortal plane towards death, violence and disaster. Tara is born again in this sequence, given a new life even as her old one travels ponderously towards its end. We had to come up with a means to illustrate this that would sink in deeper than words alone. We'd initially planned to have this sequence done by another artist, but Mukesh's work outshone all the other visualizations.

PAGE TEN
(four panels)

Panel 1
Dreamstate. Tara is suspended in an ethereal plane, shifting soft colours behing her. Strange shapes float around; stars in the background, planet-like things far away, smoky, wispy trails across everywhere. If possible, have suspended objects, strange geometric shapes with swirling colours, nearer her. Whatever strikes your fancy – magical, mysterious, cosmic/mystic icons,. Tara doesn't seem to be aware she's suspended in nothingness – her posture is tense.

Tara:　　　　　　　WHERE AM I?

Caption:　　　　　　WELCOME, THRICE-BLESSED TARA,
　　　　　　　　　　TO THE THRESHOLD OF A NEW LIFE.

Panel 2
Different angle. Her new reality is beginning to sink in, and she's afraid

Tara:　　　　　　　　　I FEEL...STRANGE.

Caption:　SOMA, THE NECTAR OF THE
　　　　　GODS, HAS BEEN MINGLED
　　　　　WITH YOUR BLOOD. THE
　　　　　STRANGENESS WILL
　　　　　SOON PASS.

Panel 3
Closer on Tara. She's looking around, utterly confused, helpless, anything that indicates mind-boggling insecurity, amazement, awe. Around her, symmetrically, five hazy, glowing wisps.

Tara:　　WHAT'S HAPPENING TO ME?

Caption:　DON'T BE AFRAID, TARA.
　　　　　I WILL BE WITH YOU SOON

Panel 4
The wisps are growing, lengthening, becoming clearer. Tara watches them, too amazed to react

Caption:　BUT BEFORE THAT, A FEW
　　　　　FRIENDS WISH TO MEET YOU.

This page is one that meant a lot to me when I saw it executed because it illustrated again that this medium, a new one for me, was so dependent on trust and collaboration. Mukesh took the script and worked out his layout, and I was jubilant, because the new way worked better than mine, sacrificing the sense of scale to show the alternate Tara characters more clearly. Also, my deep, unresolved feelings for Bollywood Tara were born here.

PAGE ELEVEN
(two panels)

Panel 1
The wisps solidify, take human form...and they're all identical to Tara at some point of time in her life. Let's say New Tara 1 is a childhood version, a little girl, New Tara 2 is a young, androgynous man with Tara's features, NT3 a plump, complacent-looking Gujarati housewife, NT 4 a glamorous movie star, NT5 a frail-looking old-woman. Identical pose, standing straight, arms at side, slightly raised. All looking at Tara, surrounding her. Tara's wide-eyed.

New Tara #1:   HELLO, TARA.

Tara: WHO ARE YOU?

One aspect of mainstream comics I've always loved is the existence of alternate universes and storylines for the same character, where each continuity, each possibility is explored. I wanted to bring this in to our story early on, to give readers a glimpse of other Taras, of other lives sacrificed for the sake of this story, to underline the fact that a hero's journey is largely a matter of chance.

Panel 2
They move closer to her, no longer identical postures. For convenience, here's the key again; New Tara 1 is a childhood version, a little girl, New Tara 2 is a young, androgynous man with Tara's features, NT3 a plump, complacent-looking Gujarati housewife, NT 4 a glamorous movie star, NT5 a frail-looking old-woman.

New Tara #2:   WE ARE TARA.

N. Tara #2:   TARA AS YOU MIGHT HAVE BEEN.

N. Tara #1:   TARA AS YOU WERE.

N. Tara #3   TARA AS YOU ARE NOT.

N.Tara #4   TARA AS YOU DREAM OF BEING.

N. Tara #5   TARA AS YOU'LL NEVER BE.

I love where we went from the script I'd sent in. We'd decided the borders for panels in this page would be wispy, drifting; the panels would blend in lazily, non-linearly. This is, after all, a dream; physical continuity yields to vision, expression, surprise. By constantly shifting scale, perspective and background, I think we achieved the mood we'd set out to create. No, that sounds far too grown up. It was the first time I'd seen my writing visualized; I was thrilled.

PAGE TWELVE
(three panels)

Panel 1
Closer on Tara, amazed, from an angle where NTs 3 and 4 are visible.

Tara: I'M DREAMING.

N. Tara #1:   No.

N. Tara #4:   YOU'RE CHANGING.

N. Tara #5:   AS WE DID. OR MIGHT HAVE.

Panel 2
Wider. They're fading away, and she's watching them leave. Let's enhance the strangeness of the background here; more celestial shapes, closing in, shifting.

Tara: WHAT?

N. Tara #2:   THIS IS WHERE OUR TARAS MEET.

N. Tara #4:   AND WE CAME HERE TO SAY GOODBYE. AND HELLO.

N. Tara #5:   AND THANK YOU FOR
                   HAVING BEEN WITH US.
                   FOR HAVING BEEN US.

Panel 3

NTs 4 and 5. Close up, intense. We need to feel a sense of both anticipation and tension. Something big is about to happen.

N.Tara #4:   AND TO SAY – WE'LL
                   SEE YOU SOON,
                   TARA-THAT-IS

N. Tara #5   WHEN YOU JOIN
                   US IN THE REALM OF IF.

Caption: IT IS TIME.

Devi was a challenge. She had to come across as divine, seductive and strong. Devi literally means goddess, but what do modern gods wear??? In the series, there have been many Devis and I thought of them as sporting a design in tune with the times in which they were incarnated.

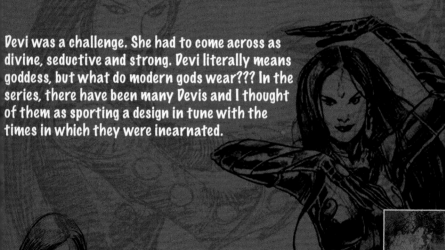

Image 1 was the first sketch where I felt I was on my way to cracking her design. The black leather seemed to push her in the right direction.

Image 2 was a full body exploration of the same, and, as you can see, the shapes around her arms added a nice pattern...but something still wasnt right.

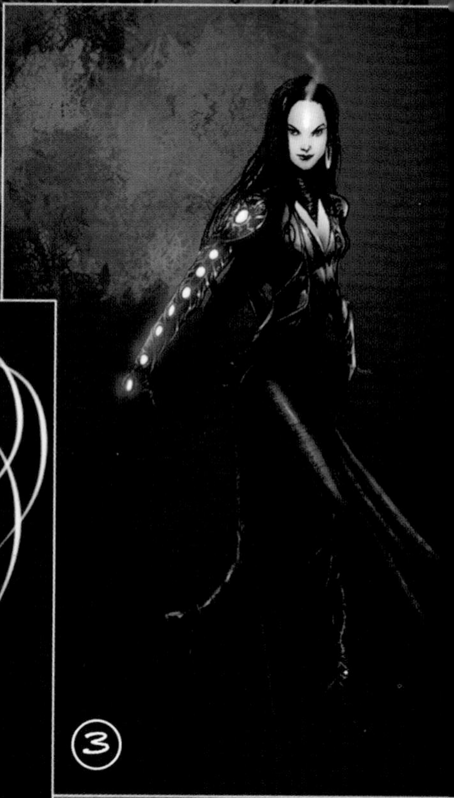

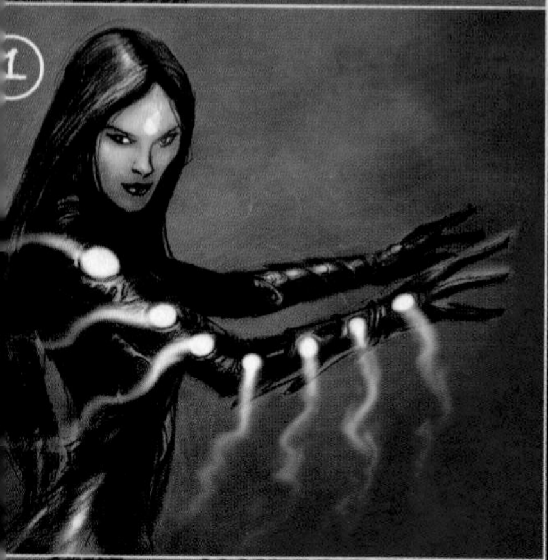

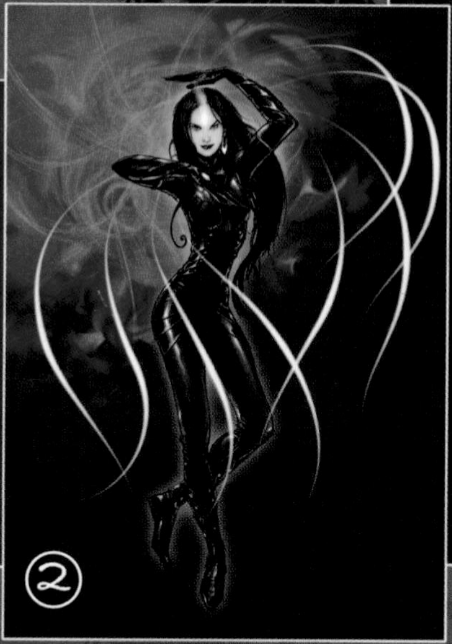

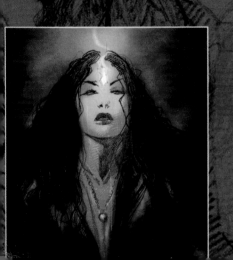

In image 3, I gave her a costume that was looser (to reflect the traditional Indian costumes, which are not tailored, but rather, are pieces of cloth arranged together). But still something was missing...then I thought "I have left her hair untouched." After looking at a few images of Shiv (with Ganga flowing out of his hairdo), I hit upon the final design, which you can see in Image 4.

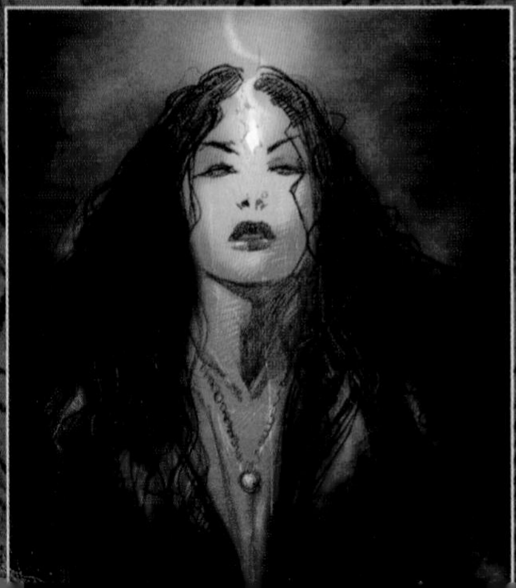

SKETCH BOOK

COMMENTARY BY ARTIST MUKESH SINGH

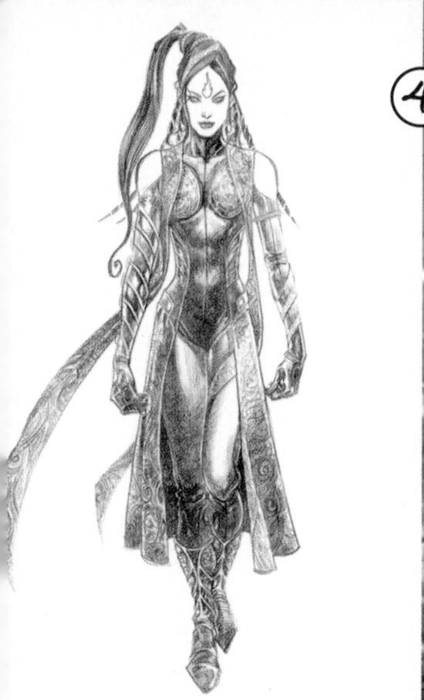
4

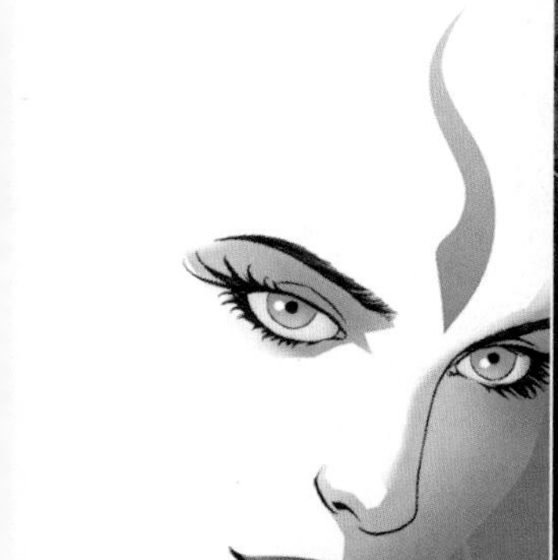

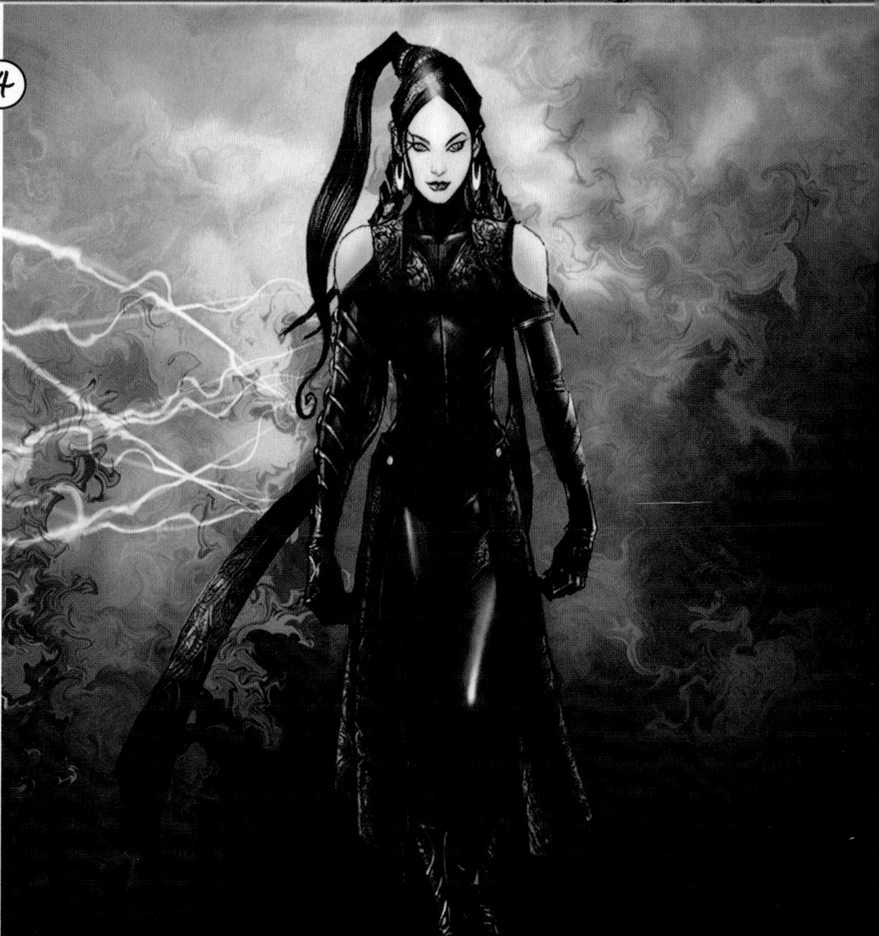

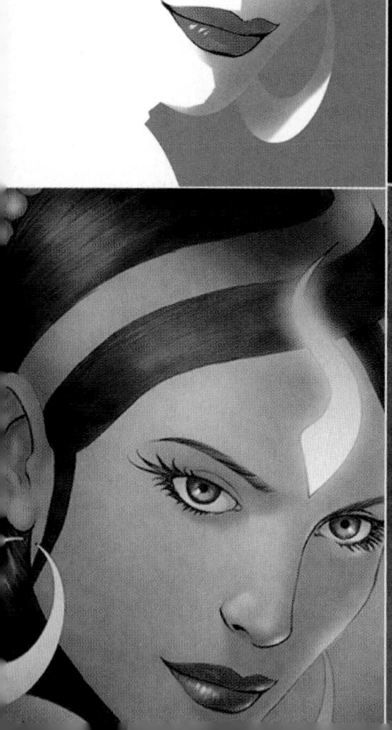

Devi sports seven spots on her right arm, with energy radiating out of them. This serves as a nice element to play with when we see her in action. The flaming bindi is more than a decorative feature: it is a living flame to signify that she is energy. The flame will reflect her mood...a cooler, softer shape when she is calm, but becoming hotter and more violent as she gets angry.

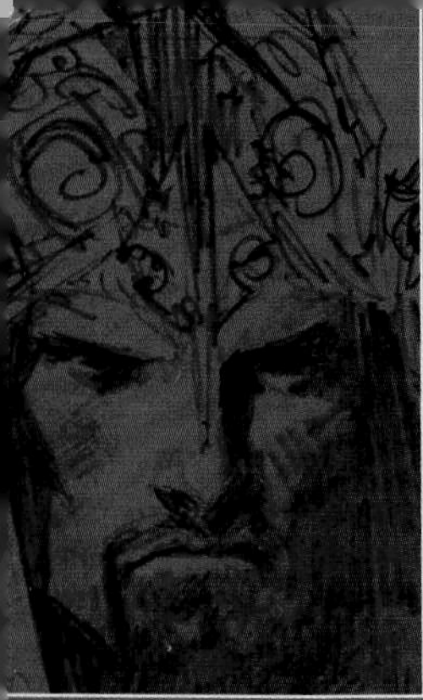

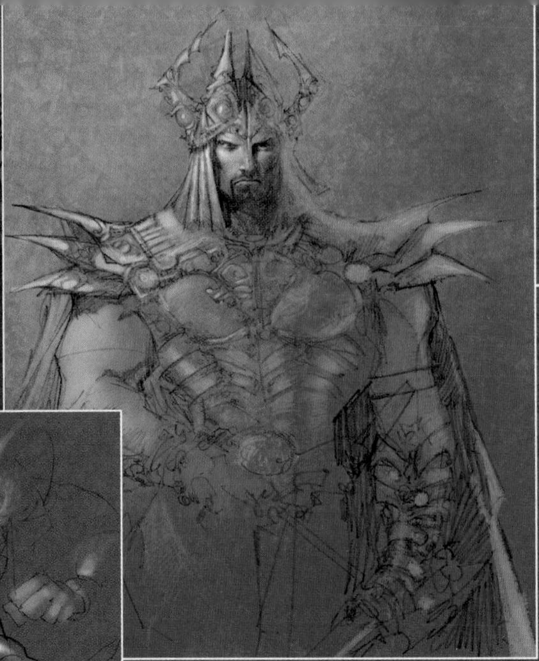

Ah Yes!!
The baddies. The most interesting of the bunch...What would we do without them?

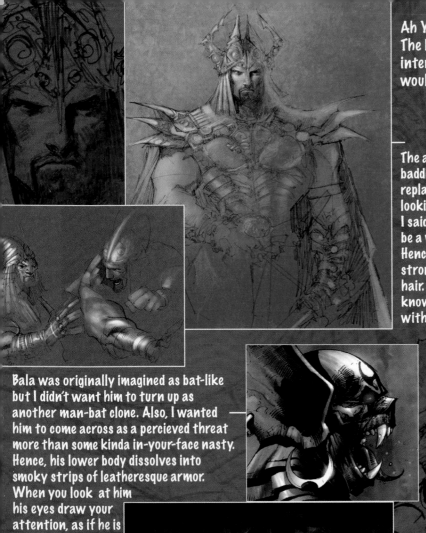

The absence of Bala as the main baddie in the first story required a replacement of equal threat. After looking at the first issue script, I said well, Iyam, his general, can be a worthy replacement. Hence the towering physique, strong jaws and flowing locks of hair. I think he is not a bad guy to know, he just comes across as one with a case of misplaced loyalties.

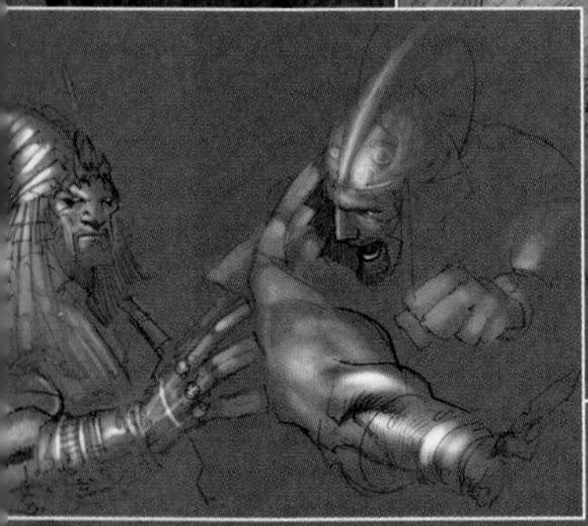

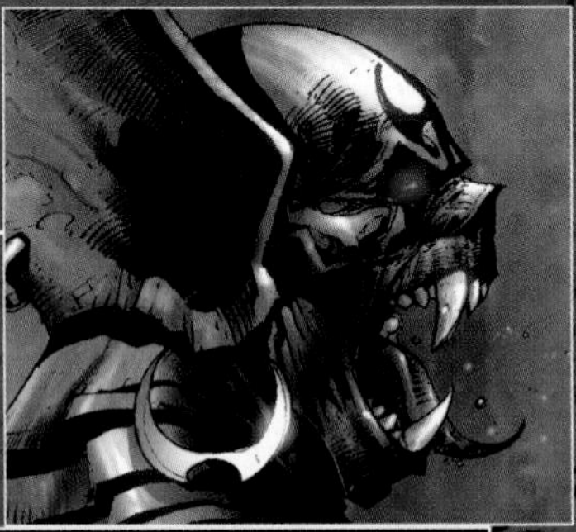

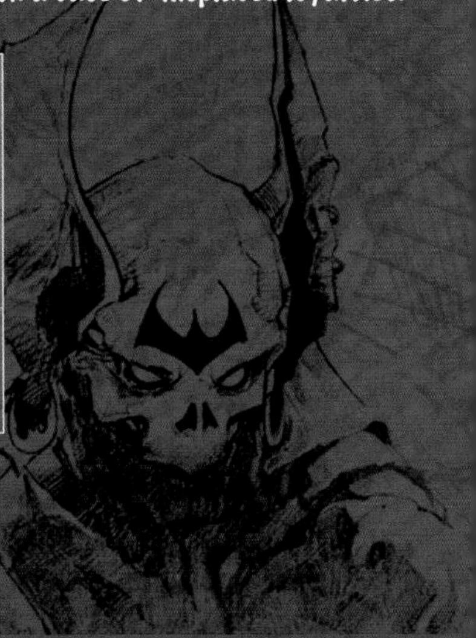

Bala was originally imagined as bat-like but I didn't want him to turn up as another man-bat clone. Also, I wanted him to come across as a percieved threat more than some kinda in-your-face nasty. Hence, his lower body dissolves into smoky strips of leatheresque armor. When you look at him his eyes draw your attention, as if he is mesmerizing you...

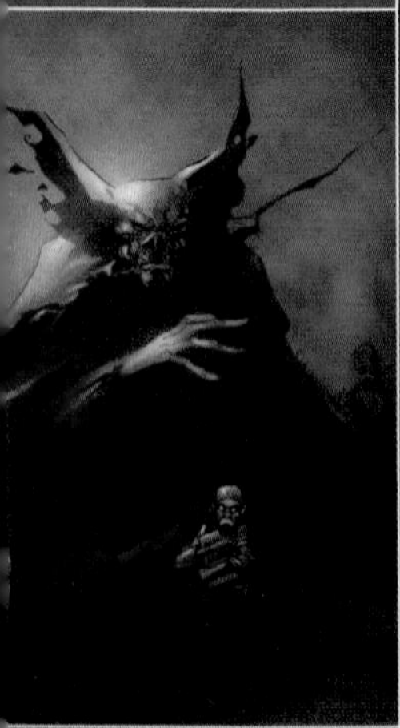

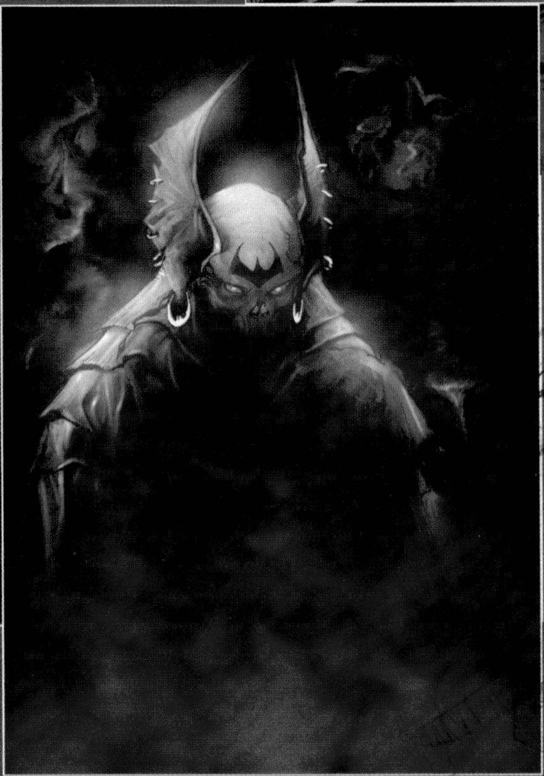

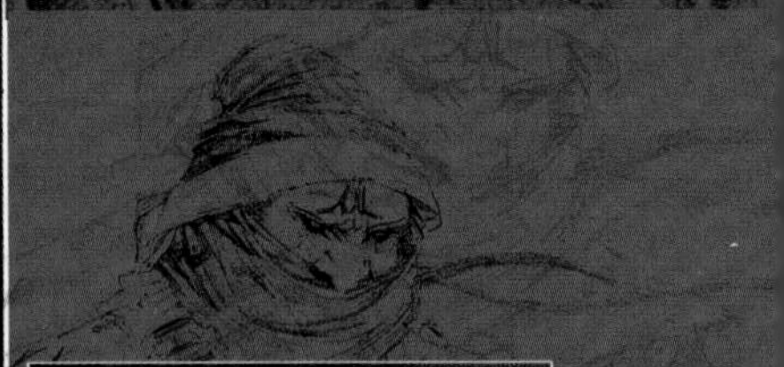

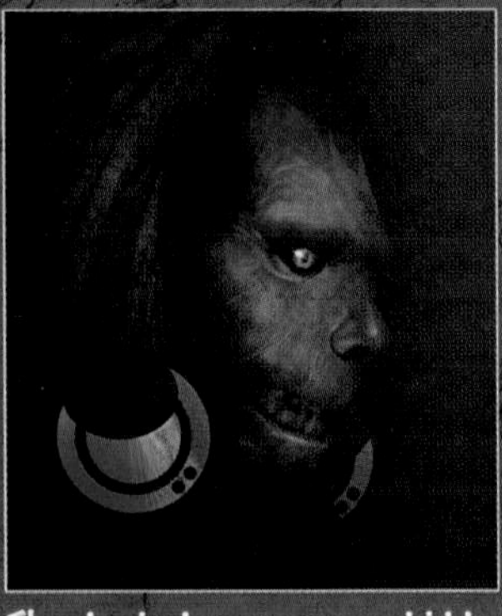

The darindes are a morbid bunch of good-for-nothings ! A rag-tag lot. They were inspired by the dacoits who once infested central India - as tough, hardy and ruthless as the unforgiving environment in which they thrived...